Visitor's Guide
NEW ZEALAND

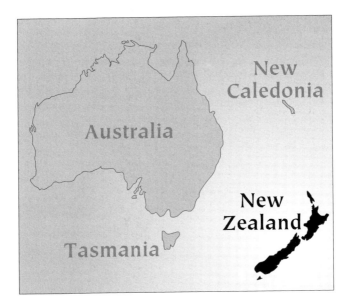

New Zealand

N
W **E**
S

1
2
3
5
4

6

7

10

8

9

Chatham Islands
(895 km west of Christchuch)

VISITOR'S GUIDE
NEW ZEALAND

Grant Bourne & Sabine Körner-Bourne

MPC®
HUNTER

Published by:
Moorland Publishing Co Ltd,
Moor Farm Road West, Ashbourne,
Derbyshire DE6 1HD England

Published in the USA by:
Hunter Publishing Inc,
300 Raritan Center Parkway, Edison, NJ 08818

ISBN 086190 569 5

British Library Cataloguing in Publication Data:
A catalogue record for this book is available from the British Library.

Colour origination by: GA GRAPHICS, Stamford, Lincs. ☎ 01780 56166

Printed in Spain by: GraphyCems

Cover photograph: Mount Taranaki from Lake Mangamahoe Domain
Rear Cover: Mount Ngauruhoe, an active volcano in
Tongariro National Park, North Island
Page 3: Auckland harbour

Illustrations have been supplied by:
Grant Bourne & Sabine Körner-Bourne

MPC Production Team:
Editor: Christine Haines
Assistant Editor: Tonya Monk
Designer: Ashley Emery
Cartographer: Mick Usher
Typesetter: Stella Porter

CONTENTS

FEATURE BOXES

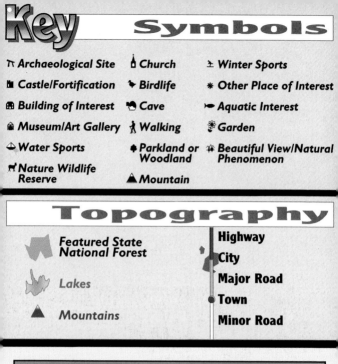

Key Symbols

π Archaeological Site
🏰 Castle/Fortification
🏛 Building of Interest
🏛 Museum/Art Gallery
⚓ Water Sports
🦌 Nature Wildlife Reserve

⛪ Church
🐦 Birdlife
🦭 Cave
🚶 Walking
♣ Parkland or Woodland
▲ Mountain

⛷ Winter Sports
✳ Other Place of Interest
🐟 Aquatic Interest
🌸 Garden
🏞 Beautiful View/Natural Phenomenon

Topography

Featured State National Forest

Lakes

▲ Mountains

Highway
City
Major Road
Town
Minor Road

How To Use This Guide

This MPC Visitor's Guide has been designed to be as easy to use as possible. Each chapter covers a region or itinerary in a natural progression which gives all the background information to help you enjoy your visit. MPC's distinctive margin symbols, the important places printed in bold and a comprehensive index enable the reader to find the most interesting places to visit with ease.

At the end of each chapter an Additional Information section gives specific details such as addresses and opening times, making this guide a complete sightseeing companion.

At the back of the guide the Fact File, arranged in alphabetical order, gives practical information and useful tips to help you plan your holiday before you go and while you are there.

The maps of each region show the main towns, villages, roads and places of interest, but are not designed as route maps and motorists should always use a recommended road atlas.

Introduction

Luxuriant rainforests, spectacular fiords, volcanoes, snow-capped mountains and long empty beaches of golden sand are just some of the ingredients that go to make New Zealand one of the most breathtakingly beautiful places in the world. No other country can boast such a variety of landscapes within such easy reach of one another. In some places the ski slopes and the seaside may be separated by no more than an hour's drive.

New Zealand is a land that offers lovers of the great outdoors all they could wish for. Outdoor activities include jet boating, white water rafting, kayaking, tramping and skiing. You can watch whales and swim with dolphins at Kaikoura or fish for a trout dinner at Taupo.

Apart from the enjoyment of sea, sun and sand another attraction for many visitors is the fascinating culture of the country's first inhabitants, the Maori. Strongholds of Maori culture are the East Cape and Northland but it is probably Rotorua that provides the best introduction to the traditional Maori way of life. Excellent museums in places like Wanganui, Auckland and Wellington offer further insight into the history of this Polynesian people. But what perhaps, in the end, makes a

above: New Zealand's beaches are second to none (Abel Tasman National Park)

holiday in New Zealand into something really special is simply the friendliness and hospitality of the Kiwis (colloquial name for all New Zealanders) themselves.

HISTORY

Arrival of the Maori

Around AD800, centuries before Columbus discovered America, Polynesian adventurers boarded simple outrigger canoes and sailed across the vastness of the Pacific Ocean to find a group of isolated islands now known as New Zealand. These ancestors of the modern Maori called their new home *Aotearoa* and they immortalised their epic migrations in the legend of the 'Great Fleet', a colonising expedition that set out from the mythical homeland of Hawaiki. Here, in the most remote corner of Polynesia, they evolved a flourishing culture, where the art of carving reached heights of accomplishment hitherto unknown anywhere in the Pacific.

The seeds of human history on New Zealand's virgin soil were sown; the next great phase of settlement was not to have its beginnings until centuries later when, in the wake of European colonial expansion, the Dutch East India Company sent Abel Janszoon Tasman off in search of new markets and new lands.

European Explorers

Tasman sighted the west coast of the South Island in 1642 but was prevented from landing by hostile Maori who attacked one of the ship's boats and killed several of the crew. No doubt discouraged by this bloody encounter Tasman did not make another attempt to go ashore and soon left the islands believing that they might be part of an unknown continent that stretched as far as South America. However the Dutch showed little interest in his discovery as this wild land did not promise any great treasures and over a hundred years were to pass before Europeans were again to visit these distant shores.

Captain James Cook's first voyage into the South Pacific was a scientific expedition that had, among other things, the task of finding out whether or not the Terra Australis Incognita (Southern Continent) really existed. In 1769 Cook's ship the *Endeavour* sailed within sight of the east coast of New Zealand, which was at that time still known by the Dutch name of Nieuw Zeeland. During the next six months he circumnavigated both main islands and charted the coastline. Cook was, after a few initial skirmishes, able to establish friendly relations with the Maori and apart from gathering valuable information on the geography, as well as the flora and fauna of the islands, his voyage proved beyond doubt that New Zealand was not the fabled Southern Continent.

Cook's voyages (he visited New Zealand again in 1772 and 1776) along with those of later explorers like the Frenchmen Jean de Surville (1769, two months after Cook) and Marion du Fresne (1772) stimulated a great deal of interest in the South Pacific. For New Zealand centuries of isolation from the rest of the world were at an end; the phase of European colonisation was no longer far away.

British Colonisation

The first arrivals were sealers and they were followed by whalers, traders and adventurers. In 1814 the Reverend Samuel Marsden arrived in the Bay of Islands to establish the country's first mission. Other missionaries soon followed but in the beginning the Maoris saw Christianity less as a means of salvation than as a way to acquire European skills and goods. The most valued item of trade among the Maori was the gun and it was not long before it was put to devastating effect in inter-tribal conflicts.

Up until 1840 the settlement of New Zealand had been sporadic and mainly limited to the Bay of Islands but that was to change when in 1837 Edward Gibbon Wakefield formed the New Zealand Association (it later became the New Zealand Company) in England. This company was the main driving force behind the organised colonisation of New Zealand in the first half of the nineteenth century.

A condition of lawlessness prevailed in the Bay of Island's settlement prior to 1840. Demands grew louder, both in New Zealand and at home, that Britain should annex the country and thus make it subject to British law. With enough problems in the colonies it already had Britain was initially reluctant to take the step of making New Zealand officially a part of the British Empire. However growing pressure and fears that France might have its own plans for colonisation made Britain finally act. Captain William Hobson was sent to New Zealand as the Governor-designate and the Treaty of Waitangi, under which the Maori accepted British sovereignty over the country, was signed at the Bay of Islands on 6 February 1840.

The first boatload of immigrants organised by Wakefield's company arrived shortly after the signing of the treaty and with them came a growing European hunger for land. Already by 1858 there were more Europeans in the country than there were Maori. In the Treaty of Waitangi it was stated that only the government could buy Maori land. This was meant to protect the Maori from being swindled by speculators. However speculation took place just the same and even the government was guilty of paying ridiculously low prices for land which was then sometimes resold to settlers for twenty times the original purchase price. On top of all this the Maori considered that even if they had sold the land they had not sold the resources that grew upon it. Armed conflict was quickly becoming inevitable.

Mount Ngauruhoe has, like
Mount Egmont, a nearly
perfect volcanic cone

In 1860 a shady land deal in Taranaki caused the outbreak of fighting between government troops and local Maori. This was the beginning of the New Zealand Land Wars, a series of localised conflicts which flared up in various parts of the North Island over the next twelve years. But in the end the Maori, who were often divided among themselves, could not hope to prevail against the vast resources of the British Empire. Those tribes that fought against the Crown lost not only the war but also much of their land, which was confiscated by the government.

An Agricultural Nation

In the South Island the problems between Maori and Pakeha (Maori name for white settlers) never developed to the point of serious warfare. Already by the middle of the nineteenth century sheep farming had established itself here as an important part of the economy. The discovery of gold in Otago and Westland in the 1860s gave an added boost to the South Island's prosperity. In the 1870s the colonial government's policy of overseas borrowing to finance the building of roads and railways sparked off an economic boom which also brought a measure of prosperity to the war-torn North Island. Unfortunately the good times soon came to an end. In 1878 the prices for wool and grain fell and the government was left wondering how it was going to pay its massive overseas debts. Before long the country was in the depths of recession, thousands of unemployed workers left the colony to seek new opportunities in America and Australia.

The colony's first long depression had, however, its positive side: it provided the impetus for a series of wide reaching social reforms that made New Zealand one of the pioneers of the welfare state. They included the introduction of free, compulsory education in 1877 and a small pension for the aged poor in 1898. In 1893 New Zealand became the first country in the world to grant women the vote.

In 1882 a possible end to the depression was signalled by the first successful shipment of frozen meat to England. Though it took a few years this trade eventually developed into a bonanza for New Zealand's farming industry. During the early years of the twentieth century markets for dairy products also expanded and dairy farming soon became as important for the New Zealand economy as the raising of sheep for wool and meat. For the moment the country's problems seemed solved, the time of the prosperous and influential farmer had arrived.

The Twentieth Century

The Great Depression of the 1930s brought hardship once again but prosperity returned with the world-wide economic recovery in 1935. In the same year the newly formed Labour Party was swept into power; the earlier reforms were extended and New Zealand now had one of the most comprehensive social welfare systems in the world. From the 1950s onwards, however, it was to be the conservative National Party, which had been formed during World War II, that dominated the political stage.

In 1947 New Zealand was granted full independence from Great Britain. Again the nation went through a period of economic boom which was to end when Britain joined the EC in 1973. The loss of the country's main overseas market (the trade barriers erected against non-EC countries made it difficult for New Zealand to be competitive) dealt a severe blow to the strongly export-oriented economy. Now many politicians began to perceive the welfare state as a luxury the land could ill afford. Even the liberally-minded Labour Party, who were in power between 1985 and 1990, began to cut back on social legislation and introduced a scheme of privatisation whereby formerly state owned enterprises were sold to the private sector. The presently ruling National Party has continued with the economic reforms inaugurated by Labour. In recent years the economy has shown definite signs of recovery.

One of the most important trends in modern New Zealand is the renaissance of Maori language and culture. The country is becoming increasingly aware of itself as a bicultural society which has its cultural roots both in Polynesia and Europe. There is also a growing awareness of the country's role as a Pacific nation and New Zealand is slowly but surely loosening its ties to 'Mother England'.

Arts, Culture and Entertainment

At least in the cities New Zealand can boast a lively arts and entertainment scene with regular exhibitions of national and international art in the galleries, performances of classical music, theatre and so on. Auckland and Wellington are probably the most interesting places as far as cultural activities are concerned but other main centres like Christchurch and Dunedin also have much to offer. Dunedin, for instance, has a reputation for producing some of the country's best rock bands, though good live music, including jazz, can be heard in pubs and discos all around the country. For details of cultural events consult one of the free city guides published by the city tourist information offices.

The arts and crafts scene also flourishes; potters, carvers, weavers and trinket-makers can be found offering their wares all over the country, from north to south. The work is often of a very high quality and can range from a simple bowl carved from beautiful native wood to an original piece of pottery that is more an *objet d'art* than a practical utensil. Good places to go shopping for handicrafts include Nelson and Kerikeri.

Though the literature and art forms of European culture are still dominant in New Zealand the last few decades have nevertheless shown a growing awareness for the achievements of *Maoritanga* (Maori culture). However the activities of Maori artists are by no means limited to such traditional crafts as wood carving or weaving but extend into all fields of modern artistic endeavour. Dame Kiri Te Kanawa is a world famous opera singer and in the pictorial arts painters like Gordon Walters and Robyn Kahukiwa have drawn on Maori rather than European sources for their inspiration. The influence of Maoritanga on subject, imagery and meaning is especially notable in the field of literature where Maori, or part Maori, writers like Keri Hulme (Bone People) and Patricia Grace have earned themselves recognition not only at home but also abroad. Other important names in New Zealand literature are Witi Ihimaera, Katherine Mansfield, Ronald Hugh Morrieson, Frank Sargeson and Janet Frame.

Those with an interest in traditional Maori culture will find Rotorua, as commercialised as it may be, the best and easiest place to study it. Meeting houses are found in many places in the country but are especially common in areas with large Maori communities such as Northland, East Cape and the Auckland area. Visitors should bear in mind however that the *marae* (strictly speaking the place in front of a meeting house but the term is often used more loosely to refer to all the buildings around it) is sacred to the Maori and permission must be obtained before entering. In some tourist centres tours are offered to local marae, thus allowing visitors a unique insight into contemporary Maori culture. Inquire at the tourist offices for details of such visits.

Maori Art

Though not proved beyond any doubt it is now generally accepted that the ancestors of the Maori people came from the coastal fringes of Southeast Asia. In a series of migrations, over a period of many centuries, these

Traditional Maori carving

Rugby Union

New Zealanders have a passion for outdoor sports and in winter (April to September) the most popular sport of all is Rugby Union football. A rugby team consists of 15 men and the game lasts 80 minutes (40 minutes for each half, not including injury time). It is played on a rectangular field and the oval ball may be carried by the players, in contrast to soccer. The object of the game is to get the ball across the other team's goal line, whether by kicking it over the goal posts or by touching it down behind the goal line. The rules are a bit complicated and those who want to know more will probably find that they are best explained by a local over a beer in the pub.

Children (boys) begin playing the game almost as soon as they can tie up their bootlaces and they all love it — well at least the stronger ones do. Physical contact with the opponent is not only allowed, it is desired and this can lead to tensions that quite often explode in fights during the game. Physical strength or speed combined with clear tactical thinking are among the most important qualities of a good rugby player. The biggest players in the team are the 'forwards' and it is their job to dominate the opponent which, admittedly, does not always occur in a fair manner. It can sometimes happen that not only the ball but also a player, with the aid of a giant fist, goes flying through the air. If the referee has not noticed anything then play continues, the ball generally being passed to quicker players known as 'backs'.

The most exciting games to watch are the international matches. New Zealand's national team, one of the best in the world, is known as the All Blacks and the best introduction to the game would be to see them in action against such arch-rivals as the British Lions (UK), the Springboks (South Africa) or the Wallabies (Australia). A good place to see such a test match would be Auckland's Eden Park but tickets have to be bought well in advance if you want to be certain of a place.

Southeast Asian peoples eventually reached the Pacific region and brought with them cultures which had been influenced by the Chinese. Therefore it is now believed that the origins of classical Maori art are to be found in China. This theory is supported by the similarity of the spiral motifs found in Maori art with curvilinear motifs in the art of the late Chou and Han dynasties. Among the oldest known examples of early

Maori art are the fifteenth-century rock drawings which are mostly found in the South Island.

Spiral motifs occur just about everywhere in Maori art but can be seen at their most complicated in the intricate wood carvings at which the Maori excel. Some of the most elaborate of these wood carvings are those decorating the façades of pataka (storehouse) and meeting houses. Spirals or curvilinear patterns are also prominent in Maori tattoos. Today the moko (tattoo) is painted on and is usually only seen during official ceremonies or during Maori folklore concerts.

Along with the spiral the most important element of traditional Maori carving is the human form, which can be portrayed in either a highly stylized or fairly realistic fashion. Characteristic of these carved figures or tiki are the large heads, the three-fingered hand and the outthrust tongue which was an expression of defiance and warded against evil.

Perhaps the best known of all Maori ornaments is the *hei-tiki*. This neck pendant (*hei* 'hanging', *tiki*, the human form') portrays an embryo-like figure with prominent eyes, tongue and a head that is turned to one side. In Maori tradition *tiki* figures symbolise an ancestor or series of ancestors and are still considered by many Maori as sacred. They were, and still are, carved from wood, stone, bone and, most prized of all greenstone (jade). Cheap plastic tikis are sold in just about every souvenir shop.

The crowning achievement of traditional Maori culture was the *whare whakairo* (carved meeting house). No other Polynesian culture has ever produced ·such a magnificently decorated building; intricate carvings covered almost all the wooden surfaces of the façade and interior, the gaps between the carved interior wall posts were filled with woven reed panels known as *kotukutuku* and painted *kowhaiwhai* patterns decorated the rafters. But the purpose behind all this was by no means purely decorative; the carvings, and indeed the building as a whole, symbolised the tribal ancestors and were a way of preserving tribal history and legends. A particularly fine example of a *whare whakairo* is the meeting house at Waitangi, in the Bay of Islands.

Song and dance also form an essential part of Maori culture. The action songs that are commonly staged for tourists in places like Rotorua combine, as the name suggests, elements of both. The rhythmic actions in these songs help to convey the meaning of the words. During the famous *poi* dance the musical rhythms are complimented by the graceful swinging of a ball attached to a length of string, the *poi*. In contrast to the poi dance the *haka taparahi* is only performed by men. The dance consists of vigorous movements accompanied by a shouted chant and this is the famous haka that is performed by the All Black rugby team before a match. It is not a war dance as many people assume. The true war dance is the *peruperu* and though similar to the haka taparahi it is always performed with weapons — something that would no doubt have given the All Blacks an unfair advantage at the start of a game.

Environmental Issues

It took European settlers little more than a hundred years to cut down and burn vast tracts of native forest in order to win land for settlement and farming. Where green pastures dotted with fluffy white sheep (60 million of them!) now extend as far as the eye can see were once dense forests filled with the sound of birds. Some of these birds are now either extinct or extremely rare as they could neither cope with the rapid loss of habitat nor with the introduction of predatory animals (cats, weasels). Today seven species of native bird are listed as endangered.

Deer, wild pigs, rabbits and opossums (plant-eating marsupial native to Australia) were also introduced by the early settlers and, in the absence of their natural enemies, they have multiplied to the point where they are pests. The large populations of red deer and opossums, for instance, have had a particularly devastating effect on the native forests. Hunting of these, and other introduced animals, is therefore encouraged.

In spite of the sins of the past there is still much worth protecting in New Zealand and New Zealanders are becoming more and more conscious of the need to save what is left of their unique and often breathtaking natural environment. Large areas of land are protected as national or forest parks and laws have been passed that force developers to consider the ecological aspects of any projects they are planning. Recycling is becoming more commonplace throughout the country and environmentally friendly products are appearing more frequently on supermarket shelves. Unleaded petrol has been available in New Zealand since 1988.

New Zealand follows an anti-nuclear policy and refuses to allow nuclear-powered or armed ships into its harbours. The government has also protested against nuclear testing by the French in the Pacific. The greenhouse effect and the destruction of the ozone layer in the earth's atmosphere are also matters of grave concern. New Zealand is relatively close to Antarctica where ozone depletion is especially dramatic.

Flora and Fauna

Flora

New Zealand's unique flora and fauna evolved in the course of millions of years of isolation. When the first Polynesians arrived they found a land almost entirely covered by evergreen rainforests. The far north of the North Island was dominated by impressive forests of giant kauri whereas much of the rest of the island was covered by equally impressive podocarp forests. Podocarps like rimu, totara and miro belong to an extremely ancient family of conifers that first appeared around 190 million years ago, when dinosaurs still roamed the earth. In the South Island the southern beech forests dominated but large areas were also covered by tussock grasslands.

Kowhai flowers

One of New Zealand's 180 species of fern

Today native forests cover only around 20 per cent of the total land area. Characteristic of the New Zealand forest or 'bush', as the locals prefer to call it, are the many different species of fern. There are in fact around 180 different species of fern to be found here but one of the prettiest is the ponga or silver fern, a large tree fern that is found in most New Zealand rainforests. The prettiest of New Zealand's flowering trees are the kowhai with its delicate yellow flowers and the pohutukawa which flowers bright red around Christmas time. New Zealand's only native palm tree is the Nikau. It is mainly found in the North Island but there are also significant stands on the South Island's west coast.

Fauna

New Zealand was originally a land that was virtually devoid of mammals. Except for two species of native bats the tree tops and forest floors were dominated by birds. In the absence of ground dwelling predators flightless birds such as the now extinct giant moa were able to flourish but the advent of man and the animals he introduced were to prove to be the nemesis of many. Of the flightless birds that still survive it is New Zealand's national bird, the kiwi, that is most well-known. Some of the more common birds that visitors are likely to see when walking through the native bush are the flightless weka, the insect eating fantail and the colourful native pigeon. Among New Zealand's rarest birds are the flightless takahe, a flightless parrot known as the kakapo and the kokako, a member of the wattle-bird family which can fly, but only just. Several species of penguins are found along the coasts of both main islands.

There are no snakes in New Zealand but the reptiles are represented by about 30 species of lizard and the remarkable Tuatara (*Sphenodon punctatus*). Though it looks like a lizard the tuatara is in fact the last survivor of an ancient family of reptiles that reached its peak during the age of the dinosaurs, some 200 million years ago. Once found on the mainland it now only survives on a few scattered off-shore islands.

A variety of marine mammals frequent the country's coastal waters and visitors have a good chance of seeing fur seals, dolphins and, in the vicinity of Kaikoura, even whales. All of New Zealand's land mammals have been introduced. Red deer, wapiti, chamois and wild pigs are just a few of the introduced animals that may be hunted for sport.

New Zealand's only poisonous spider is the katipo. It is found on beaches all over the North Island (but mainly on the west coast of the North Island) and as far south as Dunedin. Though its bite can be fatal relatively few deaths have ever been recorded. Like the North American black widow spider, to which it is related, the katipo is black with a red mark on its back. Only the female is dangerous and as the spiders are shy it is unlikely that you will have any unpleasant encounters.

Food and Drink

In recent years the quality and variety of restaurants in the larger towns and cities has improved greatly. Auckland, Wellington and Christchurch have a particularly cosmopolitan range of restaurants; Italian, Indian, Mexican, Thai and Chinese are just a few of the international cuisines to choose from. However in the smaller centres the basic sausage and chips establishments, where the price is right but the ambience non-existent, are still quite common.

The traditional take-away foods are fish and chips (French fries) and meat pies. Meat pies are sold in dairies (small corner shops which sell milk, bread and a little bit of everything else) and also in some pubs and tearooms. Chinese takeaways are also very popular and can be great value for money. American fast food chains such as McDonald's and Kentucky Fried Chicken are found in many of the larger towns and cities.

Some excellent seafood is available in New Zealand and it is worth trying such local delicacies as whitebait, oysters, paua (abalone) and crayfish (lobster). Among the tastiest fish caught in New Zealand coastal waters are snapper, tarakihi and a deep-sea fish known as orange roughy. Not a seafood but a New Zealand classic is roast lamb with mint sauce.

Those who are catering for themselves will find the shops well stocked with a wide variety of fresh foods. Fruit and vegetables are quite cheap during the summer and invariably of excellent quality. Try the kumara, a delicious variety of sweet potato that many Kiwis like to serve with their roast meals. The large supermarket chains such as New World, Pak 'n Save and Write Price are of course the cheapest places to go shopping.

A strong cup of tea in the morning and a cold beer after work is still a fairly accurate summary of the drinking habits of most New Zealanders. Though there used to be a lot of private breweries almost all the local beer is now brewed by just two companies. Among the more popular brands are DB and Lion but it is worth seeking out the such famous local brews as Black Mac (a dark beer) and Pink Elephant, both of which come from the Nelson-Marlborough area. Places where beer is brewed and consumed on the premises include the Purangi Winery near Whitianga on the Coromandel and Shakespeare Tavern & Brewery in Auckland. Ask the locals for other tips.

Wine consumption is growing in New Zealand and some of the country's white wines rank with the best in the world. Good places to go wine tasting include the Blenheim region in the South Island and the Hawke's Bay region in the North Island.

A worthwhile investment for all those who like to conclude an evening with a nice glass of wine and an appetising meal is *Michael Guy's Eating Out & Wine Guide*, which is updated annually. Another useful book is *The Great NZ Restaurant Guide* by Denis Robinson. Both are available in local bookshops.

Thermal activity, Rotorua

Geography and Geology

New Zealand is located in the South Pacific, approximately 2,000km (1,243 miles) to the south-east of Australia from which it is separated by the Tasman Sea. Stretching 1,600km (994 miles) from north to south New Zealand consists of two main islands (North Island and South Island) and a number of smaller islands, the largest of which is Stewart Island at the southern end of the South Island. The country's total land area exceeds that of Great Britain and the North and South Islands have altogether nearly 7,000km (4,350 miles) of coastline.

According to the theory of plate tectonics the earth's surface is divided up into a number of separate plates which are constantly moving. New Zealand lies in a region where the Pacific plate collides with the Indo-Australian plate. The tremendous pressures that are built up in this collision zone are released in the form of sometimes violent seismic and volcanic activity. This explains New Zealand's susceptibility to earthquakes and the impressive volcanoes and geothermal activity which visitors can see in the area of Rotorua and Tongariro National Park.

The colliding tectonic plates are also responsible for the formation of the South Island's most distinctive geographical feature; the Southern Alps or Main Divide, New Zealand's highest range of mountains. The Southern Alps extend along virtually the entire length of the South Island and are continuing to rise at the rate of about 10mm per year. The hills and mountain ranges that extend through the North Island from Wellington to East Cape are also a part of this mountain building process but the North Island's highest mountain, Mount Ruapehu, was formed by volcanic activity.

During the Ice Ages much of the country was covered by a thick mantle of snow and ice. Relics of those times are most clearly evident in the South Island. They include the beautiful lakes near Queenstown and the magnificent fiords of Fiordland National Park which were, like the lakes, gouged out by vast rivers of ice. Among the most well-known of the glaciers that still exist in the South Island are Fox and Franz Josef Glaciers on the west coast and the mighty Tasman Glacier, which is New Zealand's largest.

National Parks

New Zealand's first national park was created in 1887 and at present there are twelve, each of which is discussed in the main text. It is intended that a thirteenth, Kahurangi National Park will be gazetted in November 1995. The central purpose of these parks is to preserve New Zealand's remaining wilderness areas in their natural state but public access is allowed and encouraged insofar as it is consistent with the aims of preservation.

New Zealand's twenty forest parks offer a lesser degree of protection for some of the country's most beautiful forest and mountain scenery. As is the case with the national parks they are open to the public for recreational purposes but a certain amount of selective logging for native timbers and other, strictly controlled, commercial activities are also allowed.

The forest parks and above all the national parks are a major attraction for outdoor enthusiasts from all over the world. Most of the parks offer a well marked network of hiking trails and provide accommodation in the form of simple huts. A visit to one of these parks is a must for all those who want to appreciate New Zealand's natural beauty in its most untouched form.

Politics and Economy

Politics

New Zealand is a constitutional monarchy with Queen Elizabeth II of Great Britain as head of state. Her representative in New Zealand is the Governor-General who is appointed on the recommendation of the New Zealand government for a 5 year period. However the governor-general's functions are only ceremonial, real power lies in the hands of the Prime Minister and his cabinet of government ministers.

The two main political parties are National (conservative) and Labour. Elections take place every 3 years and all those who are over 18 years of age are eligible to vote. New Zealand's government is modelled on the British parliamentary system but in New Zealand the upper house was abolished in 1950. All legislation is now passed through the House of Representatives (formerly the lower house of parliament) which has 99 members. The leader of the political party that wins a majority of seats in the House of Representatives automatically becomes Prime Minister.

Growing dissatisfaction with what has in effect been a two-party system of government has greatly increased the desire for electoral reform. In the 1993 elections the question of proportional representation was put to the vote and the public decided overwhelmingly in its favour. The next elections will be held using the proportional system which will mean that smaller parties will now have a far greater chance of winning a seat in parliament. The National Party led by Prime Minister Jim Bolger won the 1993 general election by a one seat majority.

Economy

New Zealand is an agricultural country and its highly mechanised farms are among the most efficient in the world. The main exports are meat, wool and dairy products. However there has been an effort in recent decades to diversify exports and commodities produced by the forestry, horticultural, manufacturing and fishing industries are of growing significance. The principal trading partners are Australia, the European Community, Japan and the USA. Trade with the Middle East, Eastern Europe and Asia is also important. The influence of tourism on the economy has increased dramatically in recent years and the tourist industry is now one of the main earners of overseas funds.

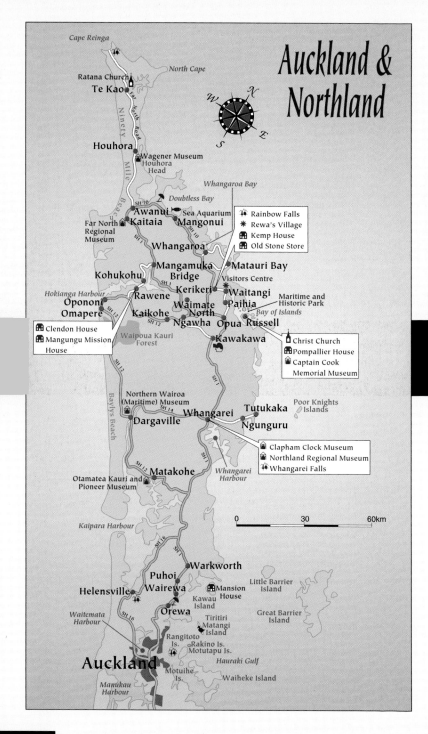

Auckland & Northland

Cape Reinga

North Cape

Ratana Church
Te Kao

Houhora

Wagener Museum
Houhora
Head

Ninety Mile Beach

Far North Road

Whangaroa Bay

SH 10   Doubtless Bay

Awanui   Sea Aquarium
Kaitaia   **Mangonui**
Far North Regional Museum

SH 1

Whangaroa

	Rainbow Falls
	Rewa's Village
	Kemp House
	Old Stone Store

Mangamuka Bridge   **Matauri Bay**

Kohukohu   SH 1   Visitors Centre

Hokianga Harbour   **Kerikeri**

Rawene   **Waitangi**

Opononi   **Waimate North**   **Paihia**   Maritime and Historic Park

Omapere   SH 12   **Kaikohe**   Bay of Islands

| | Clendon House |
| | Mangungu Mission House |

Ngawha   **Opua**   **Russell**

Kawakawa

	Christ Church
	Pompallier House
	Captain Cook Memorial Museum

Waipoua Kauri Forest

SH 12

Northern Wairoa (Maritime) Museum

SH 14   **Whangarei**   **Tutukaka**

Poor Knights Islands

Dargaville   **Ngunguru**

	Clapham Clock Museum
	Northland Regional Museum
	Whangarei Falls

Bayly's Beach

SH 12   **Matakohe**   Whangarei Harbour

Otamatea Kauri and Pioneer Museum

Kaipara Harbour

0   30   60km

SH 16

Warkworth

Puhoi   Little Barrier Island

Helensville   **Wairewa**   Mansion House

Kawau Island

SH 16   **Orewa**

Great Barrier Island

Waitemata Harbour   Tiritiri Matangi Island

Rangitoto Is.   Rakino Is.
Motutapu Is.

Auckland   Hauraki Gulf

Motuihe Is.   Waiheke Island

Manukau Harbour

Auckland & Northland

1

For most foreign visitors Auckland is the gateway to New Zealand. It is also the country's largest city and has the largest Polynesian population of any city in the world. But the city is not just a sprawling metropolis of concrete and glass; Aucklanders are blessed with two beautiful harbours and there are more than 100 beaches within an hour's drive of the city centre. With the sparkling waters of the Hauraki Gulf more or less lapping at the doorstep it is not surprising to find that many of the locals are keen yachtsmen or -women, a fact that has earned Auckland a nickname as 'the City of Sails'.

Northland is the region stretching north of Auckland. Not only is it one of the most picturesque parts of New Zealand but the subtropical climate makes its superb beaches attractive even in winter. Among the many scenic attractions are the Bay of Islands, Ninety Mile Beach and Waipoua Kauri Forest. Boat trips around the Bay of Islands, yachting, scuba diving and big game fishing are favourite activities of visitors to this region.

above: Auckland harbour

Auckland

A good place to start a walk around the city centre is on Queen Elizabeth II Square at the foot of Queen Street. There is a branch of the Auckland Visitor Centre located here where visitors can arm themselves with a free map and whatever other information they might need before setting off. Just a little north of the square is the waterfront from where boats depart on a variety of cruises around the harbour and into the Hauraki Gulf.

Not far from the information kiosk, on Hobson Wharf, is the **Maritime Museum**. This interesting 'hands-on' museum offers visitors a fascinating insight into the country's seafaring history. There are exhibits explaining how the Maori migrated across the Pacific to New Zealand as well as on the country's European discoverers Abel Tasman and Captain James Cook. On display here is the world's first jet boat, the *Hamilton Jet*, which was invented by the New Zealander William Hamilton in 1957. In the museum workshops sailmakers, woodturners and boatbuilders can be seen at work. Next door on Princes Wharf are the **Dockside Markets**. This large covered market offers arts and crafts as well as tasty food from various snack stalls.

Looking towards Auckland's busy main shopping street from Queen Elizabeth Square it is hard to imagine that in the 1840s Queen Street was no more than a bush-covered gully. It is certainly worth the stroll uphill from the harbour area if only to browse through Whitcoull's Bookshop with its good selection of New Zealand literature or one of the various souvenir shops. Only a short way up the street, on the left hand side of the road is Vulcan Lane. If it is time for a cup of coffee then one of the sidewalk cafés here might be just the thing.

Continuing on up hill one eventually passes Aotea Square where the main Auckland Visitor Centre is situated. From here the road climbs somewhat more steeply past the palms of Myers Park (right-hand side of road) and a few very inviting little ethnic restaurants, on the left-hand side. Of these the Caravanserai Tea House and Hasan Baba have the more atmospheric interiors but the Baan Thai, though not so nicely decorated, offers good Thai food at reasonable prices.

Apart from this section of Queen Street there are many other areas in Auckland where it is possible to try good food, in conducive surroundings and at a reasonable price. What is rather astonishing is the sheer number of restaurants offering exotic cuisine in a country where only a decade before a portion of crinkly *pommes frites* with steak was considered the culinary non plus ultra. Whether Middle Eastern, Vietnamese, Mexican, Turkish, Indian or Japanese; it is all here.

More of Auckland's cosmopolitan character can be discovered by turning right near the top of Queen Street into Karangahape Road (also known simply as 'K. Road'). Here it is possible to find greengrocer's shops catering to the taste-buds of the city's Asian and Polynesian population as well as a few seedy sex shops and massage parlours. At 283 K. Road the Polynesian Bookshop has some excellent titles for those with a deeper interest in Polynesian culture. Popular cafés in K. Road include Urbi et Orbi and the Verona Café. The Vesuvio restaurant has been recommended for its good Italian food.

To reach the peace and quiet of the **Auckland Domain**, which is the largest area of parkland close to the city centre, continue back along Karangahape Road, cross the Grafton Bridge, and follow Park Road. Buses to the Domain (Nos 63, 64 or 65) leave from the Downtown Bus Terminal on Commerce Street, only a short distance from the information kiosk at the foot of Queen Street.

Located within the Domain is the excellent **Auckland Museum** which houses the largest collection of Maori artefacts in the world, along with some fine displays of art and culture from the South Pacific region. Of particular interest in the Maori section is a magnificent 25m (82ft) war canoe and a carved meeting house which originally stood near Thames on the Coromandel Peninsula. A highlight of the natural history section is a model of the extinct giant moa.

If possible it is a good idea to try and make sure a visit to the museum coincides with one of the concerts put on by the Pounamu Cultural Group. These performances of traditional Maori songs and dances take place at 11.15am and 1.30pm. Visitors who arrive early enough can combine the concert with one of the very informative guided tours of the Maori galleries that take place at 10.30am and 12.45pm.

To the north-east and east of the Domain is the old suburb of Parnell. Here a number of Auckland's historic buildings have managed to escape the developers' bulldozers and the energetic might like to continue the walk through Parnell Village before returning to Queen Street via the University and Albert Park. Otherwise Parnell can be saved for later as it is only a short bus trip from the inner city.

If, however, the legs allow it then leave the Domain along Domain Drive and head for Ayr Street, just off Parnell Road. Situated here are **Ewelme Cottage** (1864) and **Kinder House** (1858), two fine old Victorian homes that are both open to the public. Further along Parnell Road the **Holy Trinity Cathedral** is also worth a look and from here it is not far to **Parnell Village**.

The village is a cluster of colonial buildings along Parnell Road that have been restored as a trendy shopping complex complete with a quaint Victorian atmosphere. There are a number of handicrafts shops here as well as some nice, if somewhat pricey, cafés and restaurants. An additional plus for all those who are spending the weekend in town is that all the shops are open seven days a week. From the village it is about half an hour on foot back to Queen Street.

Those who have not continued through Parnell can leave the Domain via Stanley Street and then follow Grafton Road and Alfred Street through the university grounds to **Albert Park**. Next to the park, on the corner of Kitchener Street and Wellesly Street East, is the **Auckland City Art Gallery**. The gallery's collection of New Zealand art is the largest and most comprehensive in the country and includes works by such important New Zealand artists as Toss Woollaston, Colin McCahon and

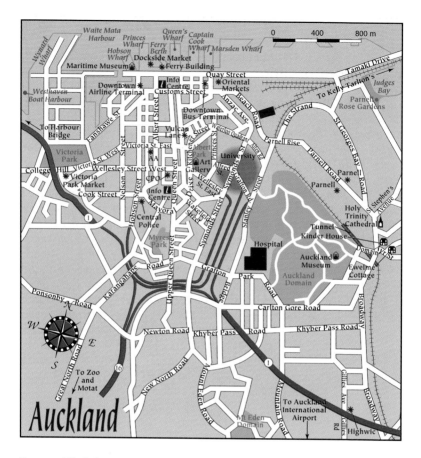

Auckland

Frances Hodgkins. Among the more important names in the gallery's European collection are Gainsborough, Turner and Bassano. From Albert Park it is no longer far to Queen Street and the start of this walk at Queen Elizabeth Square.

Because Auckland sprawls over a huge area that includes most of the islands of the Hauraki Gulf as well as the Auckland isthmus itself it is not surprising that a number of attractions lie outside the scope of an inner city walk and are best visited by either bus, car or boat. With this in mind it is worth considering getting either a Busabout Pass or the United Airlines Explorer Bus Pass. Both these all day bus passes are available at a modest price and save the hassles of parking. Fullers Cruises offer an all day boat pass they call the Harbour Explorer which is also good value (see Additional Information).

The **Museum of Transport and Technology** (MOTAT) on Great North Road, is a 10 minute drive from downtown Auckland via the North Western Motorway. Among the many machines on display are two aircraft designed by pioneer aviator Richard Pearse, who some claim became airborne in 1902, ahead of the Wright Brothers. At MOTAT 2, a separate site a short distance away, there is an impressive collection of historic aircraft. A vintage tram links MOTAT with **Auckland Zoo** where the local stars are the kiwis and tuataras but lions, elephants and other old favourites are also present.

For many an even greater attraction than the zoo is **Kelly Tarlton's Underwater World,** only 6km (3¹/₂ miles) from the city centre on Tamaki Drive. Here one has the unique opportunity of experiencing what it is like to go diving in New Zealand's coastal waters and to travel in Antarctica without getting wet or freezing in the process! In the main aquarium section a moving walkway goes through a clear acrylic tunnel that allows visitors to experience the sensation of having schools of fish and even sharks swim around them. The Antarctic Encounter is a recent addition. In this experience a trip through the south polar ice is vividly simulated with animated killer whale and a snow storm adding to the thrills. All in all Kelly Tarlton's is probably the closest most of us will ever come to one of the world's most extreme environments.

Though it may not look like it now the narrow neck of land over which Auckland spreads itself was also what one might call an extreme environment. Only a few tens of thousands of years ago the Auckland isthmus was formed by the ash and lava spewed forth by over 60 volcanoes.

*Auckland
Harbour*

Though, in the course of time, many of the smaller cones have since disappeared the larger peaks have been preserved and today they provide excellent viewpoints over Auckland and its surroundings.

Perhaps the best known of Auckland's extinct volcanoes is **One Tree Hill** 183m (600ft). Like many of the other volcanic cones it was once the site of a fortified Maori settlement or *pa*. It has been estimated that this *pa* could hold around 4,000 defenders and its massive earthworks are still clearly visible. The lone pine tree that now stands on the summit was planted to replace the original totara tree that gave the hill its name. This totara, which was sacred to the Maori, was cut down by vandals during the early period of settlement.

At the foot of the hill, in Cornwall Park, is **Acacia Cottage**. Built in 1841 it is the city's oldest building. Though not as old two other Victorian homes worth visiting are **Alberton**, to the north-west of One Tree Hill at 100 Mt Albert Road, and **Highwic**, at 40 Gillies Avenue, a short distance south of the Auckland Domain. Further afield more of Auckland's colonial past can be seen at Howick Historical Village, a restored military settlement about a twenty minute drive south-east of the city centre.

A bit further north of One Tree Hill and only a five minute drive from Queen Street is the volcanic cone of **Mount Eden** 196m (643ft). Though there are also the remains of a *pa* on the hill's slopes it is the best view in Auckland that leads most people to the summit. From here one can look out over the entire Auckland isthmus and towards the islands of the Hauraki Gulf beyond.

Hauraki Gulf Maritime Park

The sheltered waters of the Hauraki Gulf are dotted with islands, forty-seven of which fall within the boundaries of the maritime park. Though a number of the islands can be easily reached from Auckland some require special permission from the Department of Conservation (DOC) before they can be visited and others are strictly off limits. The reason for such restricted access is that a few of the more remote islands serve as a last refuge for plants and birds that are now very rare or no longer present on the mainland.

Most boats to the islands leave from near the Ferry Building on the Auckland waterfront, not far from the foot of Queen Street. Fullers runs regular trips to Waiheke, Rangitoto, Great Barrier, Motuihe and Rakino Islands. Gulf Trans operates from Wynyard Wharf to Great Barrier and the schooner Te Aroha sails during the summer from Captain Cook Wharf to Little Barrier and Tiritiri Matangi Islands — both wharfs are within walking distance of the Ferry Building.

Not included in the park but only half an hour away from Auckland is **Waiheke Island**. Its accessibility, great beaches, and a good range of accommodation make this the most visited island in the Gulf. Sea kayaks can be hired on the island and there are some good walking trails for those who prefer to stay on dry land. The small resident population consists of artists, farmers, pensioners and a few enviable business people who commute to Auckland City.

Included within the maritime park and joined to each other by a causeway are **Rangitoto** and **Motutapu islands**. Of the two it is Rangitoto that is the more interesting. This bush-clad island was formed by a series of volcanic eruptions, the most recent of which took place only 250 years ago. But since then the volcano has been a picture of tranquillity and people have been coming here for picnics and to walk through a beautiful forest of red-flowering pohutukawas for close to a century.

A 'must' when on the island is the walk from the wharf to the island's summit which takes about an hour. The views from the crater rim are spectacular. Another track branches off the summit walk to some interesting lava caves (30 minutes return). As the volcanic terrain is very rough, good walking shoes are essential. For those who want to stay longer the only accommodation is a simple camp-site on Motutapu Island.

About a two hour boat trip from Auckland **Great Barrier** is the largest island in the Gulf. With its fine beaches and unspoiled stands of native forest this sparsely inhabited island is the perfect escape for all those who love the outdoors. Favourite activities on Great Barrier, or Aotea as it is known by the Maori, include mountain biking, tramping, scuba diving, surfing and sea kayaking. Though a wide range of accommodation is available the eating out possibilities are mainly limited to Tryphena, the island's main town. There are, however, a few stores (at Tryphena, Claris and Whangaparapara) where foodstuffs and other basic necessities can be bought.

Whereas only parts of Great Barrier are included within the maritime park **Little Barrier Island** enjoys complete protection as it has the last significant area of native forest unaffected by introduced animals in the country. Among the rare native birds that have found refuge in Little Barrier's virtually undisturbed rainforest are the flightless kakapo parrot and the stitchbird. As there is no ferry service, and access is anyway very restricted, it is probably easiest to get there on a nature tour with the schooner *Te Aroha* (see Useful Information section: Auckland page 47).

More easily accessible is the island of **Tiritiri Matangi**. This wildlife sanctuary offers the unique opportunity of seeing some of New Zealand's, and the world's, rarest birds in the wild. Endangered native birds that may be spotted here include the flightless takahe, saddlebacks, red-crowned parakeets and New Zealand's rarest species of duck, the brown teal.

Motuihe and **Rakino islands**, with their fine sandy beaches, can be visited on Fullers' very popular mail run. This leisurely cruise takes you around the islands and bays of the inner gulf and lasts the whole day. For a description of Kawau Island see the following section on Northland.

Now if one has had one's fill of Auckland but not of beaches, sea and sun then there is only one thing for it: cross Auckland's harbour bridge with its 'Nippon Clippons' (two extra lanes on both sides added by Japanese engineers) and head for sunny Northland.

Route 1 • Northland

State Highway 1 (SH1) winds its way north in a leisurely fashion, passing through small farming towns and pockets of forest, with brief forays to the coast, on its unhurried path to the sun-soaked Bay of Islands and Kaitaia in the far north of Northland. Not far from Auckland both **Orewa** and **Waiwera** on the Hibiscus coast beckon with lovely white-sand beaches but Waiwera can offer thermal springs as an additional attraction. To get to the excellent beaches on Whangaparaoa peninsula leave the highway at Silverdale.

Only a bit further up the road from Waiwera **Puhoi's** atmospheric pub with its photographs and memorabilia from the pioneer days is a great place to quench the thirst after a day on the beach. From tiny Puhoi it is another 50km (31miles) to Warkworth.

Warkworth is not much bigger than Puhoi but the satellite station located near here gives the place a certain degree of importance. Once again there are plenty of nice beaches in the vicinity but it is the possibility of an excursion to **Kawau Island** that recommends a longer stop. The boat leaves from Sandspit, just east of Warkworth. The island was once home to the colonial Governor and later Premier Sir George Grey and his old residence, Mansion House (1844), can be visited.

From Warkworth the road turns inland to Wellsford, after which it continues north, briefly skirting the coast between Waipu and Ruakaka, before arriving in Whangarei.

With a population of 44,000 **Whangarei** is already a city by New Zealand standards and is Northland's largest and most important commercial centre. Less reliant than other towns in this region on tourism the city is a deep-sea port with oil refining, glass-making and ship building belonging to its main industries. The best views over the city and harbour are from Mount Parahaki.

Downtown the Clapham Clock Museum has a collection of over 500 clocks, the oldest of which date back to the seventeenth century. The Northland Regional Museum lies about 6km (3¹/₂ miles) south-west of town on the road (SH14) to Dargaville. Of interest here is a colonial homestead, a kiwi house and a vintage steam train which puffs its way through the museum park in summer. Popular beaches within reach of Whangarei are at Ngunguru and Sandy Bay. On the road to Ngunguru it is worth stopping for a look at the picturesque **Whangarei Falls**.

An excursion to the **Poor Knights Islands** can be thoroughly recommended for scuba diving enthusiasts. Departure point is **Tutukaka**, only a short distance north of Ngunguru. The waters around these islands are teeming with exotic, brightly coloured fish and offer a diving experience scarcely to be rivalled anywhere else off the New Zealand coast.

Some 55km (34 miles) north of Whangarei the town of **Kawakawa** is unusual in that it shares its main street with the railway. In summer a vintage steam train does regular trips from here to Opua. An attraction only a few kilometres south of town are the glow-worms in the Waiomio Caves. From Kawakawa a secondary road leads to the coast and Paihia.

Sunset over the Bay of Islands

The Bay of Islands

The Bay of Islands was named by Captain Cook in 1769 and it was not all that long before it became the site of New Zealand's first European settlement; a rough, brawling port known as Kororareka (Russell). The brothels and grog shops of yore have of course long since disappeared and the Bay townships are now characterised by the bustling activities of boat tour companies, kayak hire firms and the thousands of tourists they serve. And who can blame them all for coming? With its sheltered waters being ideal for boating, fishing and swimming, and with a wonderful climate on top, the Bay is the kind of place that many a tourist dreams of.

A large number of the 150 or so islands to be found in the Bay are included within the **Bay of Islands Maritime and Historic Park**. For information about walks and camping in the park, which not only includes the islands but also stretches of coastal land, it is best to contact the park information centre in Russell or the DOC office in Kerikeri.

Paihia is the traditional base for tourists who wish to explore the Bay of Islands. From here one can either embark on a big game fishing trip or simply enjoy a leisurely island cruise. Probably the best of these cruises out of Paihia or Russell is the daily Cream Trip, a $5^1/_2$ hour tour of the lovely Bay and its many islands. The tour recalls the days when milk and cream was collected by boat from isolated island farms. Other tours that can be recommended are the Cape Brett Trip and a romantic cruise aboard the sailing ship *R. Tucker Thompson*.

There is not a great deal to see in Paihia itself, though Kelly Tarlton's Shipwreck Museum is certainly worth a closer look. The museum is housed appropriately enough in an old sailing ship and displays an interesting assortment of booty salvaged from the many wrecks to be found in New Zealand waters. The café on board offers light meals but is rather expensive.

Waitangi lies across the bridge over the Waitangi River, a short distance north of Paihia. It was here, in 1840, that the controversial Treaty of Waitangi was signed and New Zealand became a part of the British Empire. In return for handing over sovereignty to the British Crown the Maori chiefs were granted the rights of British subjects and were also guaranteed continued possession of their lands and other resources. Unfortunately the promises in print were not carried out in fact and the treaty has been a point of contention between Maori and Pakeha (New Zealander of European descent) ever since. Although the signing of the treaty is still celebrated as Waitangi Day (6 February) many Maori people feel little cause to rejoice over past injustices. Ironically enough the name 'Waitangi' can be translated as 'weeping water'.

The treaty was signed on the lawn in front of the Treaty House, which was built as a home for the British government official James Busby in 1833. Kept inside the lovely old colonial dwelling are various historical artefacts, photographs and a copy of the treaty. Nearby is a Maori meeting house, the interior of which is decorated with superb carvings. Also a tribute to the Maori wood-carver's skill is the huge carved war canoe, which is lowered to water once a year on Waitangi Day. The whole complex is entered via a visitor's centre where it is possible to view a half hour audio-visual on the history of the place.

Thoroughly to be recommended for those with an interest in natural history is the Waitangi Mangrove Walk. This nature trail goes through one of the few mangrove forests in New Zealand. The trail leads to the pretty Haruru Falls and requires about 2 hours. A brochure describing the walk is available at the visitor's centre.

Russell can be reached by launch from Paihia but those who want to take their cars have to travel a little further south to **Opua**, where there is a car ferry (daily 6.40am-8.50pm. Friday until 9.50pm). There is an unsealed road that goes via Karetu and Waihaha to Russell but the trip takes much longer along this route.

Once known as Kororareka Russell was New Zealand's first European settlement. The earliest settlers, who began arriving around 1809, were a rough, brawling mixture of whalers, sealers, escaped convicts and adventurers. Such was the state of lawlessness in those wild colonial days that Kororareka was soon known as the 'Hell Hole of the Pacific' and one shocked missionary described it as 'a dreadful place — the very seat of Satan'. Rather than have the nation's first capital in a town more noted for its grog shops than law and order Captain William Hobson (who became New Zealand's first governor) decided on a spot further south at Okiato. Hobson chose the name of Russell for his new capital but it was not long before he transferred it to the more favourable site of Auckland (1840) — the capital was finally moved to Wellington in 1865 because of its more central location. The original Russell was eventually abandoned and in 1845 it was decided that Kororareka should shed the stigma attached to its old name by assuming that of Hobson's first short-lived capital.

Today this picturesque township flourishes as a centre for yachting and big game fishing. Those visitors who prefer it a bit quieter will find it makes a good alternative to Paihia as a base. Not many buildings from the original settlement are left to recall the colonial days but the few that still remain can be discovered in the course of an easy stroll. One reminder of more violent times are the bullet-holed walls of Christ Church, which survived the destruction of town by the Maori chief Hone Heke in 1845. Built in 1835 it is the country's oldest surviving church. Down on the waterfront Pompallier House (1842) was originally built to house the printing presses of New Zealand's first Catholic mission. Now the house functions as a working museum with its own vintage printery and tannery.

For the great Maori leader Hone Heke, and other chiefs who had quickly become disenchanted with the Treaty of Waitangi, the Union Jack flying from Flagstaff Hill (Maiti Hill) behind Russell was a symbol of exploitation and broken promises. Hone Heke chopped down the flag-pole four times and conducted a spirited resistance against British troops before he was finally defeated. A short, steep path leads up to this historic site from where a lovely panoramic view unfolds over the Bay.

Still on the theme of history the Captain Cook Memorial Museum has a large-scale model of the great navigator's ship *Endeavour* as its most interesting exhibit. The Duke of Marlborough Hotel also has a lot of history behind it but visitors who have worked up a healthy thirst need not despair, it is still a fully functioning pub and no museum. As a place to eat many people recommend the venerable old Gables restaurant which was founded way back in 1847.

The road onward leads north from Paihia to **Kerikeri**. The town is set near a picturesque inlet and is surrounded by orchards growing kiwifruit along with a mouth-watering variety of other subtropical fruits. Apart from its orchards Kerikeri is also renowned as an arts and crafts centre. Anybody looking for original souvenirs might well strike it lucky in a local handicraft shop. Two of New Zealand's oldest buildings are situated a couple of kilometres further north right next to the inlet. Kemp House was built in 1821 as a mission house and is the country's oldest surviving building. Still furnished in the style of the nineteenth century it is open to the public. Next door the Old Stone Store was built in 1833. It has retained its function as a shop but also has a small museum upstairs.

Other things to see around Kerikeri include Rewa's Village, a very interesting reconstruction of a pre-European Maori village on the other side of the inlet from the Stone Store, and Rainbow Falls, roughly 4km (2¹/₂ miles) outside of town.

Continuing along SH10 pass through Waipapa and Kapiro but then, if time allows, turn off before Kaeo for an excursion to **Matauri Bay**. The asphalt road soon changes to gravel but then the bumps and jolts are a small price to pay for a chance to get off the beaten track.

The road down to the coast from Matauri Bay township offers some terrific views, while the bay itself is graced with a lovely sandy beach. On a nearby hill is a memorial to the Greenpeace ship *Rainbow Warrior*. In an attempt to prevent the testing of nuclear bombs by the French at Mururoa Atoll the boat had regularly taken part in protest actions within the testing zone. On 10 July 1985 French agents sabotaged and sank it in Auckland harbour. A camera-man was killed in the incident. Now that the French have resumed testing this has once again met with spirited resistance on the part of Greenpeace and the New Zealand Government.

The coastal road passes close to a number of secluded beaches at Wainui and Tauranga Bay before arriving at **Whangaroa**. Lacking the crowds of the Bay of Islands this little town and its pretty harbour is the ideal place to get away from it all for a few days. Big game fishing fans can try their luck here but a relaxing pleasure cruise around the harbour can also be highly recommended.

Mangonui lies further north, beautifully situated at the southern tip of **Doubtless Bay**. The sea aquarium has an interesting display of living corals, sponges and other aquatic life from local waters. Doubtless Bay is lined with some magnificent beaches, though it is Coopers Beach that is most popular with the holiday crowds. The beach is fringed by ancient pohutukawa trees which make a stunning backdrop when, at Christmas, they flower bright red.

Awanui on SH10 is the point where the tour buses from Paihia or Kaitaia turn off for the trip to Cape Reinga and Ninety Mile Beach. The road is tar-sealed as far as Te Paki but it is not recommended that inexperienced motorists attempt the trip along the sands of Ninety Mile Beach.

The road to the Cape skirts Aupouri Forest on its way up the narrow Aupouri Peninsula. This man-made forest is composed of fast growing pine trees that were planted to secure drifting sand-dunes. Shortly before Houhora a road branches off to **Houhora Heads**. The 5km (3 miles) detour is especially worth it in good weather as there are some nice picnicking areas around the inlet. Another reason for this side trip is the excellent Wagener Museum, which has an extensive collection of Maori artefacts among its many interesting exhibits. Nearby is a camping ground and an old homestead built in the 1850s. At the old kauri gum digging town of **Houhora** is New Zealand's northernmost pub — an excuse for a drink if ever there was!

Over half-way to the Cape **Te Kao** is the largest Maori settlement on the peninsula. The town's humble skyline is dominated by the twin towers of the Ratana temple. Though derived from the Christian faith the Ratana church is deeply imbued with elements of Maori culture and pre-European spiritual belief. Further north the entrance to Parengarenga Harbour is the site of an impressive natural spectacle. In late February and early March thousands upon thousands of bar-tailed godwits gather here before leaving on their epic 12,000km (7,456 mile) journey to Siberia.

After Te Paki Station (the surroundings are managed by the government as Te Paki Coastal Park), where there are some simple camping

Bay of Islands

Stone Store, Kerikeri

sites, there is no other sign of human habitation until the lighthouse at ❋ **Cape Reinga**. Though the lighthouse is not open to the public visitors are compensated by the beautiful panoramic views; in good weather it is possible to see as far as the Three Kings Islands, which were sighted by Abel Tasman in 1643.

Below the lighthouse on a wave-battered promontory of rock is an ancient pohutukawa — it is said to be over 800 years old. Maori tradition has it that the spirits of the dead depart through the roots of the tree, into the ocean, on their final journey to the spiritual homeland of Hawaiki.

There is plenty of good walking in the area of the Cape and Te Paki Coastal Park. Information about the latter can be obtained from the Ranger, Waitiki Landing or at the information centre in Kaitaia. The Cape 🚶 Reinga Walkway is described in the book *Guide to Walkways — North Island*, published by the AA.

Despite the name **Ninety Mile Beach** stretches 'only' some sixty miles from west of Kaitaia to a point just short of Cape Maria Van Diemen in the far north. An unbroken stretch of white sand facing the Tasman Sea, the beach is also home to the toheroa, a prized New Zealand delicacy. These shellfish are protected and can only be harvested when populations have reached a satisfactory level.

The most comfortable way to appreciate the beautiful coastal scenery is on one of the bus tours starting from Kaitaia or the Bay of Islands. Private motorists must inform themselves about the tides before setting out. It should also be noted that most car rental firms do not allow their vehicles to be driven along the beach.

The town of **Kaitaia** is situated near the southern end of Ninety Mile Beach and is a good base for trips in the far north of the Northland region. Originally a Maori village Kaitaia started to expand with the arrival of Dalmatian (Croatian) gum diggers towards the end of the nineteenth century. More information about the gumfields is available at the Far 🏛 North Regional Museum which features an impressive display of polished kauri gum. Apart from the Cape Reinga tours there are also organised excursions to the historic gumfields starting from Kaitaia.

The route back to Auckland follows SH1 as far south as **Mangamuka Bridge** from where it takes a more scenic road to Kohukohu on the north shore of Hokianga Harbour. However those who wish to visit the historic ❋ mission station at **Waimate North** will have to continue along SH1 in the direction of Ohaeawai. This alternative also allows a dip in the hot springs near **Ngawha**, a few kilometres north-east of Kaikohe.

❋ A good place to get first impressions of the giant kauri tree is Omahuta Forest Sanctuary. The signposted access road is just a kilometre south of Mangamuka Bridge — from the turn off it is 13km (8 miles) to the car 🚶 park) . A half hour walk through native bush leads from here to a grove of kauris the largest of which, 'Hokianga', rises to a height of 54m (177ft). This sanctuary, along with the neighbouring Puketi Forest, is also home 🐦 to rare native birds such as kokakos, kaka parrots and kiwis. A splash of colour is sometimes provided by rosella parakeets, originally natives of Australia.

The road to Kohukohu enters a part of Northland virtually untouched by tourism. Here the clocks seem to tick slower, though Hokianga Harbour was once the scene of a lively kauri timber industry. However the majority of trees had already been felled by the early 1900s and with them went the region's prosperity. Once an important timber settlement **Kohukohu** now sits somewhat forgotten on the harbour shore. A car ferry links this small town to Rawene on the opposite side.

Rawene has a lovely setting near the harbour and is worth a brief stop if only to see Clendon House, a colonial building dating from the 1860s. Those with an interest in colonial history might also find the trip to Mangungu Mission House well worthwhile. Built by Wesleyan missionaries around 1838 it occupies an elevated site commanding wonderful views over the harbour. The mission house lies between Horeke and Rangiahua at the northern end of Hokianga Harbour.

The road south continues via the beach resorts of **Opononi** and **Omapere** before it enters **Waipoua Kauri Forest**, the largest remnant of the great forests that once covered Northland. Waipoua Kauri Forest is justly famed for the huge kauris that are still plentiful here. One veritable forest giant is known as *Tane Mahuta* (God of the Forest), an immense tree with an estimated age of 1,200 years, a girth of over 13m (42ft) and a height approaching 52m (171ft). It is the largest known tree in New Zealand. No less impressive is *Te Matua Ngahere* (Father of the Forest) which is 30m (98ft) high, has a girth exceeding 16m (52ft) and could be close to 2,000 years old. Both trees are signposted from the main road. A bit further south more kauri trees can be seen in the course of a walk through the smaller **Trounson Kauri Park**.

Dargaville is yet another Northland town that owes its origins to the kauri gum and timber industry. The main point of interest is the Northern Wairoa Museum (Maritime Museum) with its displays from the pioneering days, Maori artefacts and maritime exhibits. For a dip in the briny follow the road west to **Baylys Beach**.

SH12 follows the Wairoa River south of Dargaville before swinging east around Kaipara Harbour. The harbour is in fact a system of drowned river valleys and its shores are worth exploring for those seeking that pretty little spot away from it all. At **Matakohe** is one of Northland's best kauri museums, the Otamatea Kauri and Pioneer Museum. It boasts the world's largest collection of kauri gum in all its various forms; from unpolished lump to finely crafted ornament.

At Brynderwyn SH12 joins SH1 but rather than return directly to Auckland it is much nicer to ease one's way back into the big city by branching off at Wellsford and following SH16 along the eastern reaches of Kaipara Harbour. Near **Helensville** Parakai Hot Springs is the ideal place to relax after a long day's sightseeing. To Auckland it is only another 50km (31 miles) through the fruit and wine-growing country around Kumeu.

The Kauri
Giant of the Forest

The giant kauri (Agathis australis) can live for over 2,000 years, attain a girth of more than 20m (65ft) and exceed 50m (164ft) in height. Together with the American red woods (sequoias) it is not only one of the largest coni fers on earth but also one of the largest trees that has ever existed. Ancestors of the kauri already dominated the primeval forests of the Mesozoic era, over 200 million years ago. In New Zealand the kauri is only found in the north of the North Island but related trees of the same genus, Agathis, are also found in Southeast Asia and elsewhere in the South Pacific.

Though the Maori valued the mighty kauri for their dug-out canoes large-scale commercial exploitation did not begin until the arrival of the Europeans. The tree's long straight, branchless trunk was used for ship's masts and the durable timber was also highly prized for building and furniture. By the 1820s the kauri timber industry was well established and the trees were felled on a scale that would have left any of today's environmentalists in a state of nervous shock. The rainforests (the kauri forest' was actually a mixed forest made up of many different species, not just kauris) which once covered nearly all of Northland were devastated. In this region the original kauri forests now cover only 1 per cent of their former area.

Apart from the wood the kauri was also valued for its gum, which was used in the production of varnishes and linoleum. It provided the basis for a flourishing export industry and at the height of the gum boom (late nineteenth century) hundreds of gum diggers flocked to the gumfields of the Coromandel and Northland. They either tapped the gum directly from the tree or dug for fossilised gum that had been deposited by ancient forests many thousands of years ago. The gum trade reached its peak around 1900 and then slowly petered out as synthetically based varnishes began to dominate the market.

Additional Information

Accommodation & Eating Out

ACCOMMODATION

Auckland
International Backpackers Parnell *
8 Maunsell Rd, Parnell
☎ (09)358 4584

Aachen House **
(Bed & Breakfast)
39 Market Rd, Remuera
☎ (09)520 2329 Fax: (09)524 2898

Freeman's Travellers' Hotel **
(Bed & Breakfast)
65 Wellington St
☎ (09)376 5046 Fax: (09)376 4052

Hyatt Auckland Hotel ***
Cnr Princes St & Waterloo Quadrant
☎ (09)366 1234 Fax: (09)303 2932

Paihia
Lodge Eleven *
Cnr Kings Rd and MacMurray Rd
☎ (09)402 7487

Abba Villa **
21 School Rd
☎ (09)402 8066 Fax: (09)402 8066

Russell
Russell Lodge, Motel & Backpackers *
Chapel St
PO Box 33
☎ (09)403 7640 Fax: (09)403 7641

Duke of Marlborough Hotel ***
The Strand
PO Box 52
☎ (09)403 7829 Fax: (09)403 7760

Whangarei
Hatea House Hostel *
67 Hatea Drive
☎ (09)437 6174

Aaron Court Motel **
22 Wolfe St
Tel & Fax (09)438 9139
Freephone (0800)730 731

EATING OUT

Auckland
Caravanserai Tea House *
(Middle Eastern)
430 Queen Street
☎ (09)302 0244

Baan Thai **
(Thai)
456 Queen Street
☎ (09)366 4746

Poppadom **
(Indian)
55 Customs Street
☎ (09)379 8661

Vesuvio Restaurant **
(Italian)
501 Karangahape Road
☎ (09)379 4769

Paihia
Blue Marlin Diner *
Waterfront
☎ (09)402 7590

Café Over the Bay **
Waterfront
☎ (09)403 7080

Bistro 40 ***
40 Marsden Road
☎ (09)402 7444

Russell
The Gables ***
The Strand
☎ (09)403 7618

Whangarei
A'Fare Restaurant *
25 Water Street
☎ (09)438 8329

Café Monet ***
144 Bank Street
☎ (09)438 6282

Places to Visit: Auckland

Entry fees are payable unless otherwise stated.

HISTORIC PLACES

Alberton
100 Mt Albert Rd

Ewelme Cottage
14 Ayr St, Parnell

Highwic
40 Gillies Ave, Epsom
Open: the above are open daily
10.30am-12noon, 1-4.30pm, except Xmas and Good Friday.

Howick Historical Village
Bells Road, Lloyd Elsmore Park
Pakuranga
Bus: Howick bus from Downtown Bus Terminal.
Open: daily 10am-4pm.

Kinder House
2 Ayr St
Open: Monday-Friday 12noon-3pm.

Parnell Village
Parnell Road, Parnell
A picturesque cluster of shops in colonial style.
Bus: Busabout, United Airlines Explorer and buses 63, 64 & 65 from Downtown Bus Terminal.

MARKETS

China Oriental Markets
Cnr Quay St & Britomart Place
A great place for an oriental lunch in Downtown Auckland. Fashion, arts/crafts, souvenirs, herbalists and healers.
Open: daily 10am-6pm.

Dockside Markets
Princes Wharf, Quay St
Food stalls, crafts, souvenirs.
Open: Friday, Saturday, Sunday 9.30am-6pm.

Otara Markets
Newbury St (off East Tamaki Rd)
Otara
Unique Polynesian atmosphere. Food, clothes, arts & crafts.
Open: Saturday 6am-12 noon

Victoria Park Market
Opposite Victoria Park
Victoria St West
Art galleries, fashion boutiques, jewellery, souvenirs, cafes & restaurants.
Open: daily 9am-7pm.

MUSEUMS

Auckland City Art Gallery
Cnr Kitchener & Wellesley Streets
Open: daily 10am-4.30pm Entry to Ground Floor collection is free. Free guided tours 2pm Wednesday-Sunday.

Auckland Museum
Auckland Domain
Open: daily 10am-5pm (except Xmas day and Good Friday).
Perfomances of Maori Songs and Dances on most days at 11.15am & 1.30pm. Admission is charged for concerts. Further details ☎ 838 7876.
Admission to museum is free.

Hobson Wharf Maritime Museum
Hobson Wharf
Intersection of Quay & Hobson Streets
Open: Monday-Thursday 10am-6pm.
Friday-Sunday 10am-9pm.

MOTAT & NZ Science Centre
Great North Road
Western Springs
Bus: ARC (Pt Chevalier) bus 045 departs Customs St, downtown Auckland approx. every 15 minutes.
Open: Monday-Friday 9am-5pm (except Xmas Day). Weekends and public holidays 10am-5pm.
☎ 846 0199

OTHER ATTRACTIONS

Kelly Tarlton's Underwater World
23 Tamaki Drive
Orakei
Bus: No 72, 73, 74 & 75 departing Downtown Terminal. Also Busabout bus and United Airlines Explorer Bus.
Open: daily 9am-9pm.
☎ 528 0603

Pavilion of New Zealand
Montgomerie Road
Mangere (near International Airport)
Audiovisual shows provide an introduction to New Zealand's past and

present. Also live entertainment, kiwi fruit farm tours, horse riding and fishing — they guarantee you will catch one!
Bus: Airporter buses depart Downtown Airline Terminal and stop at Montgomerie Rd, only 3 minutes walk from Pavilion.
Open: 10am-4pm.

Zoo
Motions Road
Western Springs
Bus: Busabout bus or Pt Chevalier bus 045 from Customs St.
Open: daily except Xmas Day 9.30am-5.30pm (last admission 4.15pm)
☎ 378 1620

Useful Information: Auckland

Area Code: (09)

Consulates
Australia
Union House, 32-38 Quay St
☎ 303 2429

Canada
9th Floor, Jetset Centre, 48 Emily Place
☎ 309 3690

USA
General Building, Cnr Shortland & O'Connell Sts
☎ 303 2724

UK
Fay Richwhite Building, 151 Queen St
☎ 303 2973

Important Telephone Numbers
Emergency Chemist: ☎ 520 6634
Emergency Dental: ☎ 520 6609
Emergency Medical: ☎ 524 5943
Taxis: ☎ 300 3000

Post Offices
The main post office and poste restante service is located in the Bledisloe Building, Wellesley Street. Post offices are open Monday-Friday 9am-5pm.

Transport
Airport Transport
The Airbus departs from the Downtown Airline Terminal, cnr Quay and Albert Streets. The first bus leaves at 6.20am, the last bus at 9pm. From

Auckland International Airport the first bus leaves at 6.20am and the last one at 8.20pm. The journey takes about 40mins. For timetables ☎ (09)275 7685.
There are also shuttle buses offering door-to-door service: Super Shuttle ☎ 307 0500, Airport Shuttle ☎ 576 8904.

Bus Tours & Services
The Downtown Bus Terminal is between Commerce St & Britomart Place. Airport and Sightseeing buses depart from Downtown Airline Terminal and Old Ferry Building, Quay St.
     Apart from the Explorer and Busabout buses mentioned below many other companies also offer sightseeing tours around Auckland and further afield.
United Airlines Explorer Bus: includes a number of Auckland's major attractions on its route and passengers can get on and off whenever they wish. The Explorer All Day Bus Pass may be purchased at the Ferry Building, end of Queen St.
Departs: Ferry Building on an hourly basis, 10am-4pm daily.

Busabout All Day Bus Pass: valid on Auckland's Yellow Buses. Information and timetables available from information kiosk, Downtown Bus Terminal or ☎ Buz-A-Bus 366 6400. The Busabout Pass is available from the driver. It allows unlimited travel from 9am weekdays and at all times on the weekend and public holidays.

Harbour Trips & Hauraki Gulf Cruises
Most harbour services and cruises depart from Quay St, next to Ferry Building.

Fullers Cruises offers a variety of trips around the harbour and to various islands in the Hauraki Gulf (Rangitoto, Waiheke, Great Barrier and a few smaller islands). Boats depart from the piers near the Ferry Building. Tickets and information are available from Fullers Cruise Centre, ground floor of Ferry Building, Quay St. ☎ 373 3776 for information or 377 1771 for reservations.

Fullers *Harbour Explorer* is an all day or half day boat pass that allows passengers to get on and off at the various stops. The boat stops at Kelly Tarlton's, Rangitoto Island and Devonport. Boats depart daily at 9.30am, 11am, 2pm and 4pm.

Fullers *Mail Run* is an all day trip that takes in many of the islands and bays of the inner gulf. The boat departs Saturday, Sunday and Wednesday at 9.30am and arrives back in Auckland at 5.45pm.

Devonport Ferries are also operated by Fullers and depart daily from the city to the picturesque suburb of Devonport, on the other side of Waitemata Harbour. The scenic crossing takes 15 minutes. Boats depart from the Ferry Terminal, Quay St on a half hourly basis from 6.15am-7pm.

Gulf Trans, Wynyard Wharf, Auckland operates a ferry service three times per week to Great Barrier Island. For details ☎ 373 4036.

Natural history cruises of the Hauraki Gulf are offered by Adventure Cruising Co Ltd, PO Box 338, Auckland 1. ☎ 444 9342. The cruises take place aboard the historic schooner *Te Aroha* and vary in length from a single day to four days. Cruises are offered from November to April and depart from Captain Cook Wharf, Downtown Auckland.

Trains
Long distance trains and coaches depart from Auckland Central Railway Station, Beach Road. Freephone: 0800 802 802. Reservations are taken from 7am-9pm every day.

Places to Visit

ROUTE 1
Dargaville
Northern Wairoa Museum (Maritime Museum)
Harding Park
Open: daily 9am-4pm.

Helensville
Parakai Hot Springs (Aquatic Park)
4km south of town at Parakai
Open: daily 10am-10pm.

Horeke
Mangungu Mission House
Open: 12noon-4pm weekends and summer school holidays.

Houhora Heads
Wagener Museum
Open: daily 8am-5.30pm.

Kaitaia
Far North Regional Museum
Commerce Street
Open: Monday-Friday 10am-5pm. Weekends 1-5pm.

Kawau Island
Ferry departs several times daily. Earliest sailing is at 7.45am and last sailing at 2pm. Fullers Kawau Ferries Ltd also offers a variety of longer cruises on a daily basis in summer. The Royal Mail Run (New Zealand's longest by boat) departs at 10.30am daily. Departure point is Sandspit, east of Warkworth. For further information and reservations
☎ (09) 425 8006. Fax (09) 425 7650.

Kerikeri
Kemp House and Old Stone Store
Kerikeri Basin
Open: daily 10am-12.30pm, 1.30-4.30pm except Xmas and Good Friday.

Rewa's Village
Kerikeri Basin
Open: daily.

Matakohe
Otamatea Kauri & Pioneer Museum
Open: daily 9am-5pm. Refreshments at Gumdiggers Tearooms.

Paihia
Kelly Tarlton's Shipwreck Museum
Next to bridge, 500m south of Treaty House
Open: 10am-10pm. Café.

Rawene
Clendon House
Open: daily 10am-4pm except Xmas and Good Friday

Russell
Pompallier House
Open: daily 10am-5pm except Xmas and Good Friday.

*Russell Museum (Captain Cook Memorial
   Museum)*
York Street
Open: daily 10am-4pm.

Waimate North
Te Waimate Mission House
Open: daily 10am-12.30pm, 1.30-4.30pm
except Xmas and Good Friday.

Waiwera
Waiwera Thermal Pools
Open: daily 9am-10pm, Friday and
Saturday until 11pm.

Waitangi
National Reserve
Open: daily 9am-5pm. Admission for
children is free.

Whangarei
Claphams Clock Museum
Water Street (in Cafler Park rose gardens)
Open: daily 10am-4pm.

Northland Regional Museum
On Road to Dargaville, SH14
Clarke Homestead (1885)
Kiwi House
Steam Train
Open: daily 10am-4pm.

Travel Tips

BOAT TRIPS
What follows is just a selection. For
Hauraki Gulf cruises and Auckland
harbour cruises see Useful Information:
Auckland.

Bay of Islands
The following cruises are offered by
Fullers Northland but a wide variety of
other trips are offered by smaller
operators as well. Cruises start from
Paihia and Russell. Departures from
Russell are usually 10-15 minutes later.
Trips can be booked at Fullers offices in
Paihia ☎ (09)402 7421, Russell ☎ (09)403
7866 or Auckland, Bay of Islands Travel
Centre in Downtown Shopping Centre
(Shop 2 facing Customs St) ☎ (09)358
0259.
The Cream Trip (5¹/₂ hrs): daily from
October-May. Departs Paihia 10am.
June to September departs Monday,
Wednesday, Thursday and Saturday.

Cape Brett (Hole in the Rock) Cruise
(4hrs): daily October to May. Departs
9am & 1.30pm. Boat is a high speed
catamaran.
R. Tucker Thompson (6hrs): daily
November to May. Departs 9.30am.
This cruise takes place aboard a sailing
ship. Lunch included.

Kerikeri
Kerikeri River Cruise on M.V. Belfast:
Departs Stone Store Wharf hourly.
☎ (09)407 8276

BUS TOURS TO NINETY MILE BEACH
From Kaitaia and Doubtless Bay: Being
closer to Ninety Mile Beach the bus
tours are cheaper from either Doubtless
Bay or Kaitaia than from the Bay of
Islands. Operating from Kaitaia are
Sand Safaris (☎ (09)408 1778) at 221
Commerce St and Tall Tale Travel 'N
Tours (☎ (09) 408 0870) at 123B Com-
merce St. Nor-East Coachlines (☎ (09)
406 0244) operate from Mangonui.
Travel 'N Tours also offers a tour to Te
Rarawa Marae, a unique opportunity to
learn a bit about modern Maori culture.
From Paihia and Kerikeri: Fullers Cape
Reinga — Wanderer trip is an all day
trip and is available all year round.
Buses depart Paihia at 7.30am and
Kerikeri at 8am.

DOLPHIN SWIMMING
Swims with the dolphins are offered by
Fullers Northland and Dolphin Discov-
eries (☎ (09)403 7350), both of which
operate out of Paihia and Russell.
Season: all year.

SEA KAYAKING
Kayak hire and sea kayak trips are
offered at a number of places in
Northland. They include Paihia and
Russell in the Bay of Islands and
Whangaroa. For addresses contact the
local tourist offices.

STEAM TRAINS
Kawakawa to Opua (45 minutes): daily
except Friday in summer. In winter Saturday, Sunday, Monday and Tuesday.
Glenbrook Vintage Railway (Waiuku,
south-west of Auckland): Sundays from
October to June. Trip takes 45 minutes.

Tourist Information &
Park Visitor Centres

Auckland
(Main office):
Aotea Square
299 Queen Street
Auckland 1
Open: Monday-Friday 8.30am-5.30pm.
Saturday, Sunday and public holidays
9am-5pm.
☎ (09)366-6888

Queen Elizabeth Square
1 Queen Street
Open: Monday-Sunday 9am-5pm
☎ (09)366 0691

Auckland International Airport
Auckland Airport Visitor Centre
Ground Floor International Terminal
Open: Monday-Sunday from 5am until
last flight.
☎ (09)275 6467

Bay of Islands Maritime Park
Visitor Centre
The Strand
PO Box 134
Russell
☎ (09)403 7685

Dargaville
Normanby Street
☎ (09)439 8360

Kaitaia
Northland Information Centre
Jaycee Park
North Road
☎ (09)408 0879

Paihia
Information Bay Of Islands
Marsden Road
PO Box 70
☎ (09)402 7426
Open: daily 8am-5pm.

Whangarei
Tarewa Park
Otaika Road
Open: daily 8.30am-5pm
☎ (09)438 1079
Also info. about scuba diving around
Poor Knights Islands.

Waipoua Kauri Forest
Waipoua Forest Visitor Centre
Private Bag
Dargaville
☎ (09)439 0605

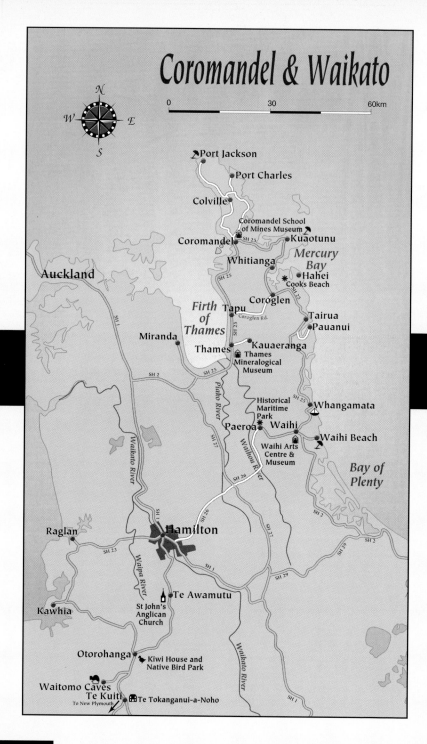

Coromandel & Waikato

Port Jackson

Port Charles

Colville

Coromandel School of Mines Museum

Coromandel
SH 25
Kuaotunu

Whitianga

Mercury Bay

Hahei
Cooks Beach

Auckland

SH 25

Coroglen

Firth of Thames
Tapu
Coroglen Rd.

Tairua
Pauanui

Miranda
SH 1

Kauaeranga
SH 25

Thames
Thames Mineralogical Museum

Piako River

Historical Maritime Park
SH 25
Whangamata

SH 2

Paeroa
Waihi

SH 27

Waihi Arts Centre & Museum
Waihi Beach

Bay of Plenty

Waikato River

Waihou River

SH 26

Raglan

SH 23

Waipa River

Hamilton
SH 1

SH 26

SH 2

SH 29

SH 1

SH 29

SH 2

SH 27

Te Awamutu
St John's Anglican Church

Kawhia

Waikato River

Otorohanga
Kiwi House and Native Bird Park

Waitomo Caves
Te Kuiti
Te Tokanganui-a-Noho
To New Plymouth

SH 1

Coromandel & Waikato 2

Rugged, wild and densely forested the Coromandel Peninsula pokes into the sea like a gnarled finger raised admon-
ishingly at the urban sprawl of Auckland on the other side of the Hauraki
Gulf. Settlement on the peninsula is relatively sparse and limited to the
ragged coastal fringes where, especially on the east coast, the visitor can
find some excellent beaches.

Though the peninsula has retained much of its natural grandeur and is
now protected as a forest park it did not escape nineteenth-century New
Zealand's hunger for gold, kauri gum (used in varnish) and timber. The
gold and gum booms were relatively short-lived but the tree-fellers only
stopped after they had decimated the once extensive kauri forests. The
peninsula still has large deposits of gold, silver, zinc and lead and some
locals fear that commercial interests could once again threaten an ecosys-
tem that is still recovering from the excesses of the past.

The Waikato encompasses the area to the south of Auckland and the
Coromandel Peninsula. In contrast to the Coromandel it is an area of
broad fertile plains which support some of the richest farmlands not only
in New Zealand but in the world. Though mostly famed for its highly
productive dairy farms horticulture has also become important in recent

above: sea kayaking is an ideal way to explore the lovely Coromandel coastline

years. Hub of the region is Hamilton on the banks of the Waikato river which, with a total length of 425km (264 miles), is the longest river in New Zealand.

The King Country, which lies to the south of the Waikato, gets its name from the Maori King Movement. This movement was formed by a number of North Island tribes who felt that the only way to stop further European encroachment on their lands was to stop feuding among themselves and to unite under a common leader. Potatau I was proclaimed the first Maori king in 1858. Today the movement is led by Queen Te Ata-i-rangi-kaahu, who has her base at Ngaruawahia.

During the land wars the King Country was a refuge for those Maori who were struggling against colonial rule and for many years afterwards it was strictly off-limits for any Europeans. It was not until the 1880s that local chiefs finally allowed the region to be surveyed and the first European settlers were able to enter the area without fear for their safety.

Physically the King Country has more in common with the Coromandel than the Waikato. The terrain is very rugged with many areas still covered by a luxuriant blanket of native forest. The principal towns are Otorohanga, Te Kuiti and Taumarunui.

Route 2 • Around the Coromandel Peninsula

From Auckland the route to Coromandel follows SH1 over the Bombay Hills then turns east along SH2 and SH25 to Thames, gateway to the Coromandel.

Thames, the largest settlement on the peninsula, can look back on an eventful history as a gold rush town. In 1867 the rich 'Shotover' strike on the nearby Kuranui stream initiated a rush to the Thames area that reached its peak in 1871. For those who want to look for reminders of the gold rush days the Information Office in Queen Street can give tips about gold-mining relics in the vicinity. In view of the wide variety of gemstones that are to be found on the peninsula an interesting place to visit is the Thames Mineralogical Museum. It claims to have the most comprehensive collection of mineral samples in the country. Roughly 30km (18$^1/_2$ miles) west of Thames, at **Miranda**, is a popular thermal springs complex.

A good place to start exploring the rugged hill-country of Coromandel Forest Park is the **Kauaeranga Valley**, a few kilometres south-east of Thames. There is an information centre here where visitors can learn about the old kauri logging industry and ecology of the area. Some of the shorter signposted tracks in the valley can be walked in 20 minutes, others would require 5 hours or more.

Avoiding the rugged interior the road to Coromandel hugs the coast, passing on its way enticing sandy beaches and idyllic little bays dotted with yachts. At **Tapu** a narrow, largely unsealed scenic road branches off the main route to traverse the Coromandel Range in the direction of Coroglen. This route would make an interesting short-cut to Whitianga for those in a hurry to get to the peninsula's nicest beaches. The many tree-ferns and nikau palms lining the road give a real subtropical feeling to the forest here. One signposted walk leads off the road to a 1,200 year old kauri that is something of a curiosity with its nearly square trunk. Also worth a stop along the way are the beautifully landscaped Rapaura Water Gardens.

Coromandel township has managed to retain some of its colonial character in a few lovely old buildings from the Victorian era. It was here that gold was first discovered in New Zealand in 1852 but today the town's prosperity rests in its function as a service centre to the surrounding dairy farms and as a popular holiday resort. Stores selling handicrafts, along with potter's workshops hint at the alternative lifestyle that has attracted many artists and craftspeople to this quiet part of the country. Not that 'dropping-out' means being impractical: the potter Barry Brickell originally built himself a little railway to transport clay to his workshop but now helps make it pay by offering rides to tourists. The Coromandel School of Mines Museum recalls the gold rush days and a working stamper battery just north of town shows how gold was separated from quartz.

The area north of Coromandel is only sparsely settled. The last chance to buy supplies for those travelling to the tip of the peninsula is at **Colville**. A dusty gravel road skirts the flanks of Mount Moehau which lies within an area sacred to the Maori. The strenuous climb to the top (8 hours return) begins by Te Hope Stream and is rewarded with the best views on the entire peninsula. In the course of this hike there is a (slight) chance of spotting a very rare native frog, *Leiopelma archeyi*. It is the most primitive of all known frogs and is strictly protected, on no account should it be disturbed!

At the end of the peninsula **Port Jackson** greets visitors with a fine beach and camping site. Camping is also possible at **Fletchers Bay**, just a little further on at road's end. Sheltered by pohutukawa trees this pretty cove is the starting point for the Coromandel Walkway to Stony Bay (6 hours return).

To get to the beaches at **Port Charles** on the east coast branch off the Port Jackson road at Whangaahei, a short distance north of Colville. The road back to Coromandel goes via Waikawau and Kennedy Bay.

The main route (SH25) continues from Coromandel to Whitianga. On the way the township of **Kuaotunu** is worth a mention as it is popular for its beaches and fishing spots. A scenic drive known as Black Jack Road leads from here to secluded Opito Bay.

Whitianga is especially favoured as a holiday resort among big game fishing enthusiasts. For other holiday-makers the town offers fine beaches, seafood restaurants, launch trips and lots of sunshine. A ferry regularly crosses the narrow harbour mouth to **Ferry Landing**, the site of an old stone wharf built in 1837. From the wharf it is possible to do a few pleasant walks.

Ferry Landing and a number of other interesting places can also be

A rugged chain of hills forms the backbone of the Coromandel Peninsula

Coromandel landscape

View from the Paku Summit, Tairua, at early evening

reached by road via Coroglen, the turn-off is a few kilometres further on at Whenuakite. **Cooks Beach** (follow Purangi Road north) is so named because it was here that Captain Cook hoisted the British flag and formally took possession of the country in the name of King George III. The purpose of Cook's stay was not, however, merely to expand the British Empire. While here he and his party observed the transit of Mercury and to mark the significance of these scientific investigations he named the bay Mercury Bay. There is a memorial to Cook's visit on Shakespeare Cliffs. You can drive to the top of the cliffs and the view is simply magnificent.

Further east **Hahei** not only has a lovely beach but also offers a chance to stretch the legs in the course of a 40 minute scenic walk to Cathedral Cove. The cove lies to the north of Hahei beach and is only accessible at low tide. **Hot Water Beach** is situated to the south and is not to be missed! At low tide bathers dig shallow holes and then bask in the thermally heated water which rises through the sand. It helps if you can get a spade.

Further south along SH25 is **Tairua**. This beautifully located beach resort looks across Tairua harbour to the more expensive resort of **Pauanui**. The drive, or walk, up to Paku summit is a must when in Tairua as the views are fantastic. Guided tours starting from Pauanui include trips into the Coromandel Range and to abandoned gold mines. Visitors who simply want to give themselves a real treat could spend a night or two at Pauanui's luxury Puka Park Lodge.

The next resort on the coast is perhaps the liveliest of them all. **Whangamata** has the best surfing on the entire peninsula and in summer half the population seems to be made up of bronzed, board carrying surfies. With the emphasis on the outdoors holiday-makers can choose between scuba diving, cycling, canoeing and fishing trips. Those without the gear can hire it here.

After Whangamata the road winds inland to **Waihi**. This is the last major stop on the Coromandel Peninsula and in view of the region's gold mining past it is perhaps appropriate that the tour ends here at the site of the biggest gold find in New Zealand's history. The original Martha Mine was discovered in 1878 and by 1908 it was one of the world's richest. After closing down in 1952 the mine was reopened in 1988 as new techniques made the extraction of gold profitable again. It is estimated that over a period of 12 years the new Martha Mine will produce about 300,000 ounces of silver and 55,000 ounces of gold annually.

The Waihi Arts Centre and Museum illustrates the history of the mine with photos, maps and models. The mine itself can be visited as part of a conducted tour. During the summer months an added attraction is provided by the Goldfields Steam Train Society which runs a vintage railway between Waihi and Waikino.

An excursion to the highly popular **Waihi Beach** can be done as part of a round trip. Follow the signposted road east to Waihi Beach, where there is excellent swimming and surfing, then return via Athenree Gorge and Waimata. Route 4 can be joined by following SH2 south via Waimate and Katikati to Tauranga.

The Karangahake Gorge links Waihi to Paeroa and was once alive with gold mining towns that have since faded or vanished completely. Following a disused railway through the gorge is the Karangahake Gorge Historic Walkway, a great way to come in closer contact with the history of the area.

Paeroa is best known in New Zealand as the home of 'Lemon and Paeroa', a soft drink made using the waters of a local mineral spring. North of town it is worthwhile visiting the Historical Maritime Park. A number of old boats have been restored here to their former glory, including a vintage paddle steamer. Otherwise Paeroa serves as departure point for an exploration of the Waikato: follow SH26 south-west to Hamilton.

Route 3 • Through the Waikato and King Country

The main road south from Auckland (SH1) leads direct to **Hamilton**, New Zealand's largest inland city. At the heart of rich farming country the city has grown rapidly along the banks of the Waikato River. Lovely riverside parks and a lake near the city centre belong to the city's chief attractions.

Recalling the days when the Waikato River was an important transportation route is the Rangiriri riverboat in Memorial Park, near the river's eastern bank. However the best way to experience some of the romance of the old riverboat days is to take a trip on the paddle steamer *MV. Waipa Delta* which departs from Parana Memorial Park.

Further insight into the region's past is offered by the Waikato Museum of Art and History. Along with its collections of fine art the museum's most interesting exhibit is the magnificent Maori war canoe *Te Winika* (1838). Contemporary Maori carving is also on display and there is a museum shop offering work by local craftspeople.

The direct route to Te Kuiti at the end of this tour follows SH3 south from Hamilton. However a more scenic alternative is to make a detour to the west coast via Raglan and Kawhia and to rejoin SH3 at Otorohanga. Of interest on the direct route is the National Agricultural Heritage complex at **Mystery Creek**. Signposted from the main road this museum complex presents a fascinating panorama of New Zealand farming from the earliest days to now. Visitors can try their hand at milking cows, stroll through a colonial village or take rides on wagons drawn by huge Clydesdale horses.

Further south **Te Awamutu** is also worth a longer stop. St John's Anglican Church (1854) is one of the oldest churches in the country, while next door the modern New Parish Church of St John (1965) can claim an original and interesting interior. An excellent, if small museum, is the Te Awamutu and District Museum. Exhibits deal with the Waikato Land Wars between Maori and European settlers and the pioneer days in general. At the Aotearoa Centre visitors can not only watch Maori carvers at work but also have the opportunity to buy their finished products. Tours of the Otawhao meeting house, where there are more examples of contemporary Maori carving to be admired, are arranged by the Aotearoa Centre.

First stop for those who have decided on the longer scenic route is **Raglan**, nearly 50km (31 miles) to the west of Hamilton on SH23. Outside the busy holiday season this seaside resort is a haven of peace with a pretty, natural harbour providing lots of additional charm. The road to Kawhia goes south from Raglan via Te Mata — please note that this road is sealed only as far as Te Mata. An attraction on the way is Bridal Veil Falls. The waterfall is signposted from the road and is accessible along a short track through dense bush.

Kawhia, on the natural harbour of the same name, is a wonderfully isolated little town. According to revered Maori tradition the town's history begins with the arrival of the Tainui canoe, one of the legendary eight canoes that brought the ancestors of today's Maori from their mythical homeland of Hawaiki to New Zealand. Today Kawhia is mainly visited by local holiday-makers who value the picturesque seclusion of the place. A special attraction is Te Puia Beach where hot water springs rise up through the sands. Friends of down-to-earth food might like to know that Kawhia Takeaways is acclaimed for the best fish and chips in the area. If you like your fish fresh then fishing trips start from the wharf.

From Kawhia SH31 winds its way through rugged hill country to join

SH3 at **Otorohanga**. A must for those with an interest in wildlife is the Kiwi House and Native Bird Park. Here it is possible to get close up views of the shy and semi-nocturnal kiwi. Other native birds can be seen in a walk-through aviary.

Near Hangatiki turn west off SH3 to **Waitomo Caves**. This extensive system of limestone caves is one of New Zealand's most famous attractions. Most of the attention focuses on the Waitomo Cave with its glow-worm grotto which is entered by boat on an underground river. Unrelated to their European counterparts the glow-worms (Arachnocampa luminosa) use light to trap insects on long sticky threads they dangle below themselves. Though found throughout the country it is only at Waitomo that they shine in such impressive numbers. Nearby Aranui Cave is mainly interesting for its spectacular limestone formations. To avoid crowds during the holiday season it is best to plan a visit for the early morning or late afternoon.

For thrill-seekers Waitomo has a few other unique attractions in the 'not to be missed' category. The Lost World trip consists of being lowered 100m (328ft) by rope into the depths of the Mangaopu Cave. Those who have not fainted on the way down can then take part in a 5 hour walk through an awe-inspiring subterranean world. If that was not enough to still the thirst for adventure then a bit of black-water-rafting in Ruakuri Cave might be just the thing. Equipped with protective hat, torch and rubber tube you are whisked through the cave by a swift flowing stream.

Among the less strenuous alternatives to the above activities is a visit to the Waitomo Museum of Caves. The museum has a collection of fossils found within the caves along with very informative displays offering a fascinating insight into the natural history of the area. Unrelated to the topic of caves but nonetheless interesting is Ohaki Maori Village and Weaving Centre. Here it is Maori culture that takes pride of place; traditional weavers can be watched at work and visitors can wander through a reconstructed pre-European Maori *pa*.

Visitors who have decided to spend a day or two at Waitomo could consider an excursion to the spectacular Marokopa Falls, further west of Waitomo on the road to Marokopa. Closer at hand is the Waitomo Walkway. This half-day walk starts by the museum and goes through some beautiful bush scenery.

Te Kuiti lies 20km (12¹/₂ miles) south of Waitomo Caves on SH3. Of particular interest here is the beautifully carved meeting house Te Tokanganui-a-Noho. It was built in 1878 by followers of the famous Maori guerilla leader Te Kooti (around 1830-93) who found refuge here from colonial troops. Permission must be obtained before entering the building but it is worth the effort as one seldom has the chance of seeing a carved meeting house of such historical and artistic significance. Inquire at the tourist office.

South-east of Te Kuiti Pureora Forest Park encompasses one of the North Island's last significant stands of podocarp forest; in other words a forest made up of native trees like miro, rimu, totara, and matai. It is also home to a large variety of native birds, including the very rare kokako. A good place to see kokakos is at the end of Bismarck Road, though this means rising very early in the morning. The park visitor centre is on the Waimiha Road which branches off SH30 between Te Kuiti and Mangakino. The Totara Walk nature trail, as well as other walks, can be undertaken from here.

From Te Kuiti there are a number of possibilities for the onward journey: SH3 provides a very scenic connection to New Plymouth on Route 5, SH30 leads to the thermal region of Rotorua and SH4 leads directly south to the volcanoes of Tongariro National Park.

Additional Information

Accommodation & Eating Out

ACCOMMODATION
Hamilton
*Hamilton East Tourist Court **
61 Cameron Road
☎ (07)856 6220
Also camping.

*Parklands Travel Hotel/Motel ***
Bed & Breakfast
24 Bridge Street
☎ and Fax (07)838 2461

Thames
*Sunkist Lodge **
506 Brown street
☎ (07)868 8808 Fax: (07)868 7426

"The Thames" Backpacker's Resort
*Dickson Holiday Park **
Victoria Street
☎ (07)868 7308 Fax: (07)868 7308
Also camping.

*Brian Boru Hotel ****
Pollen Street
☎ (07)868 6523 Fax: (07)868 9760

Waitomo
*Juno Hall **
1km before Waitomo
☎ (07)878 7649

*THC Waitomo Hotel ****
Middle of town
☎ (07)878 8228 Fax: (07)878 8858

Whitianga
*Buffalo Beach Tourist Resort **
Cnr Eyre St and Buffalo Beach Rd
☎ and Fax (07)866 5854

*Anne's Haven ***
Bed & Breakfast
119 Albert Street
☎ (07)866 5550

*Cosy Cat Cottage ***
Bed & Breakfast
41 South Highway
☎ (07)866 4488
Eccentric decor!

EATING OUT
Coromandel
*Coromandel Café **
36 Kapanga Road
☎ (07)866 8495

*Success Café ***
Kapanga Road
☎ (07)866 7100

Hamilton
*A Museum Café **
1 Grantham Street
☎ (07)838 1480

*Passage To India **
(Indian)
66 Bryce Street
☎ (07)834 0660

*Left Bank Café ****
Marlborough Place
Victoria Street
☎ (07)839 3354

Thames
*Majestic Family Restaurant ***
640 Pollen Street
☎ (07)868 6204

Old Thames Restaurant ***
705 Pollen Street
☎ (07)868 7207

Waitomo
Roselands Restaurant ***
Fullerton Road
☎ (07)878 7611

Whitianga
Cooks Cove Licensed Restaurant **
20 The Esplanade
☎ (07)866 4833

PJ's Bistro & Bar ***
31 Albert Street
☎ (07)866 5249

Places to Visit

ROUTE 2
Coromandel
Driving Creek Pottery & Railway
Driving Creek Road
Open: Trains run daily at 2pm and 4pm.
During summer also at 10.30am.

School of Mines Museum
Rings Road
Open: daily 10am-12noon and 2-4pm
during summer.

Miranda
Hot Springs
Front Miranda Road
Open: daily 10am-9pm.

Paeroa
Historical Maritime Park
Located on SH2
Open: daily all year except Christmas Day.

Tapu-Coroglen Road
Rapaura Water Gardens
Open: daily 10am-5pm. Refreshments
are available.

Thames
Mineralogical Museum
Cnr Brown and Cochrane St
Open: Wednesday & Saturday 11am-4pm.

Waihi
Waihi Arts Centre & Museum
Kenny Street
Open: Monday & Friday 10am-4pm,
weekends and public holidays 1.30-4pm.

Waihi Gold Mining Co. Ltd
PO Box 190
Open: weekday tours by prior arrange-
ment. Tours start from Information
Centre, Seddon Street.
☎ (07)863 8192

Whitianga
Purangi Winery
On road to Cook's Beach
Open: daily 9am-9pm.
Fruit wine tastings and a good restau-
rant. Winery also organises a 1^1/$_2$ hour
cruise on Purangi River.
☎ (07)866 3724

ROUTE 3
Hamilton
Waikato Museum of Art & History
Cnr Victoria and Grantham Streets
Open: daily 10am-4.30pm except Good
Friday and Christmas Day.

Mystery Creek
National Agricultural Heritage
Close to Hamilton Airport, on Mystery
Creek Rd
Open: daily 9am-4.30pm
This large museum complex incorpo-
rates the Clydesdale Museum, National
Dairy Museum, Heritage Village and
much else besides. Jet boat tours on
Waikato River are also offered.

Otorohanga
Kiwi House and Native Bird Park
Alex Telfer Drive
Open: daily 10am-5pm. June to August,
closes 4pm.

Te Awamutu
Aotearoa Centre
1 Factory Rd
Open: Monday & Thursday 9am-4pm,
Fri 2-4pm.

Te Awamutu and District Museum
Roche Street
Open: Tuesday & Friday 10am-4pm,
Saturday, Sunday and public holidays
2-4pm.

Waitomo
Ohaki Maori Village and Weaving Centre
1km before Waitomo
Open: daily 10am-4.30pm.

Waitomo Caves
Open: Tours of the Glow-Worm Caves
take place every hour on the hour from
9am-5pm. Tours of the Aranui Caves take
place at 10am, 11am, 1pm, 2pm and 3pm.
Admission is free for children under 5.

Waitomo Museum of Caves &
Information Centre
Open: daily 9am-5pm.

Travel Tips

AGATHA CHRISTIE WEEKENDS
Thames
Brian Boru Historic Hotel
Cnr Richmond and Pollen Streets
☎ (07)868 6523
Twice monthly guests can take part in a
murder mystery à la Agatha Christie.
The charming old hotel, established in
1868, offers the perfect background.

BOAT TRIPS
Hahei
Hahei Explorer
12 Beach Rd
☎ (07)866 3808
Also snorkeling trips.

Hamilton
M.V. Waipa Delta
Memorial Park, Memorial Drive
☎ (07)854 9415
Morning tea cruise Sundays 10am.
Daily luncheon cruise 12.30pm,
Afternoon tea cruise 3pm & Moonlight
cruise 7pm.

CAVE ADVENTURES
Waitomo
Black Water Rafting
PO Box 13
☎ (07)878 6219
Depart: Museum of Caves.

Lost World Adventures Ltd
Lost World & Haggas Honking Holes
PO Box 29
☎ (07)878 7788
Depart: Museum of Caves.

Waitomo Down Under
(Cave rafting, caving)
PO Box 24
☎ and Fax (07)878 6577
Depart: Taware House next to Museum.

DOLPHIN SWIMMING
Whitianga
Dolphin Quest
C/o Whitianga Information Centre
☎ (07)866 5555

FISHING TRIPS
Kawhia
Details at wharf
☎ (07)871 6305

Whitianga
Ocean Adventures
8 Laura Place,
☎ (07)866 5005

Waipounamu Sportfishing
Ferry Landing
☎ (025)924 899
Also dolphin & whale watching.

GUIDED TREKS AND TRACK
TRANSPORT
Pauanui Beach
Doug Johansens Adventure Treks &
Scenic Tours
Settlement Rd
☎ and Fax (07)864 8731

Waihi
Goldfield Treks & Tours
16 Clarke St
☎ (07)863 7699

Karangahake Walkway Shuttle
30 Mackay St
☎ (07)863 8511
Operates summer weekends and school
holidays, every $1/2$ to 1 hour. Runs from
Waikino Station, Owharoa Falls and
Crown Battery.

MOUNTAIN BIKE TOURS AND
RENTALS
Whangamata
All Terrain Mountain Bike Tours
652 Port Rd
☎ (07)865 8096

STEAM TRAINS
Waihi
Goldfields Steam Train
Wrigley St
Open: on weekends. Trip takes 1 hour.
☎ (07)863 8251

Brian Boru Hotel, Thames

Tourist Information Centres

Coromandel
Council Offices
Kapanga Rd
☎ (07)866 8598

Hamilton
Angelsea Street
PO Box 970
☎ (07)839 3360

Kauaeranga Valley Visitor Centre
Kauaeranga Valley Road
Open: daily
☎ (07)868 6381

Otorohanga
80 Maniapoto Street
PO Box 152
☎ (07)873 8951

Paeroa
Public Relations Office
Belmont Rd
☎ (07)862 8636

Tairua
Main Road Shopping Centre
☎ (07)864 7055

Te Kuiti
Rora Street
PO Box 404
Open: Monday & Friday 8.30am-5pm,
Saturday 9am-12noon.
☎ (07)878 8077

Thames
405 Queen Street
PO Box 545
Open: Monday & Friday 9am-5pm,
weekends 10am-3pm
☎ (07)868 7284

Waihi
Seddon Street
☎ (07)863 6715

Waitomo Caves
Museum of Caves Information Centre
Main Street
PO Box 12
☎ (07)878 7640

Whangamata
Port Rd
☎ (07)865 8340

Whitianga
66 Albert Street
Open: Monday to Saturday 8am-5pm,
Sunday 9am-3pm.
☎ (07)866 5555

The Volcanic Heartland 3

Volcanoes, hot-pools, geysers and crater lakes are the common denominators linking the tours within this chapter. The region offers much of the North Island's most spectacular and unique scenery, from the almost perfect volcanic cone of the now dormant Mount Taranaki (Egmont) to the sulphurous clouds hanging over the active volcano of White Island in the Bay of Plenty. Tongariro National Park with its three volcanoes is a popular destination for trampers in summer and for skiers in winter. A highlight for all visitors is the thermal region around Rotorua with its numerous mud-pools and geysers. Rotorua is also a centre of Maori culture and Whakarewarewa village offers a rare insight into traditional Maori society. On the other hand keen anglers will certainly want to spend a few days on the shores of Lake Taupo, as it is famed for its rainbow trout.

above: The slopes of Mt Ruapehu offer the best skiing in the North Island (Tongariro National Park)

Route 4 • From the Bay of Plenty to the Volcanic Plateau

Tauranga is situated on the lovely harbour of the same name and can be quickly reached by taking SH2 south from Waihi (Route 2) or by following state highways 1 and 29 east from Hamilton (Route 3). Near the centre of town is the Monmouth Redoubt, a fortified site that was built during the New Zealand Land Wars. Not far away on The Strand is the Te Awanui war canoe (1973). This beautiful replica of a traditional Maori war canoe (*waka*) is only paddled on the harbour on certain special occasions.

Other places of interest recalling Tauranga's early history are The Elms mission house (1847) in Mission Street and Tauranga Historic Village on 17th Avenue West. Here the colonial days are brought vividly back to life with Victorian period shops, houses, a saw mill and steam train.

A bridge over the harbour links Tauranga to the busy port of **Mount Maunganui**. In summer the town swells with thousands of holiday-makers attracted by the golden sands of Ocean Beach. As it extends for several kilometres down the coast there is plenty of room in spite of the crowds. An added attraction is the hot salt-water pool at the foot of the 'Mount', a 232m (761ft) hill that can be climbed for a splendid panorama of the bay.

The route (SH2) now continues a short distance inland into kiwifruit country. **Te Puke** claims itself to be the 'Kiwifruit Capital of the World' and this small furry fruit, once known as the Chinese gooseberry, has certainly done a great deal to boost the town's prosperity. A sub-tropical fruit that originally came from China it has been successfully grown in a number of areas in New Zealand. Although first introduced to the country in 1907 it was not until the mid-1970s that it became an export hit. In 1990 export earnings reached $450 million and although the kiwifruit boom is now over, due to strong overseas competition, it is still New Zealand's leading horticultural product. The Kiwifruit Harvest Festival is held in May.

After Te Puke the road returns to the coast which it follows to **Whakatane**. The town is mainly interesting for the excellent surfing beach at nearby Ohope but there are also a number of excursions that can be booked here which might easily justify a longer stay. Especially worth-while are the scenic flights over White (Whakaari) Island. This continuously active volcano lies about 50km (31 miles) off the coast in the Bay of Plenty. The clouds of ash and steam it belches forth are usually visible from many points along the coast but nothing can compare to the fantastic experience of actually walking on the volcano itself. Its deeply rutted, ash-covered slopes are pock-marked with boiling hot fumaroles (temperatures inside these volcanic vents can reach 800°C) and a look over the rim of one of the huge steaming craters is to get a glimpse of the titanic forces that have shaped our planet.

Though the island is a privately owned scenic reserve it can be visited by either helicopter or boat from Whakatane. Vulcan Helicopters offer a three hour excursion that includes a 40 minute flight over the Bay and a guided tour of the huge crater area. The tour by boat has the advantage of being much cheaper and includes a 1 hour guided tour of the island. Other organised trips from Whakatane include dolphin swimming, jet boat rides on the **Rangitaiki River**, white water rafting on the **Motu River** and big game fishing in the Bay.

Further south at **Taneatua** is the information centre for Urewera National Park (see Chapter 4). Trips into the park via either Ruatoki North or Matahi can be arranged at the Ranger Station in Taneatua. A bit further east Route 6 can be joined at Opotiki.

From Whakatane SH30 moves inland through pockets of lush native bush and past shimmering blue lakes to reach the famous tourist resort of **Rotorua**. The town lies directly on the shores of Lake Rotorua, the largest of eleven lakes in the near vicinity. Spectacular thermal activity, superb, if sadly depleted stands of native bush, and traditional Maori culture are the main ingredients that have made Rotorua one of New Zealand's greatest tourist attractions.

Rotorua's steaming pits and pools have been described as a 'foretaste of hell' and judging by the crowds that come to see them the Devil could do very good business if he decided to charge for his own fire and brimstone. However the first thing that strikes a visitor to Rotorua is not in fact any particular sight but rather the pungent smell of sulphur, which is often likened to the smell of rotten eggs. Caused by a perfectly harmless natural gas associated with the region's thermal activity it does not take long to get used to.

Anybody planning to spend a day or two here (to be recommended if all the attractions are to be seen at leisure) will find that Fenton Street offers the greatest range of accommodation. Visitors who want to give themselves a special treat should try and get a room with a thermally heated spa pool attached.

One of Rotorua's main sights is at the southern end of **Fenton Street**: Whakarewarewa thermal area. If visitor's only have time to visit one thermal area then Whakarewarewa is the one to choose. Boiling mud pools, hot pools and geysers draw thousands of people here every year. With a plume rising to nearly 30m Pohutu is the largest geyser in New Zealand. It is also one of the more reliable ones so there is a good chance of seeing its spectacular eruption.

However thermal activity is by no means the only reason for visiting Whakarewarewa. **Rotowhio Pa** is a model recreating the fortified settlements of the pre-European Maori. The carved gateway is especially striking. At lunchtime (12.15pm) the *pa* is the site of an excellent Maori folklore concert. The **Maori Arts and Crafts Institute** next door is also worth a look. Here Maori carvers and weavers can be watched while they work. Informative guided tours through the thermal area start from the institute. At the other end of the thermal reserve is a genuine Maori village.

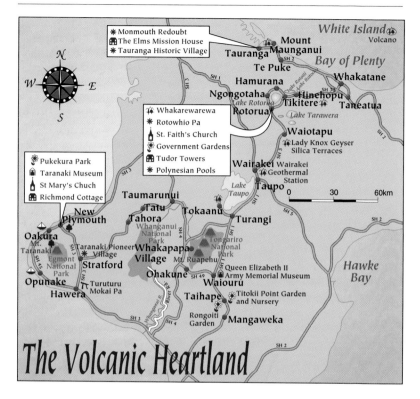

The Volcanic Heartland

Swimming with Dolphins

Dolphin swimming is becoming an increasingly popular activity in New Zealand and many visitors rave about this unique experience. Not only do participants get close enough to actually touch the dolphins as they swim about in the open sea but they are also given an informative commentary about the animals and their marine environment. Non-swimmers are welcome on these trips and the chances of getting an excellent close-up photo of a wild dolphin at sea are quite high. Swimmers are provided with wet suits and snorkels and are then taken by boat to where the dolphins normally feed. Such an excursion usually lasts about 3 hours. In Whakatane dolphin swimming is offered by Dolphins Down Under but another recommended operator is Dolphin Mary Charters in Kaikoura (South Island).

Beach near Mount Maunganui

Whakarewarewa thermal area

The villagers still use the hot pools, as the Rotorua Maori have done for countless generations, for cooking, bathing and washing. A curiosity are the graves in the village cemetery which are raised above ground because of the hot earth below.

Another pocket of Maori culture is Ohinemutu Maori village, directly on the lakefront. Of particular interest is a superbly carved meeting house (1873) and St Faith's Church (1910). The church is definitely worth entering as it is richly decorated with Maori carvings and traditional woven panels known as tukutuku.

Not far from the northern end of Fenton Street are the **Government Gardens**. What captures most attention here is the highly photogenic **Tudor Towers** (1906), a building in Elizabethan style. This former bath house is a reminder of the days when many people came to Rotorua to take advantage of the curative properties of the thermal springs. Inside the bath house is a museum with some local Maori artefacts and an art gallery. Only a short stroll from Tudor Towers the **Polynesian Pools** offer visitors a chance to ease aching limbs in hot mineral waters.

Apart from Whakarewarewa there are three other major areas of thermal activity which, however, are all some distance from the city. A drive north-east back in the direction of Whakatane leads to **Tikitere** thermal area (Hell's Gate) where a hot waterfall (Kakahi Falls) is the undisputed highlight.

On the road south to Taupo the eerily beautiful **Waimangu Valley** is the site of the Waimangu Cauldron, a large boiling lake. While here it is worth taking the launch trip across Lake Rotomohana to the Steaming Cliffs and the site of the once famous Pink and White Terraces which were destroyed in a violent volcanic eruption over 100 years ago. A popular full day excursion is the Waimangu Round Trip which includes a visit to the Waimangu thermal area as well as a boat trip across Lake Rotomohana and Lake Tarawera to the buried village of Te Wairoa.

Waiotapu thermal area is only a short distance further south and has the Lady Knox Geyser as its crowning glory. The geyser is brought punctually to life at 10.15am every day with the help of a bit of soap. The soap, it seems, reduces the surface viscosity of the water below and thus allows the super-heated steam and water deeper down to release its pent up energy by erupting through the vent. Such an eruption can last up to an hour. Also to be admired are some subtly-hued silica terraces known as The Artist's Palette, the bubbling Champagne Pool and Bridal Veil Falls.

Several other destinations can be reached from Rotorua in the course of a pleasant drive. An outing to Lake Tarawera for instance could be done in half a day. To get there head north from the city on SH30 until the signposted turn-off is reached. Along the way the Blue and Green Lakes are passed. These two lakes are famed for their contrasting colours but are best appreciated on a fine day. A little further on the road reaches Te Wairoa Buried Village, near the shores of Lake Tarawera (see also Waimangu valley).

Te Wairoa was completely buried during the catastrophic eruption of nearby Mount Tarawera in 1886. The eruption took place without any warning (the volcano was believed to be dormant!) and devastated the entire area. The world famous Pink and White silica terraces were destroyed and ash, mud and lava covered an area of approximately 8,000sq km (5,000 square miles). At least 150 people died. The village is now partly excavated and one can see the remains of a stone *pataka* (storehouse), a *whare* (Maori dwelling) and a few European buildings. The small museum displays intriguing photos that were taken before and after the eruption.

Tarawera Landing is situated a few kilometres further on from the village and this is where boats depart for the trip across Lake Tarawera. Mount Tarawera itself can be seen on the eastern side of the lake.

For the drive around Lake Rotorua itself leave the city in the direction of Hamilton on SH5. First stop is at Rainbow and Fairy Springs. The springs have a lovely bush setting and are teeming with brown, rainbow and brook trout. The trout may be hand-fed and some real monsters can be seen through an underwater viewing window. Other attractions include wallabies, kiwis and the descendants of the pigs Captain Cook introduced over 200 years ago (known as 'Captain Cookers'). Not far away is the Agrodome at **Ngongotaha**. Here visitors are entertained with demonstrations of sheep shearing and can watch sheep dogs being put through their paces. But if your taste for sheep only extends to the chops on your plate then continue on around the lake to **Hamurana Springs**. There is another trout pool here as well as a grove of giant Californian redwoods. By making a detour north at Mourea it would be possible to visit Okere Falls, otherwise continue along the lake shore to Tikitere (see above) and then follow SH30 back to Rotorua.

The last outing from Rotorua to be described here involves a bit more walking. Follow SH30 north to **Hinehopu** at the far end of Lake Rotoiti. This is the starting point of Hongi's Track, a beautiful walk through magnificent native bush scenery to the shores of Lake Rotoehu, only $1^{1}/_{2}$km (1 mile) away. Hongi Hika (1777-1828), after whom the track was named, was a famous warrior chief of the Ngapuhi tribe. On his way to attack an enemy tribe he and his warriors had to carry their canoes along this track between the two lakes. On the way back to Rotorua a detour could be made to Lake Okataina. This is the Rotorua region at its most unspoiled. No roads circle the shore of this lake which is hugged in a green embrace of sub-tropical forest. One has no choice but to leave the car and to follow one of the tracks, shaded by the delicate fronds of giant tree ferns.

If SH30 and then SH1 are taken south to Taupo a detour could be made to the fascinating thermal valley of **Orakei Korako**. The turn-off is signposted some 70km ($43^{1}/_{2}$ mile) south of Rotorua. Access to the thermal area is via a short boat trip across Lake Ohakuri. From the jetty a path then threads its way past geysers, mud pools and some beautiful silica terraces. Just how colourful the terraces will be at any one time depends

Carved entrance gate, Whakarewarewa village, Rotorua

The Maori Hangi

Rotorua is one of the best places in New Zealand to try a traditional *hangi* meal. A *hangi* is a Maori earth oven in which food is cooked by steam. Wood is piled over a shallow pit and then stones are placed on the wood. A fire is lit and once the stones are hot enough the remaining wood is removed. Water is then sprinkled over the stones and the food is placed in containers on top. Everything is now covered with a layer of leaves and dirt and left to steam for three to four hours. *Hangi* food can taste delicious if properly prepared and the *hangi* provided by Rotorua's hotels are usually accompanied by traditional Maori songs and dances. Hotels offering *hangi* meals include the THC Hotel and the Quality Hotel.

Beautifully carved meeting houses can be seen at many locations in the Rotorua area

Government Gardens, Rotorua

on whether enough hot water is flowing over them to create the conditions necessary for the growth of hot water algae. These orange, pink and green algae can flourish in temperatures of up to 60°C. Another interesting natural formation is Ruatapu Cave (Aladdin's Cave) with its hot pool. High-ranking Maori women once used the pool as a mirror while adorning themselves; hence the name Orakei Korako which means 'place of adorning'.

Those who take SH5 south will pass Waimangu and Waiotapu thermal areas (described above) and shortly before Taupo nobody is likely to miss the huge clouds of steam billowing from the Wairakei Geothermal Station — it can also be seen by those who follow SH1 as it joins SH5 just above Wairakei. At **Wairakei** geothermal energy (super-heated steam below the earth's surface that is tapped by drilling deep bores) is exploited to generate electricity and those interested in learning more should definitely visit the complex. The impressive Huka Falls are only a short drive further south. Here the Waikato River gushes through a narrow gap of rock to plunge 11m into a pool below. Other sights in the area include the Craters of the Moon, a thermally active valley where visitors can have a free look at bubbling mud pools and steaming craters, and Aratiatia Rapids. The rapids were laid dry because of a hydro-electric scheme and would have vanished for good were it not for the ensuing public outcry. They are now 'turned on' between 10-11.30am and 2.30-4pm.

Though the town of **Taupo** itself is not of great interest it does have a magnificent setting on the shores of Lake Taupo, New Zealand's largest lake 606sq km (234sq miles). Few people would suspect it but Taupo's waters actually fill a gigantic crater that was formed in a series of massive volcanic eruptions that belong to the most violent that the earth has ever known. The last great explosion in the Taupo volcanic area took place around 1,800 years ago and covered an area of some 21,000sq km (8,108sq miles) with volcanic debris.

These days the lake is better known for its excellent trout fishing than the cataclysmic events of the past and anglers come from all over the world to fish in its waters or in the streams and rivers that feed it. Especially famous among anglers is the Tongariro River which enters Lake Taupo at its southern end near Turangi. Those who are not keen on fishing can join a cruise on the steamboat *Ernest Kemp* to some modern Maori rock carvings in Mine Bay. A couple of other boats also offer a similar trip.

Though Taupo certainly makes an excellent base for an angling holiday there are also plenty of other activities in the area (jet boating, tandem skydiving, scenic flights, etc) to keep most people busy for a few days. With this in mind it is worth mentioning that many of the hotels, motels and even camping grounds in Taupo have hot pools attached. A short distance along the road to Napier (SH5) are the well-appointed De Brett Thermal Pools.

The drive down to Turangi on SH1 is especially pretty after Hatepe as the road now follows the lake shore. **Turangi** is mainly interesting for anglers as the trout-rich Tongariro river flows close to town. To the north-west at **Tokaanu** are some hot springs.

Trout, by the way, are not native to New Zealand but were introduced in the nineteenth century from North America and Europe. In spite of the fact that they seem to thrive in New Zealand waters it is necessary to maintain special hatcheries as not all New Zealand's rivers and lakes offer suitable spawning grounds. However the trout released from these hatcheries sometimes reach record sizes. A brown trout might grow to weigh as much as 16kg (35lbs)! Of the two species it is the brown trout that is more widespread. Rainbow trout are mainly found in the lakes around Rotorua and in Lake Taupo. One of the more important hatcheries is the Tongariro National Trout Centre near Turangi.

Because trout fishing is treated purely as a sport trout are not fished commercially and are not available on restaurant menus. If you want a trout meal you will either have to catch one yourself or make friends with an angler!

The direct route south is to follow SH1 to Waiouru. This stretch of the highway is commonly known as the Desert Road as it goes through a desolate yet often dramatically beautiful region of tussock grasslands bordering Tongariro National Park. There are good views of the park's volcanoes from various points along the road.

Those who want to explore the area of Tongariro National Park a bit more thoroughly should leave SH1 at Turangi and head in the direction of National Park township by following SH47 around the shores of Lake Rotoaira. If the weather is fine it might be worth stopping just before this lake for a swim in the clear waters of bush clad Lake Rotopounamu. A signposted walk (20 minutes) leads off the road to the lake which can be circled in about 2 hours. Roughly 8km (5 miles) short of National Park is the turn-off to Whakapapa village, within the boundaries of Tongariro National Park.

Tongariro National Park

New Zealand's first national park, and one of the world's oldest, was the result of a farsighted gift. To ensure that his sacred tribal lands would never fall into the hands of land hungry colonists the Maori chief Te Heu Heu Tukino IV presented the area now covered by Tongariro National Park to the Crown in 1887. In 1991 the park was recognised by UNESCO as a World Heritage site and anyone who takes the time to explore this place of active volcanoes will soon appreciate the significance of Te Heu Heu's unique gift.

Of the park's three volcanoes it is Mount Ngauruhoe 2,290m (7,513ft) that is most continually active. When it is not actually belching out steam and ash the volcano's almost perfect cone can be climbed for tremendous views over the entire plateau. Mount Ruapehu 2,796m (9,173ft) is the North Island's highest peak. On its summit is a steaming crater lake. Mount Tongariro 1,968m (6,457ft) may once have been cone-shaped like Ngauruhoe but at some time in the distant past a massive explosion blew

Emerald Lakes,
Tongariro National Park

the mountain's upper section away. On Tongariro's northern flanks are the Ketetahi hot springs.

Like all New Zealand's national parks Tongariro has an excellent system of walking tracks and if time allows **Whakapapa Village** is a good place to start off on an exploration of this magnificent, often bizarre volcanic landscape by foot. Not only is National Park headquarters located here but there is also a range of accommodation to suit all budgets. Park headquarters has all the necessary information about tracks and huts within the park as well as detailed walking maps and pamphlets describing shorter walks.

Starting close to park headquarters is the $6^1/_2$km (4 miles) circular track to Taranaki Falls. A much longer walk the authors can highly recommend takes 2 to 3 days to complete but goes through some of the parks most fascinating volcanic scenery. It starts (or ends) at the Château, skirts the nearly perfect volcanic cone of Mount Ngauruhoe and takes in the Emerald Lakes, Blue Lake, Red and Central craters and, as an essential detour, the hot springs at Ketetahi Hut. Huts along the way are Mangatepopo, Oturere and Waihohonu. The track exits the park on the Desert Road (SH1) after Waihohonu Hut and transport has to be arranged from here. This walk serves as a shorter alternative to the 4-5 day Round the Mountain Track, which it basically follows.

In winter trampers give way to skiers who flock to Whakapapa Village and the nearby ski fields on Mount Ruapehu. On the south-western flanks of the mountain **Ohakune** assumes the role of ski village for Turoa ski field. This pleasantly situated little town is also a good alternative base for walking in summer. For those who simply do not have the time to do any long walks the Ohakune Mountain Road leading up to the Turoa slopes offers some compensation as it is a beautiful drive through some of the park's finest stands of native forest. There are a number of nice spots for picnics along the way and if the hamper needs filling supplies can be bought from New World supermarket in Ohakune even on Sundays. Information about the park is available from the ranger station at the start of the road. Close to the ranger station begins the Mangawhero Forest Walk. It goes through beautiful bush scenery and takes about 2 hours to complete.

Continuing south from Ohakune it is possible to take either SH4 via Raetihi to Wanganui (see Chapter 5) or to go via Waiouru on SH1 which is the main road down to Wellington. **Waiouru** is the site of New Zealand's most important army training camp and the main point of interest here is the excellent Queen Elizabeth II Army Memorial Museum. The museum deals with the history of the New Zealand Army from colonial times to the present. There is a regular audio-visual display and refreshments are also available within the complex.

Only 28kms ($17^1/_2$ miles) further south is the small rural township of **Taihape**. Because of its central position between Auckland and Wellington on SH1 the town has long been a favourite refreshment stop for travellers. In fact in spite of only having a population of around 2,500 there are some sixteen restaurants and takeaways in town! The range of accommodation is almost as impressive with prices ranging from me-dium to low budget.

Apart from eating and sleeping Taihape offers visitors who are pre-pared to stay for a few days outdoor activities and sightseeing away from the main tourist trail. A major attraction is Titoki Point Garden and Nursery to the north-west of town which has been acclaimed as one of the finest private gardens in the country. Rongoiti Garden, which lies to the west, is also of interest with its bush walks and native birds. A good address for outdoor enthusiasts is River Valley Ventures. They organise horse treks, canoe safaris and white water rafting on the scenic Rangitikei river. Hunting and tramping is possible in the nearby Kaimanawa and Ruahine forest parks.

Another base for outdoor adventures is **Mangaweka**, further south on SH1. Right next to the main road and impossible to miss is the Aeroplane Café, an old DC-3 plane that has been fitted out as a tearoom. It is worth stopping for a snack here if only to experience more leg-room than you will ever get in the Economy Class of any modern jumbo-jet. Beside the plane is the office of Rangatikei River Adventures. They are the key to a 43m (141ft) bungy jump, jet boat trips and other outdoor activities in this rugged landscape of dramatic river gorges, walled by sheer cliffs of dazzling white papa rock.

From Taihape it is just over 200km (124 miles) down to Wellington or 1$^1/_2$ hours via Bulls to Wanganui at the start of Route 8.

Route 5 • Taranaki

Coming from the north New Plymouth in the Taranaki region is best reached from Te Kuiti (Chapter 2) but another interesting possibility for visitors coming from Tongariro National Park is to first go north via **Taumarunui** then to follow the Taumarunui-Stratford Heritage trail 150km (93 miles) south-west. The road is very winding and some stretches are unsealed but it allows travellers to see a very beautiful yet little visited area of the North Island.

Before leaving Taumarunui it is advisable to make sure the petrol tank is full as there are not many chances to fill the tank along this route. Another good idea is to get hold of the Heritage Trails booklet from the information centre or DOC office in town. It contains useful information about the various points of historic interest along the trail such as old Maori *pa* sites and abandoned coal mines. From Taumarunui the road first follows the Whanganui River west then turns south through **Tatu** to enter the picturesque Tangarakau Gorge. At **Tahora**, at the end of the gorge, there is a motor camp. Another motor camp is located at **Douglas**, not far from Stratford.

Stratford is named after Shakespeare's birthplace and many of the streets have Shakespearian names. Apart from this bit of borrowed glory the town is most interesting as an alternative base to New Plymouth for exploring the vicinity of Egmont National Park. Of interest near town is the Taranaki Pioneer Village which features fifty historic buildings. Within the complex there is a café along with a souvenir and craft shop.

Forty kilometres (25 miles) north of Stratford the small coastal city of **New Plymouth** is the first major stop in Taranaki for those travellers who have taken SH3 south from Te Kuiti. Though most people come to this part of the country to visit Egmont National Park there are a few places of interest in and around New Plymouth worthy of a closer look.

The Taranaki Museum, for instance, has a very good collection of Maori artefacts, along with exhibits on the region's colonial and natural history. The Govett-Brewster Art Gallery is not to be missed if you have an interest in contemporary New Zealand and Pacific art. A special section is devoted to the avant-garde artist and experimental film-maker Len Lye. Among the more important historic buildings in town are Richmond Cottage (1853) and St Mary's Church (1846) on Vivian Street, which is the oldest stone church in New Zealand.

New Plymouth is, however, most renowned for its exceptionally beautiful parks. Perhaps the most outstanding is Pukekura Park, only a short walk from the city centre. A touch of almost oriental charm is provided by the bright red bridges which arch over the park's two artificial lakes; they provide a sharp contrast to the lush green of native bush. From the lakeside tea kiosk a splendid view of Mount Taranaki (Egmont) has photographers rushing for their cameras. From mid-December to early February the park is lit up with coloured lights and hundreds of people stroll through in the evenings to enjoy the spectacles of an illuminated fountain and floodlit waterfall.

Great views over New Plymouth and the coastal surroundings can be had from the top of Paritutu hill, at the western edge of town near the power station. Visible from here are the rocky Sugar Loaf Islands which form part of Sugar Loaf Islands Marine Park. The islands are a sanctuary for birds and also for seals which are present in their greatest numbers between August and October. In summer boat trips can be made out to the islands. At the foot of Paritutu hill the Rangimarie Arts and Crafts Centre offers visitors a chance to see Maori craftspeople at work.

Difficult to miss with its 198m (650ft) chimney the thermal power station was originally built to burn coal but was converted to run on gas or oil after the discovery of natural gas off the Taranaki coast in 1969. This discovery of natural gas off-shore as well as an earlier find at Kapune has resulted in an economic boom for the region and New Plymouth in particular. The power station is open to the public on Wednesdays and Sundays.

Two beautiful parks within short driving distance of New Plymouth are the Pukeiti Rhododendron Trust and Lake Mangamahoe Domain. The Domain is one of the authors personal favourites. Not only is it a beautiful picnic spot but the view of Mount Taranaki (Egmont) with the lake in the foreground makes the heart of any photographer beat faster. Superb!

Mount Egmont
National Park

The Round the
Mountain Track is one
of New Zealand's
'Great Walks'

Egmont National Park

This national park is, as far as most visitors are concerned, Taranaki's crowning glory. It is centred around Mount Taranaki 2,518m (8,261ft), a dormant volcano with an almost perfect cone which is often compared to that of Japan's Mount Fuji. On those days when the mountain is not obscured by heavy white clouds (which can be rather often!) the sight of its snow-capped peak towering above the surrounding dairy lands is strikingly beautiful. A long-standing dispute as to how the mountain should be named was settled by deciding that it can be referred to by either its Maori name *Taranaki* or the European name Egmont. The park, which was created in 1900, is the second-oldest in the country after Tongariro and has, incidently, retained its European name.

The majority of people enter the park along one of the three mountain roads. The closest to New Plymouth is Egmont Road which leaves SH3 at Egmont village. The North Egmont Visitor Centre is located at the top of the road and provides simple accommodation, a cafeteria and displays relating to the park. Pembroke Road goes up the mountain from Stratford to the Mountain House Motor Lodge at East Egmont and the Manganui ski field. The ranger station is reached before East Egmont and this is the place to stop for park information. To the west of Stratford Manaia Road leads up to Dawson Falls Visitor Centre. Accommodation is available at the Tourist Lodge next door.

Skiing on the mountain is perhaps the most popular sport during the winter months but otherwise the park is the domain of trampers and climbers. The most popular walk is the four day Round-the-Mountain Track 55km (34 miles). It can be easily reached from the ends of any of the mountain roads which also provide convenient starting points for shorter day walks. The easiest route to the summit starts from North Egmont and requires about 8 hours return. **Please note**: This route is only 'easy' for fit trampers under favourable weather conditions. When there is a lot of snow on the summit mountaineering experience (ice axe and ropes) is essential. As the weather can quickly change anywhere in the park, even in summer, it is important to have suitable footwear and to carry warm clothing and a raincoat on any longer walks. It always pays to inquire about track and weather conditions before starting out.

There are two possibilities for the continued journey to Wanganui (Chapter 5); either follow the inland route via Stratford on SH3 or take the coastal road following SH45. **Oakura**, a few kilometres outside of New Plymouth on the coastal road, is known for its excellent surfing and windsurfing. There is also some good swimming and surfing at Opunake further down the coast.

Hawera, where SH45 merges with SH3, is interesting because of a couple of unusual private museums. Tawhiti Museum covers Taranaki's eventful history with life-size figures cast from real people living in the area, as well as colourful dioramas. Attached to the museum is a bush railway. The other private museum has been the work of New Zealand's most devoted Elvis fan: Kevin Wasley. Although a long way from Gracelands Elvis fans should not miss the Elvis Presley Memorial Record Room with its collection of rare recordings and memorabilia. A short distance north of town the Turuturu Mokai *Pa* is regarded as one of the ❋ best remaining examples of a pre-European Maori fortification. Having said that it is only fair to mention that the only visible remains are the trenches, dug-in hut sites and food storage pits. A pamphlet put out by the local tourist office helps explain the historical significance of the place and is worth getting for those who plan a visit. Just over 90km (56 miles) south-east of Hawera is the city of Wanganui.

Additional Information

Accommodation & Eating Out

ACCOMMODATION
New Plymouth
Wave Haven *
780 Main South Road, SH45
Oakura
☎ (06) 752 7800 Fax: (06) 752 7733

Aaron Court Motel & Caravan Park **
57 Junction Road, SH3
☎ and Fax: (06) 758 8712
Freephone:(0800) 101 939

Balconies Bed & Breakfast **
161 Powderham St
☎ (06) 757 8866

Rotorua
Kiwi Paka *
60 Tarewa Road
☎ (07) 347 0931 Fax: (07) 346 3167

Eaton Hall Guest House **
39 Hinemaru Street
(Bed & Breakfast)
☎ (07) 3 47 0366 Fax: (07) 348 6287

Midway Motel ***
293 Fenton Street
☎ and Fax (07) 347 7799

Taupo
Burkes Backpackers *
69 Spa Road
☎ and Fax (07)378 9292

Acacia Bay Lodge **
868 Acacia Bay Road
Tel. (07) 378 6830
Good place for anglers.

Tauranga
Bell Lodge *
39 Bell Street
☎ (07) 578 6344

Greerton Motor Inn **
1237 Cameron Road
☎ (07) 578 8164 Fax: (07) 578 3064

EATING OUT
New Plymouth
Tastings Foodcourt *
Centre City Shopping Mall
Gill Street
☎ (06) 758 4688 (bookings not taken)

Burundi Café-Bar *
55a Egmont Street
☎ (06) 458 1112

Juliana's Restaurant & Bar ***
Auto Lodge
395 Devon Street East
☎ (06) 758 88040

Rotorua
Mr India Tandoori Restaurant *
46 Amohau Street
☎ (07) 349 4940

Tastebuds Mexican Food *
93 Fenton Street
Tel. (07) 349 0591

Fish Pot Café **
Eruera Street
☎ (07) 349 3494

Rendezvous Restaurant ***
116 Hinemoa Street
☎ (07)348 9273
Great lamb dishes!

Taupo
Margarita's Tapas Bar & Restaurant **
63 Heuheu Street
☎ (07) 378 9909

Tauranga
Cheeks Family Restaurant *
64 Devonport Road
☎ (07) 578 6400

Harbourside Brasserie & Bar ***
(seafoods)
Old Yacht Club Building
The Strand Extension
☎ (07) 571 0520

Places to Visit

Hamurana
Hamurana Springs
17km north of Rotorua
Open: daily.

Hawera
Elvis Presley Memorial Room
51 Argyle Street
Open: by prior arrangement ☎ (06) 278
8599. No admission but donations
appreciated.

Tawhiti Museum
47 Ohangai Road
Open: Friday, Saturday, Sunday,
Monday 10am-4pm. June, July, August
Sunday only.

Mount Maunganui
Hot Salt Pools
Adams Avenue
Open: daily 8am-10pm.

New Plymouth
Govett Brewster Art Gallery
Queen Street
Open: Monday to Friday 10.30am-5pm,
weekends and public holidays 1-5pm.
Admission is free.

Power Station
Open: Guided tours Wednesday 10am
and Sunday 2pm. Admission is free.

Pukeiti Rhododendron Trust
Carrington Road
Open: daily 9am-5pm.

Pukekura Park
Fillis Street
Open: Display houses daily 10am-
12noon and 1-4pm. Tea kiosk closed
Tuesday.

Rangimarie Maori Art & Craft Centre
Centennial Drive
Open: 8.30am-4pm Monday to Friday.

Richmond Cottage
Gill Street
Open: (November to May) Monday,
Wednesday, Friday 2-4pm; Saturday,
Sunday, public holidays 1-4pm. (June to
October) Friday 2-4pm; Saturday,
Sunday, public holidays 1-4pm.

Taranaki Museum
Ariki Street
Open: 10.30am-4.30pm Tuesday to
Friday and 1-5pm weekends. Admis-
sion is free.

Ngongotaha
Agrodome
Riverdale Park
Western Road
Open: daily. Live Sheep Shows at 9.15am,
11am and 2.30pm. Licensed restaurant.

Orakei Korako
Thermal Region
Open: daily 8am. Last trip leaves
4.30pm (summer), 4pm (winter). Café.

Rotorua
Polynesian Pools
Hinemoa Street
Open: daily 9am-10pm. Café and bar.

Rainbow and Fairy Springs
Fairy Springs Rd, 5km from city
Open: daily 8am-5pm. Shows at
10.30am, 1pm and 2.30pm. Licensed
restaurant.

St Faith's Anglican Church
Lakefront
Open: daily 8.30am-5pm.

*Te Whakarewarewa Thermal Reserve &
    Maori Arts & Crafts Institute*
South of town centre on Fenton St
Open: daily 8.30am-5.30pm. Guided
tours hourly. Cultural Concert 12.15pm.

Tudor Towers (Bath House)
Government Gardens
Open: daily 10am-4.30pm.

Stratford
Taranaki Pioneer Village
1km south of Stratford
Open: daily 10am-4pm.

Taihape
Rongoiti Garden and Nursery
Koeke Road — Off Rongoiti Rd
13km from SH1
Open: Wednesday to Sunday 1 September to 30 April.

Titoki Point Garden and Nursery
North-west of town
(20 mins from SH1)
Open: 10am-4pm Wednesday to Sunday, October to May.

Taupo
De Brett Thermal Pools
Napier-Taupo Highway
Open: daily 8am-9.30pm.

Tauranga
Historic Village Museum
17th Avenue West
Open: daily 9am-6pm summer. Winter 5pm.

The Elms Mission House
Mission Street
Open: tours by prior arrangement. Contact tourist office.

Te Wairoa
Buried Village
Tarawera Rd, 15km east of Rotorua
Open: daily 8.30am-5.30pm. June to August 9am-4.30pm.

Tikitere
Hell's Gate
16km NE of Rotorua
Open: daily 9am-5pm.

Tokaanu
Thermal Park and Pools
Open: daily 10am-9.30pm.

Turangi
Tongariro National Trout Centre
Open: daily 9am-4pm. Entry is free.

Waimangu Volcanic Valley
SH5, 19km south of Rotorua
Open: daily 8.30am-5pm.

Waiotapu Thermal Region
SH5, 30km south of Rotorua
Open: daily 8.30am-8.30pm. In winter closes at 5pm. Lady Knox Geyser erupts daily at 10.15am.

Waiouru
Army Museum
Next to SH1
Open: daily 9am-4.30pm.

Wairakei
Craters of the Moon
Open: dawn to dusk. Admission is free.

Geothermal Station
Information Centre
Open: daily 9am-4pm.

Huka Village
Huka Falls Rd
Open: daily 9am-5pm. A colonial-style craft village.

Travel Tips
BOAT TRIPS
New Plymouth
Chaddy's Charters
Tickets: Chaddy's Boat Shed, Ocean View Parade
☎ (06)758 9133
Sugar Loaf Islands and Marine Park.

Taupo
The sailing-boats *Barbary* and *Spirit of Musick* and the steamboat *Ernest Kemp* offer 2-2$^1/2$ hour cruises on the lake. Depart daily at 10am and 2pm. Depature point is Taupo Boat Harbour, off Redoubt Rd. Contact the tourist office or book at the wharfs.

The *MV Waireka* (African Queen) does a 2 hour cruise on the Waikato River to Huka Falls. Departs daily at 10am and 2pm. Departure point is 9km (5$^1/2$ miles) north of Taupo, along Huka Falls Rd. ☎ (07) 374 8338).

Whakatane
Blue Sky Tours
'Kahurangi' Cat
☎ (07) 323 7829
Trips to White Island.

CANOE/KAYAK HIRE
Ohakune
Yeti Tours
PO Box 140
☎ (06) 385 8197
Also guided trips on Whanganui River.

Taumarunui
Wades Landing Outdoors
RD2 Owhango
☎ (07) 895 5995.

DOLPHIN SWIMMING
Whakatane
Dolphins Down Under
92 The Strand
☎ and Fax (07) 308 4636.

FISHING TRIPS
Taupo
Fly fishing guides and fishing charters can be arranged at Information Centre. Equipment is provided.

JET BOATING
Taupo
Huka Jet
☎ (07) 374 8572.

Whakatane
Kiwi Jet Boat Tours
Silver Hill, R.D.1
☎ (07) 307 0663.

MAORI HANGIS AND CULTURAL TOURS
Taupo
Maori hangis and concerts are offered by De Bretts Hotel, Spa Hotel and at Huka village. Contact information office for details.

Rotorua
Kingsgate Hotel
Eruera Street
Magically Maori Feast and Revue
(Freephone) ☎ 0800 654 685 or
(07) 347 1234
Nightly feast at 7pm, Maori Revue at 8.30pm. Free shuttle service within Rotorua.

Quality Hotel
Fenton Street
Maori Concert and Hangi
(Freephone) ☎ 0800 808 228 or
(07) 348 0199

Every night from 6.45pm. Free pick up and drop off within Rotorua.

THC Hotel
Hangi and Concert
Froude Street
☎ (07) 348 1189
Nightly 6pm. Complimentary transport within Rotorua.

Twilight Cultural Tour
Tamaki Tours
PO Box 1492
(Freephone) ☎ 0800 500 331 or
(07) 3462 823
This is a Maori-owned company. They also do tours to thermal areas.

SCENIC FLIGHTS
Tongariro National Park
Mountain Air
☎ (07) 892 2812
Offer flights over the volcanoes from Chateau Airport.

Whakatane
Vulcan Helicopters
PO Box 10 Waimana
☎ (07) 308 4188
Trips to White Island volcano. Flights depart Whakatane airport.

VOLCANIC TOURS
A few addresses:

Rotorua
Mud 'N Mountain (Wild Trax)
C/o Information Office or
PO Box 1163.

Taupo
☎ (07) 345 3264
Highlights: Waiotapu Thermal Wonderland, Mount Tarawera and a hot swim.

Tarawera Volcanic Golds Tour
C/o Information Centre
☎ (07) 347 1199
Highlights: Waimangu Valley, Rotomahana Crater Lake and Mount Tarawera.

Waimangu Round Trip
C/o Information Centre or
PO Box 402, Rotorua
☎ (07) 347 1199
This is the oldest and most famous volcanic tour.

WHITE WATER RAFTING
Taihape
River Valley Ventures
R.D.2
☎ (06) 388 1444

Tauranga
Wet 'N Wild Rafting Company
PO Box 1047
☎ (07) 578 4093

Whakatane
Motu Raft Tours
PO Box 2124
☎ (07) 308 7760

Tourist Information &
Park Visitor Centres

Egmont National Park
Department of Conservation (DOC)
Devon Street West
New Plymouth
☎ (06) 758 0433

North Egmont Visitors Centre
Egmont Road, Egmont Village
Open: daily 9am-5pm.
☎ (06) 756 8710

Dawson Falls Visitors Centre
Take Manaia Rd from Kaponga
☎ (025) 430 248

Hawera
Information South Taranaki
55 High Street
PO Box 5
☎ (06)278 8599

Mount Maunganui
Salisbury Avenue
☎ (07) 575 5099

New Plymouth
Corner Liardet and Leach Streets
Open: Monday-Friday 8.30am-5pm,
weekends 10am-3pm.
☎ (06) 758 6086

Ohakune
Ruapehu Visitors Centre
54 Clyde Street
PO Box 36
☎ (06)385 8427

Rotorua
Tourism Rotorua
67 Fenton Street
Open: daily 8am-5.30pm
☎ (07) 348 5179

Stratford
Miranda and Broadway
PO Box 320
☎ (06) 765 6708

Taumarunui
Railway Station
Hakiaha Street
PO Box 345
☎ (07) 895 7494
Information on Whanganui National
Park.

Taupo
13 Tongariro Street
PO Box 865
Open: daily 8.30am-5pm
☎ (07) 378 9000

Tauranga
The Strand
PO Box 1070
Open: Monday to Friday 8am-5pm,
weekends 8am-2pm.
☎ (07) 578 8103

Tongariro National Park
Ohakune
Ranger Station
Mountain Road
☎ (06) 385 8578

Turangi
Turangi Regional Office
Turanga Place
☎ (07) 386 8607

Whakapapa Village, Mount Ruapehu
Visitor Centre
Behind Château Hotel
☎ (07) 892 3729

Whakatane
Boon Street
PO Box 307
Open: Monday to Friday 9am-5pm,
Saturday (October to Easter) 9am-2pm.
☎ (07) 308 6058

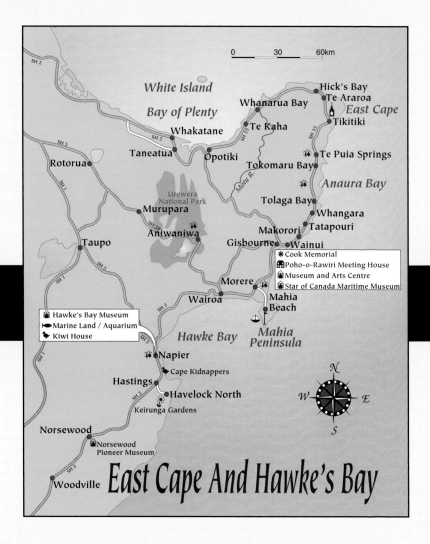

0   30   60km

White Island

Bay of Plenty

Hick's Bay
Te Araroa
Whanarua Bay
East Cape
Te Kaha
Tikitiki
Whakatane
SH 2
Taneatua
Ōpotiki
Rotorua
Te Puia Springs
Tokomaru Bay
SH 5
Anaura Bay
Urewera National Park
Tolaga Bay
Murupara
Whangara
Tatapouri
Aniwaniwa
Makorori
SH 38
Gisbourne
Wainui
Taupo

Cook Memorial
Poho-o-Rawiri Meeting House
Museum and Arts Centre
Star of Canada Maritime Museum

Morere
Mahia
Beach
Wairoa
Mahia
Peninsula

Hawke's Bay Museum
Marine Land / Aquarium
Kiwi House

Hawke Bay

Napier
Cape Kidnappers
Hastings
Havelock North
Keirunga Gardens

N
W   E
S

Norsewood
Norsewood
Pioneer Museum

Woodville

East Cape And Hawke's Bay

East Cape & Hawke's Bay

This chapter covers most of the eastern North Island, an area blessed by long warm summers and mild winters. Major attractions include the gannet colony at Cape Kidnappers, the wilderness area of Te Urewera National Park, the 'Art Deco Capital of the World' Napier and the secluded bays and beaches around East Cape. A special attraction around Christmas are the flowering pohutukawa trees along the East Cape coastal road.

Route 6 • The East Cape Road

The East Cape is an area rich in the history of the Maori people and many of the small settlements scattered along the coast still have a predominantly Maori population. The stretch of coast between Hicks Bay and Gisborne is known to the local Maori as *Tairawhiti* which means 'the coast upon which the sun shines across the water'. As much of the land along the coastal highway is privately owned (a fact which is not always immediately obvious, ie no fences or signposts) it is essential to seek permission before attempting to camp outside the designated areas.

above: Neo-Classical Bank of New Zealand building in Dannevirke

Quickly reached from Whakatane (Route 4) the small town of **Opotiki** has gone down in New Zealand history because of a particularly tragic event. In 1865 the Reverend Carl Volkner, who up until that time had enjoyed the trust of local tribes, was executed in his church by Maori belonging to the anti-European Hauhau movement. Although accounts of the killing vary one particularly gruesome version has it that Volkner was decapitated and that his eyes were gouged out and eaten. Whether or not this account of his death is true the fact is that Volkner had been guilty of spying and the killing can be seen as an act of revenge. The place of Volkner's untimely death is now known as the Church of St Stephen the Martyr and it is here that the reverend lies buried.

Organised outdoor activities that start from Opotiki include mountain bike tours through the East Cape's rugged bush covered interior and exhilarating jet boat rides on the mighty Motu river. For the even more adventurous there are also white water rafting trips through the magnificent forest scenery of the Motu river's lower gorge — one to five days of pure adventure!

A nice excursion from Opotiki, and a great spot for a picnic, is the Hukutaia Domain, about 7km (4^1/$_2$ miles) west of town. This pretty 5 hectare reserve contains a fine selection of native plants, many of which are identified with their botanical, common and Maori names. One of the domain's most impressive trees is an ancient puriri that is known to the

Puriri (*Vitex lucens*)

he puriri is a sub-tropical tree with timber as hard and as durable as teak. Unfortunately the timber has an irregular grain which makes it difficult to work and it is only used as firewood or for railway sleepers. The trees produce small flowers throughout most of the year and can reach a height of 20m (65ft). The puriri's habitat is restricted to the northern half of the North Island.

local Maori as *Taketakerau*. Over 2,000 years old its hollow trunk was once used as a place to inter the bones of important people.

From Opotiki SH35 commences its winding journey along a coastline dotted with lovely little bays and beaches. The first place of any size is the old whaling settlement of **Te Kaha**. The last whales were harpooned here in the 1930s and since then the little town has relied mainly on farming and fishing to get by. Tourism has also done its bit to help the local economy as there are a number of fine beaches, as well as good fishing, in the vicinity. Well worth a look is the magnificently carved Tukaki meeting house, though permission should be gained before entering the *marae*.

Continuing north **Whanarua Bay** is a particularly beautiful spot and those who wish to overnight can do so at the Rendezvous on the Coast Holiday Park. Apart from providing budget accommodation in the form of cabins and tent sites the holiday park also offers instruction in scuba diving and they hire out boats and kayaks. From Whangaparaoa the road goes inland before reaching the coast again at Hicks Bay, some 30km (18^1/$_2$ miles) distant.

Idyllic **Hicks Bay** was named after a member of the crew on Cook's ship the *Endeavour*. Here visitors can spend their time fishing, swimming and bush walking in the most picturesque of surroundings. A feature of the area are the many ancient puriri trees which, in contrast to the pohutukawa, flower nearly all year round.

A short journey further down the coast is the settlement of **Te Araroa**. From here it is possible to turn off along the road to the East Cape lighthouse, supposedly the most easterly in the world. The 40km (25 miles) return trip is best done early to witness the sunrise. For those who do not have their own transport the Hick's Bay Backpackers Lodge (☎ (06) 864 4731) arranges 'sunrise tours' to the lighthouse.

The road moves inland again after Te Araroa and the first place of interest is **Tikitiki**. Visitors should not miss seeing the Anglican Church here as it is beautifully decorated with Maori art. Further south **Te Puia Springs** is worth noting for its natural hot pools. **Tokomaru Bay** is only another 10km (6 miles) away and would be a pleasant spot to spend a few quiet days by the seaside.

Continuing south those who want to experience a really lovely stretch of coast, away from it all, should take the turn-off to **Anaura Bay**. A wonderful beach of golden sands and a panoramic walkway (2 hours) with views over the sea are ample reward for the trip. It was here that Captain Cook made his second landing in New Zealand and there is a plaque to mark the event.

Compared to Anaura Bay and indeed to most settlements along this road **Tolaga Bay** is a sizeable town. Not only is the beach here good for swimming it is given added distinction by the presence of New Zealand's longest wharf (660m) (722ft). It was built between 1926 and 1929 to enable ships to unload even when the tide was out. A few kilometres south of town the Cook's Cove walkway is a great chance to stretch the legs. Tupaea's Cavern, a natural rock archway linking Tolaga Bay with Cook's Cove, is a highlight of the walk. The start of the track can be reached by following Wharf Road off the main highway. Closed during the lambing season (1 August to 30 September) the walk takes roughly 2^1/$_2$ hours to complete.

The 55km (34 miles) drive down to Gisborne could be punctuated with stops at **Whangara**, where there is a nice beach, or at **Tatapouri** where the fishing is good and freshly caught crayfish are often for sale. Shortly before Gisborne are the superb beaches at **Makorori** and **Wainui**.

Not only does the small coastal city of **Gisborne** get more than its fair

Anaura Bay, East Cape

Maori traditions and folklore are still very much alive on the East Cape

share of sunshine but it is also the first place in the world to see the rising sun. This is due to its proximity to the International Dateline and extreme easterly position. Perhaps a more important fact for some is that all the sunshine, and suitable soils, have gone a long way to making the Gisborne region an important wine-growing area producing some excellent Chardonnays.

The city occupies a significant place in New Zealand history as it was here on 9 October 1769 that Captain Cook landed for the first time on New Zealand soil. The spot is marked by the Cook Memorial at the foot of Kaiti Hill, on Kaiti Beach Road. From the top of the hill a magnificent view encompasses the city with its three rivers as well as the broad expanse of Poverty Bay. Near the top is a statue of Captain Cook.

The road up to the look-out on Kaiti Hill passes the Poho-o-Rawiri meeting house, one of the largest in New Zealand. Although permission is required to enter (inquire at visitor information) it is well worth going inside to see some superb examples of traditional Maori carving.

Further insight into the Maori culture of the Gisborne region can be gained by visiting the small Museum and Arts Centre. It also deals with the period of European settlement and an old colonial cottage forms part of the complex. Next door is the Star of Canada Maritime Museum. An interesting fact about this museum is that it was originally the bridge of a ship wrecked off Kaiti Beach in 1912. Prior to becoming a museum it had served for many years as one of Gisborne's more unique homes.

Thirty-five kilometres (22 miles) to the north-west of Gisborne, via Ngatapa, is the Eastwoodhill Arboretum. It comprises the largest collection of flora from the Northern Hemisphere in the country. The best times to visit are in spring when magnolias, cherries and horse chestnuts burst into flower or in autumn when deciduous trees like oaks, maples and ash are aflame with colour. Another 15km (9 miles) further on Rere Falls is a popular picnic and swimming spot.

From Gisborne the road south continues via **Manutuke** on SH2 where there are two magnificently carved meeting houses. However the interior of Toko Toru Tapu Anglican Church is also beautifully decorated with Maori carvings. Once again visitors are reminded that meeting houses and the *marae* on which they stand are not museums but places where Maori gather socially. They are also places where ancient traditions are cultivated and preserved. It is always important to seek permission locally before entering these areas.

Another 47km (29 miles) further south at **Morere** are the Morere Hot Springs. Here it is possible to enjoy the thermal waters in a pretty setting of native bush. There are a number of pools, both public and private, to choose from but nicest is the luxury of having a pool all to oneself. Several easy walks go through the surrounding forest which contains groves of nikau palms, graceful tree ferns and an abundance of native birds.

The road to **Mahia Peninsula** leaves SH2 at Nuhaka. Hilly and sparsely populated the peninsula attracts visitors with its fine beaches and good diving and surfing conditions. The main settlement is **Mahia Beach** where there is a small golf course.

Wairoa, 33km (20^1/$_2$ miles) west of Nuhaka, is chiefly interesting as the southern gateway to Urewera National Park. A distinctive feature of the Marine Parade is a solid kauri lighthouse (1877) that was brought here from Portland Island at the tip of Mahia Peninsula.

Te Urewera National Park

Rugged, wild and unspoiled Te Urewera National Park is the third largest national park in New Zealand and protects the largest remaining area of native forest in the North Island. It is also the ancestral home of the Tuhoe people, the 'Children of the Mist', who even today live in relative isolation from the rest of the country.

State Highway 38 provides access to the park for those coming from Wairoa and also for those coming from Rotorua via **Murupara**. The northern section of the park is accessible from Whakatane via **Taneatua**. Park headquarters is located at Aniwaniwa on the shores of Lake Waikaremoana but there are also ranger stations at Murupara and Taneatua.

Surrounded by primeval bush **Lake Waikaremoana** is the main centre for activities in the park. The lake itself is not only popular for swimming, boating and trout-fishing but also provides a lovely backdrop for the Lake Waikaremoana Track which closely follows the lake for most of its length. A highlight of this 3 to 4 day walk is the splendid view over lake and forest from Panekiri Bluff.

There are many other excellent walks in the park varying in length from short strolls to trips of several days. In the category of 'stroll' is the walk to Aniwaniwa Falls, only 15 minutes from park headquarters. Especially worthwhile is the track to Lake Waikareiti, a wonderfully tranquil place that can only be reached on foot. The track starts near park headquarters and about 3 hours is needed for the return trip. There is a hut at Sandy Bay that can also be reached by row-boat (inquire at park headquarters, Aniwaniwa) and this would be a great place to stay, if only for a single night. Here, surrounded by nothing but the silent grandeur of the forest, it is possible to imagine New Zealand as it was before the coming of man; a land of birds covered by a vast cloak of primordial green. Here the still of the evening is broken only by the morepork's (a native owl) call, while a multitude of insects, among them perhaps a magnificent puriri moth, are attracted by the warm glow of lantern light.

From Wairoa SH2 continues south through picturesque countryside to the coast at Napier. The Department of Conservation (DOC) brochure *Napier-Tutira Highway: Hawke's Bay Reserves and Walkways* is worth getting for those with an interest in natural history.

Route 7 • Hawke's Bay

For $2^1/2$ minutes on 3 February 1931 both **Napier** and Hastings were gripped by one of the most devastating earthquakes ever to hit New Zealand. In that short span of time both cities were reduced to rubble and Napier was suddenly 3,600ha (9,000 acres) larger, as the titanic forces unleashed by the quake heaved up land in a matter of seconds from the seabed.

Following the earthquake Napier was mainly rebuilt in the Art Deco style of the 1930s and today the city is considered to have one of the finest concentrations of such architecture anywhere in the world. Most of the Art Deco buildings are located in the inner-city, often easily recognisable by the delicate pastel tones in which they have been painted. Good examples can be found along Emerson, Tennyson and Hastings Streets. However one particularly splendid example, the Rothman's Building, is located on the outskirts of town on the road to Gisborne and Taupo. Visitors can take themselves on their own 'Art Deco walk' using the leaflet available from the visitor information centre. There are also guided walks starting from the Desco Centre on Tennyson Street.

Lined with tall Norfolk pines Napier's lovely Marine Parade lures the visitor with a variety of attractions. Performing dolphins and seals can be seen at Marineland, while the Hawke's Bay Aquarium has a fascinating collection of marine life including sharks and piranhas. New Zealand's unique tuatara is also on display here.

Close to Marineland is the recently opened Stables Complex. The attractions here are a waxworks museum and 'Earthquake '31', a simulation of the great quake. They also show historic movie footage taken before and after the Napier earthquake.

The Napier-Hastings earthquake is also featured at the excellent Hawke's Bay Museum, further north along the Marine Parade. One of the best permanent exhibitions here is *Nga Tukemata* (The Awakening) which deals with the art of the East Coast's Ngati Kahungunu people. Other permanent exhibitions cover Art Deco, colonial history and arts and crafts in New Zealand.

North of the museum the Kiwi House is unique in that it is the only such place in New Zealand where visitors can actually touch and feed a kiwi. Other creatures kept here include bush geckoes, native land snails, moreporks and whistling frogs.

Those in search of a great view should venture to the top of Bluff Hill where the look-out offers a panoramic vista of the entire Hawke Bay coastline. To get there follow the signpost from Lighthouse Road at the northern end of town.

The biggest natural attraction in the vicinity of Napier is the colony of Australasian gannets (*Sula bassana serrator*) at **Cape Kidnappers**. This is the world's largest mainland gannet colony, the only other one being at Muriwai Beach, near Auckland. These large sea-birds usually only breed

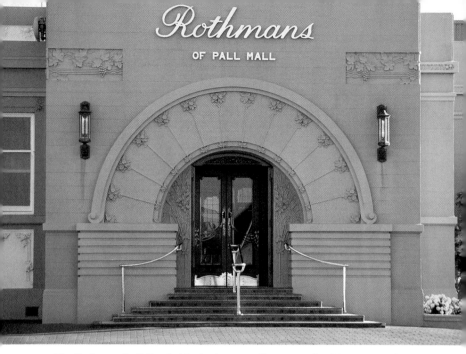

The Rothmans building in Napier is an excellent example of Art Deco architecture

Cosy little tea rooms provide a welcome respite from travel

Wayside stands offering fresh fruit and vegetables are commonplace in the region of Gisborne and Hawke's Bay

on small isolated islands so Cape Kidnappers provides a unique opportunity to see them up close. The best time to view the birds is between early November and late February.

There are organised trips out to the colony but for those who want to walk the starting point is Clifton Domain, 21km (13 miles) south-east of Napier, near Te Awanga. The 8km (5 miles) walk runs along the beach and takes about 2 hours. As this route is only possible when the tide is out it is best to start 3 hours after high tide and to return no later than $1^1/2$ hours after low tide. Tide schedules are available from the Napier information centre.

Only 20km ($12^1/2$ miles) further south of Napier, on SH2, **Hastings** is set in the middle of the Hawke's Bay fruit and wine-growing region. During harvest season roadside stalls are literally brimming over with bargain priced citrus fruits and other fresh produce. There are also several wineries producing some excellent wines to ensure that those who follow the Hawke's Bay wine trail (contact information office for details) will have a pleasurable time.

Destroyed like Napier in the 1931 earthquake the town was rebuilt in a similar fashion. There are some good examples of Art Deco architecture but it is the Spanish Mission style in particular that captures attention here. This style is fairly easy to recognise by such features as curving, rounded gables, orange roof tiles and rough-cast walls. In other words if the building looks like it belongs on a Spanish hacienda then it was built in the Spanish Mission style. A number of impressive buildings in this style can be seen along Russell, Eastbourne and Heretaunga streets.

❋   Other places to visit include the Hawke's Bay Exhibition Centre with its changing exhibitions of local, national and international art and if you are travelling with children Fantasyland leisure park. In nearby **Havelock North** Keirunga Gardens with its miniature railway is another great place to take the kids. A short drive away Te Mata Peak (399m/1,308ft) awaits with breathtaking views and a fine restaurant from which to enjoy them.

From Hastings continue south on SH2, through the sheep farming centres of Waipawa and Waipukurau, to **Norsewood**. This tiny place (population 330) was founded by Scandinavian settlers who arrived here in 1872. The few reminders of those early pioneering days are to be found in Upper Norsewood in the Norsewood Pioneer Museum. Also close by, in a glassed boat-house, is the fishing boat *Bindalsfareing*, a gift from the Norwegian government. Handy to the museum is a pleasant tearoom where a little old lady serves Devonshire teas and is delighted to have travellers sign her guest-book. Woollen garments can be bought directly from the Norsewear factory in Lower Norsewood, opposite which is an interesting crafts shop.

Further south SH2 passes through Dannevirke, another old Scandinavian settlement, and eventually reaches **Woodville**. From here the traveller can choose between two routes to Wellington: either go west though the scenic Manawatu Gorge and then via Palmerston North and Levin to join SH1, or continue on SH2 through the little visited Wairarapa region (see Chapter 5).

Additional Information

Accommodation and Eating Out

ACOMMODATION
Gisborne
Gisborne Backpackers *
690 Gladstone Road
☎ (06)867 7141

Green Gables Travel Hotel **
31 Rawiri Street
Kaiti
☎ (06)867 9872

Colonial Motor Lodge ***
715 Gladstone Rd
☎ (06)867 9165 Fax:(06)867 4099

Napier
Criterion Backpackers Inn *
48 Emerson Street Mall
☎ (06)835 2059

Pinehaven Travel Hotel **
259 Marine Parade
☎ and Fax (06)835 5575

Masonic Hotel **
Tennyson Street
☎ (06)835 8689 Fax:(06)835 2297

Opotiki
Opotiki Central Backpackers *
30 King Street
☎ (07)315 5165

Masonic Hotel **
Church Street
☎ (07)315 6115

Tokomaru Bay
House of the Rising Sun *
PO Box 100
☎ (06)864 5858

Whanarua Bay
Rendezvous on the Coast Holiday Park *
Private Bag 1114
Opotiki
☎ and Fax (07)325 2899
Hire diving equipment & kayaks.

EATING OUT
Gisborne
Café Villaggio *
57 Ballance Street
☎ (06)868 1611

Regent Restaurant **
(Seafood)
61 Gladstone Road
☎ (06)867 7457

Pinehurst Manor ***
4 Clifford Street
☎ (06)868 6771

Hastings
The Cat and Fiddle Ale House *
502 Karamu Road
☎ (06)878 4111

St George Estate Vineyard Restaurant **
St Georges Road South
☎ (06)877 5356

Napier
Golden Crown Restaurant *
38 Dickens Street
☎ (06)835 5996

Gumnuts Restaurant *
(Vegetarian available)
New Provincial Hotel
Corner Emerson St and Clive Square
☎ (06)835 6934

Mango Jack's Café **
18 Hastings Street
☎ (06)834 0405

The Tennyson Restaurant ***
(Seafood)
Clive Square
☎ (06)835 3373

Opotiki
Vo Lee Lan Restaurant **
(Oriental)
Church Street
☎ (07)315 6237

Places to Visit

ROUTE 6
Gisborne
Eastwood Hill Arboretum
Rere Road
(35km from Gisborne)
Open: daily 10am-4pm.

Museum and Arts Centre
Stout Street
Open: 10am-4pm Monday to Friday;
Saturday, Sunday and public holidays
1.30-4pm.

Poho-o-Rawiri Meeting House
Open: contact tourist office for details.

Star of Canada Maritime Museum
Stout Street
Open: same as Arts Centre.

Morere
Hot Springs
Open: 10am-5pm.

ROUTE 7
Hastings
Fantasyland
Grove Road
Open: daily.

Hawke's Bay Exhibition Centre
Eastbourne Street
Open: 10am-4.30pm Monday to Friday.
Weekends 12noon-4.30pm.

Havelock North
Keirunga Park Railway
Keirunga Park
Open: First and third Sunday of each
month 11am-4pm.

Napier
Hawke's Bay Aquarium
Marine Parade
Open: daily 9am-5pm. Feeding 3.15pm.

Hawke's Bay Museum
Marine Parade
Open: daily 10am-4.30pm.

Kiwi House
Marine Parade
Open: daily 11am-3pm. Show at 1pm.
Feeding at 2pm.

Marineland of NZ
Marine Parade
Open: daily 10am-4.30pm. Shows
10.30am and 2pm.

Stables Complex
321 Marine Parade
Open: daily 9am-5pm.

Travel Tips

Cape Kidnappers Gannet Colony
The season is October to April.

Te Awanga
Gannet Beach Adventures
Charlton Rd
☎ and Fax (06)875 0898
Depart Charlton Rd. Bookings essential.

Gannet Safaris
RD2, Hastings
☎ (06)875 0511
Depart Summerlee Station, near Te
Awanga.

FISHING TRIPS
Gisborne
East Coast Fishing Guide Service
David Dods
☎ (06)862 7850

Opotiki
Mark Draper
Fishing and Outdoors
PO Box 445
☎ (07)315 7434

JET BOATING
Opotiki
Motu River Jet Boat Tours
☎ (07)315 8107
The same company also offer white
water rafting trips.

KAYAK AND CANOE RENTALS
Gisborne
Bay Kayaks Ltd
364 Ormond Rd
☎ (06)837 3737
Also do tours on Lake Waikaremoana.

Gisborne Health and Fitness Centre
4 Whitmore Street
☎ (06)867 3977

NATIONAL PARK TRANSPORT
Te Urewera National Park
Intercity buses run between Rotorua
and Wairoa on Monday, Wednesday, &
Friday. The Waikaremoana Shuttle runs
between Wairoa, Tuai and the Visitor
Centre on Monday, Tuesday, Friday,
Saturday & Sunday ☎ (06)837 3855

Tourist Information & Park Visitor Centres

Gisborne
*Eastland and Gisborne District
    Information Centre*
209 Grey Street
PO Box 170
Open: daily 9am-6pm; December to
January 9am-9pm.
☎ (06)868 6139

Hastings
Russell Street
☎ (06)876 0205

Napier
Marine Parade
Open: Monday to Friday 8.30am-5pm,
weekends 9am-5pm.
☎ (06)835 7579

Opotiki
Corner St John and Elliott Street
Po Box 591
☎ (07)315 8484

Te Urewera National Park
Aiwaniwa Visitor Centre
Private Bag 2213
Wairoa
☎ (06)837 3803

DOC East Coast Conservancy
PO Box 668
63 Carnarvon Street
Gisborne
☎ (06)867 8531

Wairoa
Marine Parade West
☎ (06)838 7440

Wanganui, the Wairarapa & Wellington

5

Covered here is the capital city of Wellington with its beautiful harbour, the 'River City' Wanganui and a thinly populated region known as the Wairarapa. Palmerston North is the starting point for exhilarating jet boat trips through the Manawatu Gorge, Mount Bruce National Wildlife Centre is a magnet for nature lovers and Cape Palliser, the southernmost point of the North Island, is a place for those who value seclusion above all else. At the Cape there is nothing but a lighthouse, a seal colony and all the peace and quiet that anybody could ever wish for.

Route 8 • From Wanganui to Wellington

Wanganui is reached along SH3 for those coming from Taranaki (Chapter 3) but SH4 offers the most direct route if you are coming from Ohakune near Tongariro National Park. It is at Wanganui that New Zealand's longest navigable river, the Whanganui, enters the Tasman Sea and it is this river that gives the city much of its attractive character.

above: The Wanganui River

A note: According to the logic of such Maori place-names as Whakatane and Whangarei the name 'Wanganui' should be spelled 'Whanganui'. However the 'h' has only been restored to the river and the national park. On older maps they still leave out the 'h' in the river's name.

The best way to appreciate the city's location on the banks of the Whanganui is to take the elevator to the top of Durie Hill. It is reached through a long pedestrian tunnel and actually ascends through the hill itself. At the top is a look-out tower with splendid views over the city to the coast and even as far as Mount Taranaki in clear weather. Not far away there are even better views from the top of the Durie Hill War Memorial Tower.

Taking the elevator back down again the city centre is only a short walk away over City Bridge. Continue up Victoria Avenue, the main shopping thoroughfare, and before long a glance to the right will reveal a hill upon which the visitor will find Wanganui's main cultural attractions.

First and foremost is the excellent Whanganui Regional Museum. Its Maori collection, featuring a huge war canoe that could hold 70 men, is one of New Zealand's finest. Other displays deal with colonial and natural history; note the skeletons of extinct moas in the New Zealand birds section. Also not to be missed is a collection of Maori portraits by Gottfried Lindauer (1839 to1926).

Nearby the Sergeant Art Gallery houses a collection of paintings from the nineteenth and twentieth centuries. Important New Zealand artists represented here include J.C. Hoyte, John Gully and C.F. Goldie. From outside the building presents a rather Mediterranean aspect with its domed roof and surrounding palms.

Maori culture comes to the fore again at Putiki Church in Anaua Street. Though plain from the outside the interior of the church is magnificently decorated with carvings and woven wall panels (*tukutuku*). However if old river boats are more to your taste then a visit to the wreck of the paddle steamer *Waimarie*, near the Wanganui Riverboat Centre on Taupo Quay, might be of interest. The 34m (102ft) boat is being restored and should be back on the river in 2 or 3 years.

There are a number of pleasant parks scattered around the city where visitors can stretch their legs or take a picnic. Perhaps loveliest of all is Virginia Lake, about one kilometre north of the city centre along Great North Road (head in the direction of New Plymouth). Kowhai Park with its imaginative children's playground is on the same side of the river as Durie Hill. It spreads along the river bank near Dublin Street Bridge but can also be reached by crossing City Bridge and then following a path along the river.

A highlight of any visit to Wanganui, for many perhaps the highlight, is a river trip. One of the more romantic ways to do this is to board the historic paddle steamer *Otunui* (1908). The old riverboat sails to a number of destinations along the river but the trip to Holly Lodge Winery is especially popular. There are also jet boats operating on the river for those who like a faster pace.

An interesting day trip from Wanganui is the excursion to Bushy Park, ❄
some 24km (15 miles) away. To get there drive in the direction of New
Plymouth as far as Kai Iwi, then turn off to the right and follow the side
road another 8km (5 miles). The scenic reserve features a historic homestead built in 1906 and easy walks through native bush. If you want a
change from sterile motel rooms accommodation is also available at the
homestead which offers guests a unique colonial atmosphere at very
reasonable prices.

The **Whanganui River Road** follows the Whanganui River from
Wanganui to Pipiriki, 79km (49 miles) north of the city. The partly unsealed road takes visitors into a remote part of New Zealand steeped in
Maori and colonial history. Sprinkled along the way tiny Maori settlements with names like Atene (Athens) and Hiruharama (Jerusalem) act
as reminders of early missionary activity in the area. About 23km (14
miles) short of Pipiriki is the restored Kawana Flour Mill. Flour was first 🏛
ground here in 1854 and the mill operated for over 50 years before falling
into disuse. Next to the mill is a colonial style cottage that once belonged
to the miller.

Pipiriki serves as a gateway to the rugged beauty of Whanganui National Park. In the days when riverboats regularly plied the river the
settlement boasted an elegant hotel with guests from all over the world.
Fire destroyed the hotel in 1959 and at present the only place to stay is a
simple camp-site. The DOC office provides information about the park
and a small museum housed in a colonial cottage has exhibits on the 🏠
history of the river and Pipiriki. Also of interest in the village is the *MV
Ongarue*, an old riverboat built in 1903 and now displayed on land.

The return trip is made by continuing north-east to Raetihi, then following scenic SH4 back to Wanganui. The entire journey covers 180km
(112 miles) and motorists should note that there are no petrol stations
between Upokongaro at the south end and Raetihi at the north end.

If you do not have your own transport — or even if you do — a great
way to explore the River Road is with the Mail Bus which leaves
Wanganui each weekday. The driver provides a commentary on places of
scenic and historic interest and also stops at various points along the way.
If you are travelling under your own steam it is well worth getting hold
of the DOC pamphlet *The River Road Scenic and Historic Drive*, available at
the DOC office or tourist information in Wanganui. Also available at
these places is the very detailed booklet *A Motorist's Guide to the Wanganui
River Road* by Judith Crawley.

Whanganui National Park

The main attraction of this park is of course the Whanganui River, New
Zealand's second longest, which commences its 329km (204 miles) journey to the sea on the flanks of Mount Tongariro. But the park also protects
one of the most remote areas of wilderness in the central North Island.
Largely untouched tracts of podocarp-broadleaf forest, alive with native

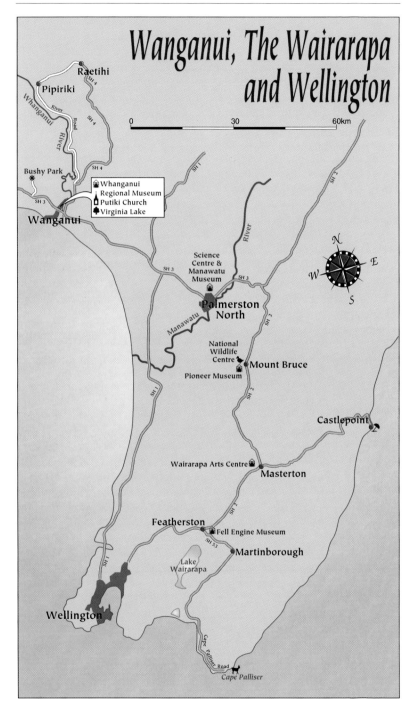

Wanganui, The Wairarapa and Wellington

Raetihi
Pipiriki

Whanganui River

Bushy Park

SH 4

Wanganui

Whanganui Regional Museum
Putiki Church
Virginia Lake

SH 3

SH 1

River

Science Centre & Manawatu Museum
SH 3

Palmerston North

Manawatu

SH 2

National Wildlife Centre
Pioneer Museum
Mount Bruce

SH 1

SH 2

Castlepoint

Wairarapa Arts Centre
Masterton

SH 2

Featherston
Fell Engine Museum
SH 53
Martinborough

Lake Wairarapa

SH 1

Wellington

Cape Palliser Road
Cape Palliser

birds, are only accessible to canoeists or to those prepared to shoulder their backpacks for several days along the park's main hiking trails.

The river has a long history as a transportation route. In pre-European times the Maori used it as a link between the coast and the North Island's rugged interior. With the arrival of European settlers a steamer service was eventually established between the two main settlements of Wanganui and Taumarunui. The first riverboat commenced operation in 1886 and before long there was a fleet of 12 boats serving isolated farming communities along the river.

Due to the magnificent scenery tourism was also quick to develop on the river and the three day trip between the two main settlements became a must for visitors to the country. To cope with the boom the luxury hotel Pipiriki House was built in 1892 and in one year (1905) 12,000 guests were recorded as having stayed here. By the 1920s however the boom was over.

The decline of the riverboat industry was coupled with several factors. Erosion, difficulty of access and the sheer ruggedness of the landscape forced many farmers along the stretch of river north of Pipiriki to abandon their farms. Rising costs and the development of road and rail dealt the final blow and steamer services ended in 1958.

Since then, however, tourism has revived on the river with jet-boating and canoeing becoming increasingly popular activities. In fact the canoe trip down the river from Taumarunui to Pipiriki, right through the

Canoes like this one, with its finely carved prow were an important mode of transportation for the Maori

middle of the park, is one of the most enjoyable outdoor experiences that a visitor to New Zealand can have. Riverside camping, narrow gorges and dense forest reaching right down to the water's edge are highlights of this 4-5 day paddle tour. Because of the river's gentle gradient the trip is also suitable for the inexperienced.

Tramping in Whanganui National Park is made somewhat complicated because of the need to arrange transport. As the two main tracks either start or end on the Whanganui River a jet boat must be arranged to pick you up or drop you off before setting out. Both the Matemateonga Walkway and the Mangapurua Track are easy 3-4 day walks. The latter is given a bit of historical interest by the 'Bridge to Nowhere'. This large concrete structure was built in 1936, at a time when many settler-farmers were already leaving the isolated Mangapurua Valley. By 1942 the valley was completely abandoned. Now regenerating forest has covered the approaches to the bridge which remains as a poignant symbol of the settlers' vain attempt to cultivate the land.

From Wanganui SH3 continues south to **Palmerston North**. This university town has no major attractions to hold the tourist's interest, though the Science Centre and Manawatu Museum is worth a brief stop. Jet-boat trips through the scenic Manawatu Gorge can be arranged here and might also justify a longer stay.

The Wairarapa region is reached by first travelling east through the Manawatu Gorge in the direction of Woodville. From here SH2 runs south through sheep and dairy farming country to the National Wildlife Centre at **Mount Bruce**. The Wildlife Centre is fascinating for anybody who has an interest in New Zealand's unique fauna. Here it is possible to see some of the rarest birds and reptiles in the world. A track leads through beautiful forest past large outdoor aviaries where the habitat of native birds is simulated as closely as possible. The visitor can see kokakos, saddlebacks, keas and kakapos; all of which are found no where else but in New Zealand. In the nocturnal house there are not only kiwis but also the rare tuatara, a lizard-like survivor from the age of the dinosaurs. One of the prize exhibits is the takahe, a large flightless bird that was presumed extinct until it was rediscovered in 1948. The breeding programmes and research carried out at the centre play a vital role in the survival of the takahe and the country's other endangered species.

Another 10km (6 miles) south of the National Wildlife Centre is the Mt Bruce Pioneer Museum. It prides itself as being Wairarapa's largest private museum with items ranging from waterwheels to gramophones.

Next stop is **Masterton**, the main centre of the Wairarapa. The biggest attraction this prosperous farming town has to offer is the annual Golden Shears shearing competition. Contestants come from all over New Zealand and overseas to demonstrate their skills at sheep shearing. A top shearer can remove the wool from a sheep in less than a minute but the judges also control the quality of the shearing and not just the speed.

Worth a longer look is the Wairarapa Arts Centre. Of particular interest here is the Stidolph Museum of Early Childhood with its collection of clockwork toys and antique dolls. There are also regular art and craft exhibitions held at the centre.

Those who want to explore a little more of the Wairarapa's rugged and sparsely populated hill country should consider making an excursion from Masterton to **Castlepoint** on the coast. The road goes via Tauweru and Tinui, a distance of 66km (41 miles). The first thing visitors will notice about this little seaside settlement is the lighthouse, built in 1913 and one of the tallest in the country 23m (75ft). There is good swimming in a sheltered lagoon known as the 'Basin' and even a golf course. The annual race meeting held in March on the sandy beach has a tradition reaching back to the nineteenth century. As there is accommodation (motel, camping grounds) and a store Castlepoint would be a nice, if very remote, place to escape the tourist crowds.

Featherston lies 36km (22 miles) south of Masterton on SH2, close to the shores of Lake Wairarapa. Railway enthusiasts in particular will want to pause here to see the town's Fell Engine Museum. The Fell engine was designed to climb the steep Rimutaka Incline over the Rimutaka Range that separates Wellington from the Wairarapa. With a gradient of 1:15 to overcome the locomotives could only manage a top speed of 5km/h for the 4.8km (3 mile) journey up. The Fell engines were operated for 77 years until the building of a tunnel in 1955 made them obsolete. The beautifully restored engine on display is supposedly the only remaining Fell locomotive in the world. A walkway (4 hours one way) now follows the incline. It can be reached by taking Western Lake Road south.

To the south-east of Featherston is a wine growing district centred around **Martinborough**. Those who want to do their own tour of the vineyards should pick up the relevant brochure at the information centre in Masterton.

A side trip for the more adventurous is to the most southerly point of the North Island at **Cape Palliser**. To get there continue on from Martinborough in the direction of Lake Ferry, a tiny fishing settlement. Shortly before Lake Ferry there is a turn-off to Whangaimoana. From now on the road is largely unsealed as it follows the rugged, exposed coastline to the Cape. Drivers should note that several streams have to be forded which can be dangerous after heavy rain. At the Cape there is a lighthouse and the North Island's largest seal colony.

From Featherston the main road winds its way over the windswept but very scenic Rimutaka Range before descending into the Hutt Valley to reach Wellington.

Tararua Ranges, Wairarapa

Sheep sheering demonstrations are a feature of agricultural (A&P) fairs throughout the country

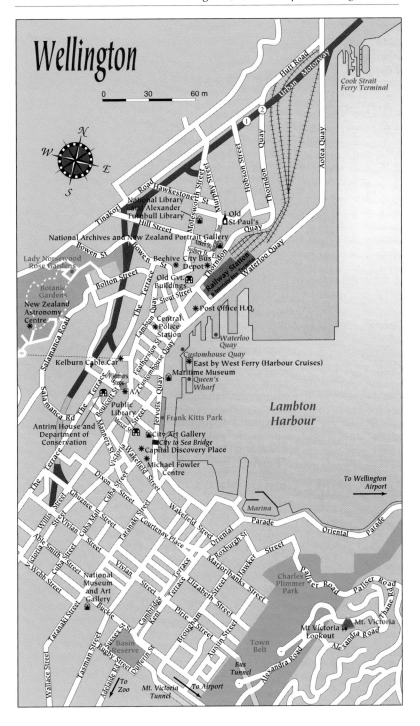

Wellington

Tucked in between steep hills and a beautiful harbour is New Zealand's capital city, **Wellington**. Nicknamed 'Windy Wellington' the weather here can be capricious to say the least, but on a fine summer's day when the sunlight reflects off the waters of Oriental Bay and on the surrounding hills the red or blue painted tin roofs of the houses form intense spots of colour in the crystal clear air, then there can be little doubt that the city is one of the loveliest in the world.

Architecturally too the city has much to offer. It is fascinating just to walk around the downtown area, through narrow canyons formed by glass-fronted skyscrapers to be suddenly surprised by a quaint relic from the Victorian era or an impressive example of post-modernist design. Steep flights of steps climb up past boutiques and snack bars, a spacious square provides unexpected respite from the chaos of city traffic; everywhere there seem to be nooks and crannies waiting to be explored. In fact a walk around the inner city is as easy as it is rewarding; Wellington's geographical situation has left little room for expansion except up and most places of interest are quickly reached on foot.

For those who have arrived by car a good place to park is near the Maritime Museum at Queen's Wharf, Jervois Quay. There is usually plenty of room here and it is not far to the city centre. Another car park that is handy is at the Michael Fowler Centre, Wakefield Street. Finding free parking in downtown Wellington is a time consuming and for visitors probably fruitless exercise.

If a walk around the city is started on Queen's Wharf then the first place of interest is the **Maritime Museum**. On display here is a large-scale model of the harbour, model ships and other maritime memorabilia. A perfect way of rounding off the museum visit is to depart on a harbour cruise with the East by West Ferry, only a short stroll away.

However land-lovers might prefer to walk through nearby **Frank Kitts Park**, a nice place to sit and just watch the boats go by. From here cross Jervois Quay not on the first footbridge but on the second, larger one. This unusually designed wooden structure is known as the 'City to Sea Bridge' and is decorated with modern sculptures. It leads to the recently completed **Civic Square**, one of the city's new architectural highlights.

The first thing to do in the square is to arm oneself with a free map and a few useful brochures from the information centre. Of interest on the square itself is the **Capital Discovery Place**, a science centre designed for children, the **Michael Fowler Centre**, where concerts are held, and the **Wellington City Art Gallery**. An interesting feature of the public library, at the north end of the square, are the 'nikau palm' columns on the outside of the building. It was designed by Ian Athfield, one of New Zealand's leading architects.

From Civic Square continue along Mercer Street, then turn left on Willis Street, one of the main shopping thoroughfares. After passing the imposing Majestic Tower building turn right, up Manners Street, to Boulcott Street. Here you can visit historic **Antrim House** (1905), an

Edwardian building that is now headquarters of the Historic Places Trust. Plimmer Steps, a short distance further on, lead down to busy Lambton Quay.

A pleasant detour can be made from Lambton Quay by taking the cable car up to **Kelburn**. At the top there is a restaurant with superb views over the city and harbour. An alternative place to have lunch or a snack is in the nearby **Botanic Gardens**. The Tea House is located in the Lady Norwood Rose Garden. Also in the gardens, near the upper cable car terminus, is the **New Zealand Astronomy Centre** with its planetarium. Return the same way.

Continue north along Lambton Quay, until you reach the intersection with Bowen and Whitmore Street. Across the intersection, on the right, is the **Old Government Building**. Built in 1876 it is the second largest wooden building in the world, only the Todaiji Temple in Japan is larger.

On the opposite side of the road is the Parliament Buildings complex with the distinctive **Beehive**. Designed by British architect Sir Basil Spence and completed in 1981 the aptly named building houses all the ministerial offices, including that of the Prime Minister. A tour of the Beehive and the House of Representatives can be arranged by telephoning 471-94577.

The **National Library** complex is only a short distance away, on the corner of Molesworth and Aitken Street. Apart from housing the most comprehensive collection of books in the country the library also has a gallery where art exhibitions are held. Incorporated within the complex is the **Alexander Turnbull Library** with its important collection of historical manuscripts and photographs relating to New Zealand's colonial past. It is based on the private library bequeathed to the nation by Alexander Turnbull, a wealthy merchant in 1918.

Continue down Aitken Street to Mulgrave street where art and the past is again the subject at the **National Archives**. Displayed here for posterity is the original Treaty of Waitangi together with other important early New Zealand documents. In the same building is the **New Zealand Portrait Gallery**. Just a few metres up the road the last stop on this walk is **Old St Paul's** (1866). The church does not look like much from outside but the magnificent wooden interior is English Gothic at its best. It is hard to believe that for a long time it was in danger of being pulled down! Today most would agree that the church that was built to replace it as a cathedral (St Paul's Anglican Cathedral, Molesworth Street) has none of the charm of its predecessor.

The slightly more direct route back to the starting point is to go via Featherston Street. Otherwise return the same way along Lambton Quay where there are several good bookshops to browse through. The Quay, by the way, really did once mark Wellington's waterfront. Lack of suitable building space in the inner-city meant that land reclamation began already in the nineteenth century and is continuing to this day.

A number of Wellington's other attractions lie somewhat further afield and are best visited either by car or bus. To the south, on Buckle Street, is the **National Museum and Art Gallery**. It is especially worth visiting for

Oriental Bay, Wellington

A modern skyscraper dwarfs one of Wellington's old wooden buildings

its excellent Maori and Pacific Island collections. A highlight of the Maori section is a carved meeting house from near Gisborne that was built around 1842. **Wellington Zoo** is 4km (2^1/$_2$ miles) from the city centre in the suburb of Newtown. Apart from typical zoo animals like lions and chimpanzees there are also some New Zealand originals here such as giant wetas and tuataras.

Probably one of Wellington's nicest excursions is the City Marine Drive. From Jervois Quay drive south towards picturesque Oriental Bay then simply follow the coastal road to Owhiro Bay where the route leaves the coast and returns to the city along Happy Valley, Ohiro and Brooklyn Roads. Popular swimming spots along the way are at Oriental and Lyall Bays. This drive also allows the possibility of an excursion up to the lookout on Mount Victoria. To get there climb the hill along Marjoriebanks Street then follow the signs (though it helps to have a good map). Once at the top, and no doubt battered by Wellington's infamous winds, you are rewarded with a panorama of city and harbour second to none.

If the day's sightseeing is to be concluded with a culinary treat then why not combine it with a dinner cruise (Bluefin Cruises) on the harbour? However if the weather makes it seem more prudent to stay on shore you can still enjoy the harbour atmosphere, together with a delicious seafood meal, at either Dockside or Shed 5 on Queen's Wharf. Otherwise take your pick; Chinese, Italian, Malaysian, Thai, Indian and even Mongolian fare can be consumed by candle-light and to a musical accompaniment ranging from classical to live jazz.

Additional Information

Accommodation and Eating Out
ACCOMMODATION
Masterton
Masterton Backpackers *
22 Victoria Street
☎ (06)377 2228

Victoria House **
(Bed & Breakfast)
15 Victoria Street
☎ (06)377 0186

Palmerston North
Peppertree Hostel *
121 Grey Street
☎ (06)355 4054

Albert Motor Lodge **
700 Main Street
☎ (06)357 3119 Fax: (06)357 3115

Wanganui
Bignell Street Budget Motels *
86 Bignell Street
☎ (06)344 2012

River City Motel **
59 Halswell Street
☎ and Fax (06)343 9107

Wellington
Maple Lodge *
52 Ellice Street
☎ (04)385 3771

Trekkers Hotel/Motel *
213 Cuba Street
☎ (04)385 2153 Fax: (04)382 8873

Tinakori Lodge **
182 Tinakori Road
☎ (04)473 3478 Fax: (04)472 5554

Harbour City Motor Inn ***
92-96 Webb Street
☎ (04)384 9809 Fax: (04)384 9806

EATING OUT
Masterton
Amble Inn **
126 Chapel Street
☎ (06)377 4159

Phoenix **
11 Church Street
☎ (06)378 2545

Palmerston North
Stads Café *
737 Main Street Terrace
☎ (06)355 2164

Redford's ***
10 Rangitikei street
☎ (06)356 8363

Wanganui
Beijing *
Corner Maria Place and St Hill Street
☎ (06)345 4889

Alberts Restaurant **
321 Victoria Avenue
☎ (06)345 8408

Wellington
Café Bodega *
286 Willis Street
☎ (04)384 8206

Chariot Indian Restaurant *
15 Kent Terrace
☎ (04)801 8205

Dockside Restaurant ***
Queens Wharf
☎ (04)499 9900

Grain of Salt Restaurant ***
1st Floor
232 Oriental Parade
☎ (04)384 8642

Places to Visit: Wellington

Antrim House
63 Boulcott Street
Open: weekdays 9am-4.30pm.

Capital Discovery Place
Civic Square
Open: 10am-5pm Saturday and Sunday
and most public and school holidays.

City Art Gallery
Civic Square
Open: 10am-6pm Tuesday to Friday,
10am-8pm Thursday, weekends 11am-
5pm. Free entry Tuesday. Closed Monday.

Maritime Museum
Queens Wharf, Jervois Quay
Open: Monday to Friday 9.30am-4pm;

weekends and public holidays 1-4.30pm.

Museum of New Zealand
Buckle Street
Bus: No 11
Open: daily 9am-5pm. Free admission.
Restaurant.
The museum will be moved to a new
site on Lambton Harbour in 1998.

National Archives and
New Zealand Portrait Gallery
10 Mulgrave Street
Open: Monday to Friday 9am-5pm &
Saturday 9am-1pm.

National Library and
Alexander Turnbull Library
Corner Molesworth and Aitken Streets
Open: Monday to Friday 9am-5pm,
Saturday 9am-1pm.

New Zealand Astronomy Centre
Botanic Garden
Open: daily 10am-5pm. Planetarium
shows from 10.15am-4.15pm on weekends and public holidays.

Old St Paul's Cathedral
Mulgrave Street
Open: Monday to Saturday 10am-
4.30pm, Sunday 1-4.30pm.

Wellington Zoo
Newtown
Open: daily 8.30am-5pm (last entry
4.30pm). Best time to see the kiwis is
10am-12noon.

Useful Information: Wellington

Area Code: (04)

HARBOUR TRIPS
East by West (Trust Bank) Ferry: From
Queens Wharf to Days Bay. Trip takes
30 mins. ☎ 499 1282

Blue Fin Harbour Cruises: Daytime and
evening cruises. Buffet meals served on
afternoon (depart 1pm) and evening
(7pm) cruises. Tea/coffee and scones
with morning cruise (10am). Depart
from Bluefin Wharf off end Whitmore
St. ☎ 569 8203.

Important Telephone Numbers
After Hours Medical: ☎ 384 4944
After Hours Pharmacy: ☎ 385 8810
Automobile Association (AA): ☎ 473 8738
Taxis: ☎ 384 4444

Main Post Office
Railway Station
Open: Poste Restante mail can be collected Monday to Friday 8.30am-5pm.

PUBLIC TRANSPORT
Airport Transport
An airport shuttle service is provided by Super Shuttle (☎ 387 8787) and Johnston's Shuttle Express (384 7654). They offer either a door-to-door service or a less expensive service from the railway station to the airport. The latter service is available Monday to Friday every half hour from 7.15am-5.45pm.

Bus Services
Most routes start beside railway station and the bus stop on Courtenay Place. Ridewell (☎ 801 7000) gives information on public transport in the Wellington region. Bus route maps and timetables are available from tourist office. Long distance buses depart from railway station.

The *Daytripper Pass* allows unlimited travel anywhere in Wellington city for one day. It can be bought on any Stagecoach bus. It is valid weekdays from 9am and at all hours on weekends. ☎ 801 7000.

Cable Car
Lambton Quay
Open: Monday to Friday 7am-10pm, Saturday 9.20am-6pm, Sunday 10.30am-6pm. Runs to Botanic Garden every 10 mins.

Trains
Long distance and suburban trains depart from Wellington Railway Station (☎ 498 3413, freephone (0800) 802 802).

Scenic Bus Tours
Harbour Capital Tours: Faultline tour (1 hour) departs 9am, Skyline tour (1¹/₂ hours) at 10.30am & Coastline tour (3 hours) at 1.30pm. Tours depart from Information Centre, Civic Centre, Wakefield St. ☎ 499 1282.

Wally Hammond's City Scenic Tours: Run 10am and 2pm daily. Depart Travelworld Holidaymakers Information Office, corner Mercer and Victoria Streets. For Hotel pick-up and return ☎ 472 0869.

Unique Tours: Tours with an accent on Maori heritage. ☎ 383 6143.

Places to Visit

ROUTE 8
Featherston
Fell Engine Museum
Middle of town
Open: 10am-4pm Saturday and school holidays. 10am-4pm Sunday (October to April). 1-4pm Sunday (May to September). Also by prior arrangement.
☎ (06)308 9777

Masterton
Wairarapa Arts Centre
Bruce Street
Open: 10am-4.30pm Monday to Friday; weekends 1.30-4.30pm.

Mount Bruce
National Wildlife Centre
On SH2
Open: daily 9am-4pm.

Pioneer Museum
On SH2
Open: most days.

Palmerston North
Science Centre and Manawatu Museum
Between Main and Church Streets
Open: daily 10am-5pm.

Wanganui
Bushy Park
24km north-west of Wanganui
Open: daily 10am-5pm.
☎ (06)342 9879

Sergeant Art Gallery
Queen's Park/Civic Centre
Open: 10.30am-4.30pm Monday to Friday; weekends 1-4.30pm.

Whanganui Regional Museum
Watt Street/Civic Centre
Open: 10am-4.40pm Monday to Saturday; Sunday 1-4.30pm.

Travel Tips

BOAT TRIPS
Raetihi
Wakapai River Trip
RD6 Raetihi
☎ and Fax (06)385 4443 or contact tourist offices in Ohakune or Taumarunui.
On a river boat through Whanganui National Park. A 5 day, 4 night adventure package.

Wanganui
Paddle Wheeler Otunui
PO Box 763
☎ (06)345 0344 or (025)432 997
Depart City Marina by town bridge at
10am, 12.10pm & 1pm.

CANOE/KAYAK HIRE
The following also offer guided trips.
National Park
Plateau Outdoor Adventure Guides
Box 29, National Park
☎ (07)892 2740

Wanganui
Paterson's Canoe Hire
RD3, Wanganui
☎ (06)343 7195

Rivercity Tours
PO Box 4224
☎ (06)344 2554 or (025)993 347

Whanganui River Experiences
PO Box 377
☎ (06)345 7933, freephone: (0800) 808 686

JET BOATING
Palmerston North
Manawatu Jet Boat Tours
☎ (06)326 8190 or (06)356 8657
Through spectacular Manawatu Gorge.
Minimum of 4 people.

Pipiriki
Bridge To Nowhere
Jet Boat Tours
PO Box 192, Raetihi
☎ (06)385 4128
On the Whanganui River.

Wanganui
River City Cruises
PO Box 314
☎ and Fax (06)343 9354
From Wanganui on Whanganui River.

MAIL BUS RUN
Wanganui
Rivercity Tours
PO Box 4224
☎ (06)344 2554 or Fax (06)347 7888
The mail bus departs Wanganui on week-
days for the trip to Pipiriki. Very popular.

PARK TRANSPORT
Whanganui National Park: To walk the
Matemateaonga from Wanganui a bit of

arranging is necessary. Take the mail bus
to Pipiriki. Catch the pre-booked jet boat
to start of track (Bridge to Nowhere Jet
Boat, address above). To get out to Stratford at other end either walk, hitch or
arrange to be picked up by Camp 'n
Canoe, Kaponga ☎ (06)764 6738.

Tourist Information &
Park Visitor Centres
Masterton
Tourism Wairarapa Visitor
Information Centre
5 Dixon Street
PO Box 814
☎ (06)378 7373

Palmerston North
The Square
PO Box 474
☎ (06)358 5003

Wanganui
101 Guyton Street
PO Box 637
Open: Monday to Friday 8.30am-5pm,
weekends 10am-2pm.
☎ (06)345 3286

Whanganui National Park
Pipiriki
DOC Office
☎ (06)385 4631

Taumarunui
Taumarunui Field Centre
Cherry Grove
☎ (07)895 8201

Wanganui
DOC Office
Corner Ingestre and St Hill Streetss
Open: Monday to Friday 8am-5pm.
☎ (06)345 2402

Wellington
Department Of Conservation (DOC)
59 Boulcott St
☎ 471 0726 Fax: 4711082
Info about Forest and National Parks.

Wellington City Information Centre
Corner Wakefield and Victoria Streets
PO Box 2199
Open: daily 9am-5pm.
☎ (04)801 4000

Marlborough & Nelson

Marlborough and Nelson belong to the sunniest regions in New Zealand. Some of the country's best wines are grown here and the local orchards can generally be counted on to produce bumper harvests of such export favourites as kiwifruit, apples and pears. Furthermore nearly all New Zealand's tobacco and hops are grown on the small coastal plain around Motueka, on the western side of Tasman Bay.

But not all the land has been given over to agriculture: both trampers and nature-lovers will find Abel Tasman National Park something akin to paradise on earth. Here it is possible to combine swimming with walking on the park's splendid coastal track. Not so well known among tourists, but places of great beauty nevertheless, are Kahurangi National Park (formerly North-West Nelson State Forest Park) and Nelson Lakes National Park further south. Over on the east coast at Kaikoura visitors have the chance of getting close-up views of gigantic sperm whales. A leisurely cruise through the labyrinth of islands, bays and inlets that make up the Marlborough Sounds is also a fascinating experience.

above: Marlborough Sounds

Route 9 • Picton to St Arnaud

Most people arrive in **Picton**, at the head of Queen Charlotte Sound, with the Cook Strait Ferry from Wellington. Accordingly this attractive little port is used by the majority of travellers only as a short transit stop on the way to or from the North Island. However there are a few things to see and do here and with a wide range of accommodation the town makes an ideal base for an exploration of the Marlborough Sounds.

The Sounds are a complex system of drowned river valleys and islands that remain as a legacy of the Ice Ages. Today large areas are protected as the Marlborough Sounds Maritime Park and though passengers on the Cook Strait Ferry will already have sailed through Queen Charlotte Sound it is only on one of the launch cruises from either Picton or Havelock that you can get a really close look at the many secluded bays and bush-clad headlands that make up the park.

One of the most popular trips on the Sounds is the 'Magic Mail Run' cruise. The *M.V. Beachcomber* departs Mondays and Thursdays, delivering mail and supplies to isolated homesteads scattered around Queen Charlotte Sound. For those who want to combine a launch cruise with a hiking trip the Cougar Line offers a drop-off service to the start of the Queen Charlotte Walkway at Ship Cove. This 3 to 4 day walk is an ideal alternative to the summer crowds on the Abel Tasman track. Ship Cove was, incidentally, a favourite anchorage for Captain James Cook who returned here no less than five times during his exploration of the Pacific. A memorial commemorates the explorer's visits.

In town itself the Smith Memorial Museum has an interesting collection of relics from the days when whaling was a profitable industry in the Marlborough Sounds. The hull of the *Edwin Fox*, a nineteenth-century sailing ship that is going to be restored to its full glory in the, hopefully, not too distant future is located next to the ferry terminal complex. Ultimately the ship will be used as a floating maritime museum. In the meantime visitors can inform themselves about the ship's fascinating history in the adjacent Edwin Fox Centre.

A pleasant excursion from Picton is the very windy but also very scenic coastal road via Waikawa to Rarangi. It can be made into a round trip by returning to Picton via Tuamarina on SH1, a total distance of 110km (68 miles). Around Waikawa there are some secluded holiday homes, tucked away in luxuriant bush and with splendid views over Queen Charlotte Sound. It is the dream of many a New Zealander to own such a holiday home which is called a 'bach' in the North Island but is also known as a 'crib' in the South Island.

Only 29km (18 miles) south of Picton, in the midst of a major wine-growing region, is the sun-kissed town of **Blenheim**. Marlborough's wines have an international reputation for excellence and the vineyards around Blenheim can offer exclusive vintages that it would be difficult to obtain elsewhere. Guided tours of the wineries with extensive tastings are conducted by Deluxe Travel Line (☎ (03)578 5467) but a wine trail map is also available from the tourist office for those who want to visit the vineyards at their own pace. Among the wineries that serve meals are Allan Scott Wines & Estates (a real tip for food, not just wine!), Hunter's Wines and Merlen Wines. A special treat for wine connoisseurs lucky enough to secure a ticket is the Marlborough Wine and Food Festival. It takes place on the second Saturday in February at Montana Wine's Brancott Estate, the largest vineyard in New Zealand.

Apart from the bacchanalian pleasures of food and wine Blenheim can also offer an edifying peek into its pioneering history at the Brayshaw ❄ Museum Park. On display are some impressive traction engines, vintage tractors and a reconstructed colonial village.

From Picton the route continues west along the scenic Queen Charlotte Drive to Havelock. A nice place for a picnic on this stretch of road is at Momorangi Bay. Shortly before Havelock the Cullen Point lookout provides magnificent views over Mahau Sound to the east and the rugged Richmond Range to the west.

Havelock, at the head of Pelorus Sound, is a nice enough little town and serves as a good base for boat trips or walks in the area. One of the more popular walks is the Nydia Track. The entire walk requires 2 days but it is possible to walk just the section between Nydia Bay and Shag Point in 5 hours. Glenmore Cruises, who also do the mail boat run (full day trip), can provide boat access to the track on Tuesdays and Fridays. Seafood gourmets might note that there are more than 200 mussel farms in Pelorus Sound and the green-lipped variety found here are a real delicacy.

The road turns inland from Havelock to pass the old gold mining settlement of **Canvastown**. Gold was discovered here in 1860 but the real rush did not take place until four years later when larger deposits were found. Many of the prospectors erected simple canvas dwellings while they worked their claims, hence the name 'Canvastown'. The rush was already over by 1865 but a few determined souls continued prospecting well into the twentieth century. Visitors who want to try their luck at gold ❄ panning can do so by inquiring at Pinedale Motorcamp (☎ (03)574 2349). It is claimed that enough gold can be sluiced in one day to pay for accommodation! The necessary equipment is provided.

After Canvastown the road heads towards Pelorus Bridge Scenic Reserve, where there are some pleasant walks, and then continues to the township of Rai Valley from where a short detour can be made to the old pioneer cottage (1881) at **Carluke**. Now it is just a matter of climbing over 🏛 the forested Rai Saddle and passing through a few more small settlements to reach the coast and Nelson.

Tobacco farming, orchards, forestry and fishing have all combined to make **Nelson** a prosperous city. Nearly surrounded by hills Nelson enjoys, as do most places in the north of the South Island, an equable climate and gets more than its fair share of sunshine. The city also has a justifiable reputation for its fine parks and an excellent beach at Tahunanui, only a few kilometres away, adds to the natural attractions.

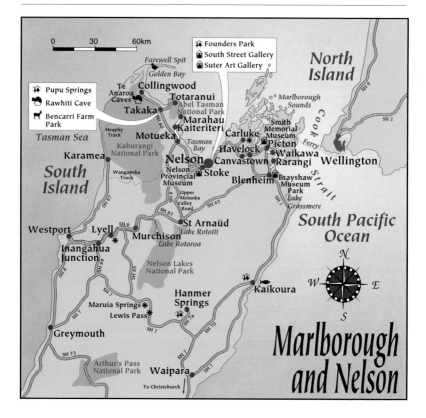

Founders Park
South Street Gallery
Suter Art Gallery

Pupu Springs
Rawhiti Cave
Bencarri Farm Park

Marlborough and Nelson

A pioneer cottage near Blenheim

Picton waterfront

Fishing boats at Picton

Focal point of the city is the rather unattractive cathedral (1925-65), which has at least a beautiful setting atop a hill at the end of the main street. Not far away the South Street Gallery serves as a display case for the work of some of Nelson's leading potters. The relative seclusion of this region, coupled with a more relaxed pace of life has proved to be a magnet for many craftspeople but especially potters have been drawn here by the excellent local clays.

Located in Queen's Gardens on Bridge Street the Suter Art Gallery is mainly interesting for its collection of paintings by important New Zealand artists such as Gully, Woollaston, Lindauer and Hodgkins. There is a nice restaurant here and the work of local potters can be seen in an attached craft shop.

Something of Nelson's history can be felt by visiting Founders Park, at 87 Atawai Drive. A few of Nelson's old buildings have been relocated here to recreate the atmosphere of a nineteenth- century village. There are some more historic buildings scattered around town with Melrose House (1876) on the corner of Brougham and Trafalger Streets being one of the most impressive.

Continuing on from Nelson to Motueka it is worth stopping at **Stoke** to have a look at the Nelson Provincial Museum. It is situated in the beautiful wooded expanses of Isel Park and houses a large photographic collection as well as an important collection of Maori artefacts. Nearby is historic Isel House (1848-1905), a lovely two-storied homestead set to advantage in the park's spacious gardens. Equally imposing is Broad Green House at 276 Nayland Road. It was built in the mid-1850s and is elegantly furnished according to the fashion of the time.

Another interesting stop can be made at the Craft Habitat complex, a few kilometres further along SH6. This is a major craft and arts centre where visitors can buy directly from the craft workers' studios. Shortly after Richmond turn right towards Appleby on SH60. From here a turn-off leads to the beach on Rabbit Island. Otherwise continue along the coastal road, passing more pleasant beaches at Ruby Bay and Tasman (Kina Beach), to Motueka.

Motueka is a relaxed little town at the centre of a hops, tobacco and fruit growing district. Apart from serving as a stepping stone to the beach and bush walks of Abel Tasman National park the town can be used as a base for a variety of organised outdoor activities such as sea kayaking, horse trekking and white water rafting.

The road to Abel Tasman goes north via Riwaka and **Kaiteriteri**, where there is a magnificent beach of golden sand. From here it is not far to **Marahau**, another fine beach with motor camp, at the entrance to the park.

Abel Tasman National Park

Named after the Dutch explorer who was the first European to discover New Zealand in 1642 Abel Tasman is one of New Zealand's most popular and idyllic national parks. Superb beaches, a rugged backdrop of bush-clad hills and lots of sunshine draw over 30,000 people a year to the park's magnificent coastal track.

Apart from the Marahau entrance the park is also accessible by road from several other points. From Takaka, in Golden Bay, a partly unsealed road leads to the Wainui and Totaranui entrances. The Coast Track can be reached by boat from Kaiteriteri or even directly from Nelson.

By far the most popular walk in Abel Tasman is the Coast Track. Classified as one of New Zealand's Great Walks it runs a distance of 51km (31 miles) between Marahau at the southern end and Wainui at the northern end. It is not even necessary to walk the track in its entirety as a water-taxi service picks people up or drops them off at various points along the coast. Once on the track hikers can lounge on magnificent beaches, cool off in the clear blue sea and no doubt spend a large amount of time scratching uncovered limbs that have been bitten by those irksome sandflies.

But the sandfly is not the only problem in paradise; all this beauty and the relative ease with which the track can be walked means crowded huts and other hikers around every corner. The solution to the accommodation problem is to bring a tent but the best way to avoid the crowds is to visit outside the peak season (November to Easter).

Another way to be (more or less) alone with nature is to follow the coast by kayak. In fact kayaking around Abel Tasman is fast becoming a popular alternative to the Coast Track as it allows you to visit small off-shore islands and to come into closer contact with the park's fascinating marine-life; seals, penguins and dolphins might all be seen in a day's leisurely paddling.

The Inland Track is rather more strenuous than its coastal equivalent but also much less crowded. It can be started from either Marahau or Wainui and would require from 3 to 5 days to complete. A detour from the track can be made to Harwood's Hole, a huge vertical shaft that is over 370m (1,214ft) deep. Visitors are warned not to approach the edge of the hole as the surrounding scree is very unstable. The hole can also be reached along Canaan Road, a rough side road that branches off SH60 en route to Takaka.

The Park Café at the Marahau end of the Coast Track is a good place to fill up on homemade cooking before or after doing the track. They also serve the excellent Nelson-brewed Mac's beer. Towards the northern end of the track the Awaroa Lodge and Café caters to ravenous hikers and day-trippers.

From Motueka SH60 winds up and over Takaka Hill 791m (2,595ft) to Golden Bay. The hill is also known as Marble Mountain because large quantities of marble are found beneath the softer limestone surface. As

Abel Tasman is one of the country's most beautiful National Parks

Abel Tasman Coastal Track

The Walk to Asbestos Cottage

n autumn the afternoon sun does not penetrate the narrow valley through which the Cobb Dam road twists, losing itself in ever deepening shadow. There is no exit for this road which, after a laborious climb to the Cobb Reservoir, can only peter out as it spent before the vastness of Kahurangi National Park. Travellers who want to venture further into this wilderness have no choice but to continue on foot.

A well-defined track skirts the valley's side in the direction of Asbestos or Chaffey's Cottage. In summer day trippers take advantage of the first short section of the track which has been developed as a pleasant nature walk with signs explaining the trees and birdlife.

The way leads past an abandoned asbestos mine with sulphurous-green tinged rocks. Asbestos was discovered here in 1889 at Grecian's Creek. This chrysolite asbestos was not high quality although it was commercially mined up until 1963. It was the asbestos and the more glamorous lure of gold which led Henry Chaffey to choose this isolated valley as an abode in 1913 and kept him here until the start of the 1950s. He was a prospector of course and in between working the asbestos he spent much of his time fossicking in secluded valleys for gold, often leaving his wife alone for long periods of time. This lonely life seemed to suit, however, as they rarely ventured out of the valley except for supplies. Anne left her home only once in all their 28 years together, to go to hospital. Cut off as they were from the distractions and comforts of town life they found solace in the chill winter evenings with the home-brew which they became addicted to. Anne nurtured a flourishing garden and blackberries and potatoes still grow by the hut. One day, while bringing provisions on foot from the outside world, Henry Chaffey collapsed and died in the winter snow. Anne reluctantly left her home for Timaru. There she died of cancer, her grip on life no doubt lessened by the unfamiliar circumstances of town living.

Trampers who spend the night at the cottage can more easily envisage how it must have been to live in such isolation. How Anne must have warmed herself before the huge open fireplace on the evenings she was alone. How she must have fussed over the few visitors she received. With its rough-hewn furniture and the history that still clings to it there is more than just a touch of romance to the hut, one of the oldest in the park.

can be expected in limestone country there are plenty of caves in the area but the Ngarua Caves on Takaka Hill belong to the most interesting and easily accessible. Cave features include beautiful stalactite and stalagmite formations together with the skeletal remains of the giant moa.

Located near a number of superb beaches **Takaka** is the main centre in the Golden Bay region. The town itself does not have a lot in the way of attractions but there are several places of interest in the vicinity. New Zealand's largest freshwater springs (Pupu Springs) bubble to the surface in a scenic reserve about 5km (3 miles) to the north-west of town. To the south-east is the huge Rawhiti Cave which is over a million years old. A guided tour to the cave and back takes about 3 hours. Five kilometres (3 miles) south of Takaka, at Bencarri Farm Park, visitors can let themselves be amazed by the spectacle of tame eels slithering out of a river to be fed.

Collingwood lies 28km (17 miles) to the north-west of Takaka. A former gold rush town (gold was discovered in 1856 in the Aorere river) Collingwood is a base for guided tours to Farewell Spit and for those who plan to walk the well-known Heaphy Track. Other attractions in the area include the Te Anaroa limestone caves and isolated Wharariki Beach where there is a seal colony.

Farewell Spit is a narrow tongue of land, composed entirely of sand, that curves around the north-western extremity of Golden Bay. A bird sanctuary and wetland of international importance it provides a vital habitat for many species of migratory wading birds. Towards the end of March huge flocks of bar-tailed godwits gather here prior to departing on their annual migration to the tundras of Siberia and Alaska. Other migratory birds that can be seen on the Spit include knots, turnstones and curlews.

Because of the Spit's protected status free public access is restricted to small areas of beach at its base. The only way to travel its entire length is to book a tour with a licensed operator like Collingwood Safari Tours. No hobby ornithologist will want to miss their 'Gannet Tour' as it provides access to the gannet colony (and lighthouse) at the far end of the Spit. The Collingwood Bus Service also runs a nature tour to Farewell Spit (☎ (03)524 8188). It takes about $6^1/_2$ hours and lunch is provided.

The other way to come to grips with nature from Collingwood is to go on a walk through the unspoiled wilderness of Kahurangi National Park (formerly North-West Nelson State Forest Park). Covering an area of about 450,000ha (1,111,500 acres) this is New Zealand's second largest National Park. Probably the most well-known walk in the park is the Heaphy Track (6 days). It can be started near Collingwood and comes out on the west coast near Karamea, a total distance of about 75km (47 miles). Transport is available to and from both ends of the track with Collingwood Safari Tours.

A highlight of the Heaphy is the coastal section where exotic-looking nikau palms fringe lonely beaches. The nikau (*Rhopalostylis sapida*) is the only palm tree in the world that grows naturally at such southerly latitudes. It is found throughout the North Island and in the South Island as far south as Greymouth.

Much less travelled than the Heaphy Track, which is part of the DOC's Great Walks system, is the Leslie-Karamea (Karamea River Track). It goes through the same forest park as the Heaphy but is longer (7 to 8 days) and, in the opinion of the authors, it is a more interesting though more difficult walk. Access to the track is along the scenic Cobb Dam Road, off SH60 near Upper Takaka. The track exits the park near Little Wanganui, a few kilometres south of Karamea. This last part of the walk follows a section of the Wangapeka Track. The very energetic could return to Golden Bay along the Heaphy. For more information about the track contact the DOC office in Takaka.

From Collingwood return along SH60 to Motueka. Now take SH61 south to the junction with SH6. A side road (Upper Motueka Valley Road) branches off SH6 via Golden Downs and Kikiwa to reach **St Arnaud**, the gateway to Nelson Lakes National Park.

Nelson Lakes National Park

On first seeing Lake Rotoiti in 1860 the explorer Julius von Haast wrote: 'It was with the greatest delight that I looked over this beautiful lake; its deep blue waters reflected the high rocky mountain chains on its eastern and southern shores, which, for a considerable height from the water's edge (from which they rise abruptly), are clad with luxuriant primeval forest. The surface of the lake swarmed with birds, giving life to this magnificent scene'.

Today the great flocks of native waterfowl have, sadly, disappeared from Lake Rotoiti, decimated by introduced predators such as rats, stoats and cats and, of course, by the encroachment of man. But otherwise, over a hundred years later, the scene has hardly changed. Dense stands of beech and podocarp forest still surround the shores of both Lake Rotoiti and its larger counterpart Lake Rotoroa. The ancient beech forests still resound to the song of native birds, even if a few species, like the kokako, have since disappeared. Bellbirds, native robins and the ever present fantail are commonly heard or seen along the hiking trail. Higher up in the alpine regions New Zealand's mountain parrot, the kea, is a frequent sight. Chamois and red deer may also be glimpsed in the park, though because they are hunted they are very shy.

Situated at the northern end of the Southern Alps the alpine regions of Nelson Lakes are more easily accessible for trampers than in the national parks further south. Without needing special alpine skills any tramper, who is reasonably fit, can enjoy the solitude and beauty of these mountains.

A popular, and very beautiful trail through the park is the Travers-Sabine Track. This 5 day trek starts near park headquarters in St Arnaud, links both main lakes via an alpine pass, and can be turned into a circular route by returning to St Arnaud from Sabine Hut at the head of Lake Rotoroa. It really is a magnificent walk and the authors can thoroughly recommend it.

To some a villain, to some a clown the kea is the world's only alpine parrot and is only found in the high country and mountains of the South Island. Its diet consists mainly of insects and berries but it will eat carrion when the chance arises. There have been cases where the kea has actually attacked live sheep and with its powerful curved beak and strong claws it is well equipped for the purpose. However this only happens very rarely and though the kea was once shot due to exaggerated reports of such behaviour it is now fully protected.

Most visitors to New Zealand are unaware of the kea's reputation as a killer among local farmers and tend to see this parrot in a completely different light: as the mischievous feathered clown of the mountains. Keas like sliding down the tin roofs of mountain huts (preferably in the early hours of the morning) and would not think twice about flying off with your

The Kea
(*Nestor Notabilis*)

watch or any other shiny object that you might leave lying about. Their natural curiosity and lack of natural enemies makes them quite unafraid of people and it is not difficult to get close to the birds.

Unfortunately the kea's curiosity is developing into a bit of a problem in those areas where it has been fed by visitors who have been charmed by its antics. More and more notices are appearing at places like Mount Cook National Park advising people 'not to feed the keas'. Feeding keas attracts them to areas of human habitation and when they are not actually eating the keas burn off their excess energy by ripping apart anything that their beak's can get hold of. This might be the rubber sealing on the windscreen of your car, your backpack or your expensive walking boots.

But more serious than the damage done to human property is the change in the kea's natural behaviour that feeding brings about. The kea's normal food has a much lower energy value than human food and a sandwich for the kea is like having breakfast, lunch and dinner all at once! Not that the conservation authorities are worried about lots of obese keas becoming yet another of New Zealand's flightless birds. What really worries them is that the kea will stop foraging for its natural foods and become dependant on human leftovers. On top of all this it is probable that human food is bad for the kea and that a kea that scavenges for scraps is living about as healthily as an adolescent on junk food. In other words: please do not feed the keas!

Alpine scenery and a mountain tarn in Nelson Lakes National Park

Among the shorter walks that start from near park headquarters is the Peninsula Nature Walk ($1^1/_2$-3 hours return), the Loop Track ($1^1/_2$-2 hours return) and the Rotoiti Lakehead Track (6 hours return). Detailed information on these and other walks in the vicinity is available from park headquarters.

However tramping is not the only activity in the park. In winter there is skiing at the Mount Robert and Rainbow ski fields, whereas in summer anglers come to try their luck fishing for brown trout in the deep, clear waters of the two main lakes. Accommodation and supplies are all available in the small township of St Arnaud, which enjoys an idyllic location right next to the shores of Lake Rotoiti.

Continue west from St Arnaud first on SH63, then on SH6, which threads its way through the picturesque Buller Gorge to reach the west coast near Westport (see Chapter 7). On the way the road passes through the settlements of Murchison and Inangahua Junction, both of which were devastated by major earthquakes in 1929 and 1968 respectively. At **Lyell** a walkway leads to an interesting pioneer cemetery and some historic gold mines.

Route 9a • West Coast via Lewis Pass

Instead of continuing west from Picton this route heads south on SH1 to Kaikoura before it turns inland to reach the west coast via Lewis Pass. Just over 30km ($18^1/_2$ miles) from Blenheim the road passes New Zealand's only solar salt works at Lake Grassmere. Sea-water is pumped into this shallow lake during the summer months where it is evaporated to obtain sea-salt. The pink colouration of some of the lake's crystallizing ponds is due to a unicellular form of algae.

Further south, after Wharanui, the road follows a wild, rocky coastline which is not only picturesque but also a preferred habitat for the spiny crayfish (*Jasus edwardsii*). This crustacean is similar in appearance to the lobster and the flesh of its tail is also valued as a delicacy. Just before Kaikoura it is sometimes possible to buy freshly caught crayfish from wayside stands.

Kaikoura has a lovely setting on a small peninsula with breathtaking views of the Seaward Kaikoura Range. The view of the mountains, which rise abruptly from the sea to heights of well over 2,000m (6,561ft), is especially beautiful in winter when snow caps the peaks. This dramatic tableau would have been enough in itself to justify a stop but it is the chance to go whale watching that now brings the tourists in their thousands.

Kaikoura is one of the few places in the world where sperm whales come in so close to shore. The deep waters directly off the Kaikoura coast offer an abundant supply of food not only for whales but also other large marine animals such as dolphins (including Hector's dolphin which is the world's rarest) and seals. Visitors have a chance of seeing all these animals if they venture out in the small boats that are operated by Whale Watch Kaikoura. But the greatest thrill is when the tiny craft approach to within 300m (984ft) of the giant sperm whales. Up to 20m (65ft) long and reaching a weight of 70 tons these behemoths of the ocean are the largest of all toothed whales. Nature lovers should on no account miss this opportunity to see at close quarters the creature immortalised in Melville's novel *Moby Dick*. Apart from sperm whales it is also possible to see killer whales (in actual fact the largest member of the dolphin family) as well as pilot, minke and humpback whales.

Because the whale watching tours only take place in good weather conditions visitors should be prepared to stay a few extra days if they want to be certain of seeing the whales. Many visitors stay longer anyway in order to go on one of the organised excursions that allow them to swim with the dolphins or seals. In winter Sea-to-Summit Safaris (☎ 319 6182) take groups up to the recently opened Mount Lyford ski field.

There are also a few things to do in Kaikoura that do not involve spending money. A nice excursion is the drive along the peninsula to Point Kean, where there is a large fur seal colony. Keen nature photographers might like to follow the walkway along the seashore which starts from the car-park. Apart from close-up views of fur seals it is also possible to see large colonies of red-billed gulls and many other seashore birds. Note that this coastal walk is only possible at low tide though. An alternative is to take the cliff-top route which allows spectacular views over the coast. A pamphlet describing various walks on the peninsula is available from the information centre.

From Kaikoura SH1 goes directly south to Christchurch at the end of Route 14 but those who want to continue on to Hanmer Springs and the west coast have a couple of possibilities open to them. The easiest road to drive is SH1 down to Waipara. From here SH7 can be followed over the Lewis Pass (863m/2,831ft) to the West Coast with a short detour to Hanmer Springs on the way. The more direct route to Hanmer Springs is along SH70 which can be joined just south of Kaikoura. However a long stretch of this road is unsealed which makes it rather slow to drive.

With their beautiful alpine setting the outdoor hot pools at **Hanmer Springs** are a glorious place to rest and soothe aching limbs. Open throughout the year the mineral waters range in temperature from 36-40°C. Visitors can choose between large pools in a landscaped setting or small private pools with their own shower and change facilities. Conveniently located within the thermal reserve is a restaurant serving snacks and light meals.

Several walks go through the surrounding forest which comprises both native and exotic trees. Particularly worthwhile is the Mount Isobel Track (5 hours) as it goes through an area with interesting sub-alpine flora. Another good walk, the Forest Walk (1 hour), leads through stands of conifers and deciduous trees; it would be particularly attractive in autumn.

Other outdoor activities around Hanmer Springs include horse treks, golf, bungy jumping, jet boating and skiing at the nearby Amuri ski field. A bit further afield there is good walking through alpine scenery at the top of Lewis Pass (contact information centre at Hanmer Springs for track information), while the hot pools at nearby **Maruia Springs** provide a place to relax afterwards.

For those who want to return north the road through the remote tussocklands of Molesworth Station provides a spectacular alternative to the coastal route. This private road is only open to the public between 1 January and 13 February and links Hanmer Springs to Blenheim. With a spread of 180,000ha (444,798 acres) Molesworth is New Zealand's largest high country cattle station. The scenery is quite magnificent and well worth the small fee payable for using the road. Those who do not want to take their own vehicles along this unsealed road can join one of the safari tours starting from either Hanmer Springs or Blenheim.

Touring Note: Travellers who have continued south to Christchurch can still join Route 10 on the west coast by crossing the Southern Alps via Arthur's Pass to Greymouth or Hokitika. From Christchurch the start of Route 11 at Wanaka is joined by following state highways 72, 79 and 8 south via Mount Hutt, Tekapo and Omarama — see also Route 14.

Swing-bridges allow safe river crossings on most national park tracks

Additional Information

Accommodation and Eating Out

ACCOMMODATION

Hanmer Springs
Northern Castle Guest House **
(Bed & Breakfast)
148 Hanmer Springs Road
☎ (03)315 7492

Kaikoura
Top Spot Backpackers *
22 Deal Street
☎ (03)319 5540
(non-smoking)

Norfolk Pine Motor Inn **
124 The Esplanade
☎ (03)319 5120 Fax (03)319 6405

Picton
Picton Lodge *
3 Auckland Street
☎ (03)573 7788 Fax (03)573 8418

Americano Motor Inn **
32 High Street
☎ (03)573 6398 Fax (03)573 7892

Marineland Guest House **
28 Waikawa Road
☎ (03)573 6429 Fax (03)573 7634

Nelson
Tasman Towers *
10 Weka Street
☎ (03)548 7950

Aloha Lodge **
19 Beach Road
Tahunanui
☎ (03)546 4000 Fax (03)546 4420

St Arnaud
The Yellow House *
☎ (03)521 1887
Alpine Lodge ***
☎ (03)521 1869 Fax (03)521 1868

EATING OUT

Kaikoura
Why Not Café *
Westend
☎ (03)319 6486

Suntrap Restaurant **
(Crayfish)
Main North Road
☎ (03)319 5743

Motueka
The Park Café *
Marahau
At entrance to National Park
☎ (03)527 8270

Gothic Gourmet Restaurant ***
208 High Street
☎ (03)528 6699

Nelson
Valeno's *
35 Bridge Street
☎ (03)547 6724

Land Of Pharoahs **
270 Hardy Street
☎ (03)548 8404

Junipers ***
144 Collingwood Street
☎ (03)548 8832

Picton
The Federal Hotel *
12 London Quay
☎ (03)573 6077

Tides Inn Restaurant **
(seafood)
33 High Street
☎ (03)573 7091

Marlborough Terranean ***
31 High Street
☎ (03)573 7122

Places to Visit

ROUTE 8

Collingwood
Te Anaroa Caves
Rockville (near Collingwood)
Open: guided tours daily during summer
(27 Dec to 23 Jan); 10.30am, 12.30pm, 2.30pm
and 4.30pm. 24 Jan to 24 Dec by appoint-
ment. ☎ (03)524 8131

Blenheim
Brayshaw Museum Park
New Renwick Road
Open: During daylight hours. Admission is
free.

Carluke
Pioneer Cottage
(Near Rai Valley township)
Open: Daylight hours. No admission charge.

Nelson
Founders Park
Atawhai Drive
Open: daily 10am-4.30pm.

South Street Gallery
10 Nile Street
Open: Monday to Friday 10am-5pm,
weekends and public holidays 10am-4pm.

Suter Art Gallery
In Queens Gardens,
Bridge Street
Open: daily 10.30am-4.30pm.

Picton
Edwin Fox Centre
Next to Ferry Terminal Complex
Open: daily 8.45am-5pm.

Smith Memorial Museum
London Quay
Open: daily 10am-4pm.

Stoke
Broadgreen House
276 Nayland Road
Open: 1 November to 30 April. Tuesday
to Friday 10.30am-4.30pm, weekends
1.30-4.30pm. 1 May to 31 October
Wednesday, Saturday, Sunday 2-4.30pm.

Craft Habitat
SH6
(shortly after Stoke)
Open: daily.

Isel House
Isel Park
Open: during summer, weekends 2-4pm.

Nelson Provincial Museum
In Isel Park, off Hilliard St
Open: Tuesday to Friday 10am-4pm,
weekends 2-5pm.

Takaka
Bencarri Farm Park
McCallum's Rd
Anatoki Valley
Open: daily 11am-4pm during summer.

Rawhiti Cave
Open: For a guided walk to this isolated
cave contact Jane Baird. ☎ (03)525 9061

Takaka Hill
Ngarua Caves
(20km from Motueka)
Open: daily August to mid-June. Guided
tours from 10am. Last tour 4pm.

ROUTE 9a
Hanmer Springs
Molesworth Station
Open: for private vehicles between 1 Jan
and 13 Feb.
Tours: Alpine Adventures, Molesworth
Station Safaris (☎ (03)315 7323), Hanmer
Springs and Back Country Safaris
(☎ (03)578 9904), Blenheim. Tours vary
in length from $^1/_2$ day to 2 days. Both
operators supply lunch and refresh-
ments. For more information contact the
tourist offices in either Blenheim or
Hanmer Springs.

Thermal Reserve
(hot pools)
Open: daily 10am-8pm.

Kaikoura
Maori Leap Cave
(A large stalactite cave)
3km south of Kaikoura
Open: Guided tours (45 mins) at
10.30am, 11.30am, 12.30pm, 1.45pm,
2.30pm and 3.30pm.

Lake Grassmere
Dominion Salt Ltd
Salt Works
Open: Guided tours Tuesday 1.30pm
and Friday 1.30pm.

Travel Tips

BOAT TRIPS
Marlborough Sounds
The Magic Mail Run
Beachcomber Fun Cruises
8 London Quay, Picton
☎ (03)573 6175
Departs: Picton, town wharf Monday,
Tuesday, Thursday and Friday at
11.15am. Returns mid/late afternoon.
Free tea and coffee, bring your own
lunch. Bookings essential.

Cougar Line
The Waterfront, Picton
☎ (03)573 7925
Offer three cruises in Queen Charlotte
Sound.
Departs: Picton, town wharf daily at
8.15am for 'Day Tripper' (drops walkers
off at Ship Cove, start of Queen
Charlotte Walkway); 11.15am for
'Luncheon Cruise' ($4^1/_2$ hours); 2.15pm
for 'Short Cruise' (3 hours).

Pelorus Mail Run
Glenmore Cruises
Havelock
☎ (03)574 2276
Departs: Havelock Tuesday, Wednesday, Thursday at 9.30am. Returns
Tuesday 5.30pm, Wednesday 6.30pm
and Friday 5pm. The boat follows a
different route on each of these days.
Free tea and coffee. Bring your lunch. In
summer bookings essential.

NATURE TOURS
Collingwood
Farewell Spit Bird Sanctuary
Collingwood Safari Tours Ltd
Tasman Street
PO Box 15
Collingwood, Golden Bay.
☎ (03)524 8257

Collingwood Bus Service
C/o Post Office
☎ (03)524 8188
Tours run daily for groups of 5 or more
people. Bookings essential.

Kaikoura
Dolphin Swimming
Dolphin Mary Charters
Booking office in town centre
☎ (03)319 6777

Seal Swimming
Ocean Experience Charters
Dive and Sports Centre
Yarmouth Street
☎ (03)319 6444

Sea to Summit Safaris
Book at visitors' centre
☎ (03)319 5641

Whale Watching
Whale Watch Kaikoura Ltd
The Whaleway Station
☎ Freephone (0800)655 121 or (03)319 5045
Season: up to 4 sailings daily, throughout the year.
Bookings are essential and should be
made at least 3-4 days in advance. In the
course of the 3 hour trip you may see
sperm whales, orcas, dolphins and seals.
A number of operators offer whale
watching from the air; Kaikoura Helicopters ☎ (03)319 6609, Whale Watch
Air Ltd Freephone (0800)655 121 or
(03)319 6580 and Air Tours Kaikoura
☎ (03)319 5986.

SEA KAYAKING
Kayaks are for hire and sea kayak trips
are offered at a number of places in the
Marlborough Sounds and Golden Bay
area. A few addresses:

Motueka
Abel Tasman Kayaks
Marahau
☎ (03)527 8022
Rentals & trips.

Ocean River
Main Road
Marahau
☎ (03)527 8266
Rentals and trips. Bookings essential.

Picton
Malborough Sounds
Adventure Company
1 Russell St
☎ (03)573 6078
Kayak rentals and trips.

Havelock
Te Hoiere Sea Kayaks
PO Box 33
☎ (03)574 2610
Rentals and trips.

TRACK TRANSPORT
Abel Tasman National Park
By Bus/Minibus: Skyline Connections,
Wallace Street, Motueka, depart from
Nelson and Motueka for Marahau daily
(entrance to park). Also depart Takaka
for Wainui/Totaranui (northern
entrances to park). ☎ (03)528 8850
Abel Tasman National Park Enterprises,
Old Cederman House, Main Road,
Riwaka have a daily bus service to both
ends of the park. Departs from Nelson,
Motueka and Takaka. ☎ (03)528 7801.
Golden Bay Tours operate on demand to
Totaranui and Awaroa. ☎ (03)525 9079
Bayway Travel, 114 Commercial Street,
Takaka also operate on demand to Abel
Tasman. ☎ (03)525 9573

By Boat: Abel Tasman Seafaris (☎ (03)527
8083) depart Marahau and drop hikers
off, or pick them up, at various points in
the park. Also day cruises.
Abel Tasman National Park Enterprises
(see above) depart Kaiteriteri. Offer similar service to Seafaris. Also day cruises.

Catalina Cruises depart Nelson and Kaiteriteri for various points in park.
☎ (03)546 9885
Spirit of Golden Bay has a daily ferry service from Tarakohe Harbour (near Takaka) to various points around coast of Abel Tasman and on to Nelson.
☎ (03)525 9135

Kahurangi National Park
(formerly North-West Nelson State Forest Park)
Collingwood Safari Tours have an on demand service from Collingwood to Heaphy Track and/or return. They can also arrange air transport. ☎ (03)524 8257
Bayway Travel (see above) also provide transport to Heaphy and Cobb (Leslie-Karamea) tracks.

Nelson Lakes National Park
Nelson Lakes Transport has a regular passenger service from Nelson to the park. Departs Monday to Saturday. Departure point is Nelson Visitor Information Centre. Bookings essential.
☎ (03)548 6858
Nelson Lakes Shuttles operate between St Arnaud, Blenheim and Picton. Departs Monday, Wednesday and Friday. Bookings essential.
☎ (03)521 1887

WHITE WATER RAFTING
A few addresses:
Hanmer Springs
Rainbow Adventures
Jack's Pass Road
☎ (03)315 7444

Motueka
Wildwater Adventures
PO Box 208
☎ (03)528 6363
Offer trips on Buller, Karamea, Motueka and other rivers.

Murchison
Go West Rafting
Chalgrave Street
☎ (03)523 9315
On Lower Buller River.

Tourist Information Centres & Park Visitor Centres

Blenheim
1c Main Street
PO Box 880
☎ (03)578 9904

Hanmer Springs
Department of Conservation
Amuri Avenue
PO Box 6
☎ (03)315 7128

Kaikoura
The Esplanade
PO Box 6
☎ (03)319 5641

Motueka
236 High Street
Open: daily during summer. Monday to Friday 8.30am-7pm, weekends 9.30am-7pm.
☎ (03)528 6543

DOC OFFICE
Corner High and Edward Streets
☎ (03)528 9117
Information on Abel Tasman and Kahurangi National Park (formerly North-West Nelson Forest Park)

NELSON LAKES NATIONAL PARK
Visitor Centre
St Arnaud
☎ (03)523 9369

Nelson
Corner Trafalgar and Halifax Street
PO Box 194
Open: daily 7am-7pm.
☎ (03)548 2304

Picton
Picton Information Centre
Auckland Street
PO Box 332
☎ (03)573 8838

Picton Information Services
Picton Ferry Terminal Building
PO Box 309
☎ (03)573 6855

The West Coast (Westland)

The west coast is a thinly populated sliver of land bounded on one side by the pounding waves of the Tasman Sea and on the other by the rainforest-clad slopes of the Southern Alps. Gold once brought a measure of prosperity to this wild, isolated coast and a touch of the old gold rush days can still be felt at Shantytown, near Greymouth and Mitchell's Gully Gold Mine. Other attractions include Franz Josef and Fox Glaciers, the sea-sculpted rocks at Punakaiki (Paparoa National Park) and Westland National Park. A useful booklet to pick up from one of the local tourist offices is *The Great West Coast Drive*. It is packed with tips on what to see and do.

Route 10 • The West Coast Highway

Established in 1861, after the discovery of gold in the Buller Gorge, **Westport** was the first European settlement on the west coast. It is therefore perhaps appropriate that this journey begins here, even though the town is bypassed by SH6 from Nelson, as well as all those tourists in a hurry to get down to the glaciers further south.

above: One of the most beautiful drives in New Zealand; the West Coast highway

Once the gold rush was over coal mining became the town's dominant industry. Though less glamorous this black gold proved more dependable than its yellow counterpart and even today it ensures the town a measure of prosperity. A good insight into Westport's coal mining history can be gained by visiting 'Coaltown', an excellent little coal museum with a simulated coal mine and audio-visuals to help bring the past to life.

In recent years Westport has become increasingly well-known as a centre for adventure tourism, which is no doubt at least partly the reason for the fresh paint on some pubs and a new found interest in preserving the town's quaint old shop verandahs. Apart from white water rafting through the Buller Gorge it is possible to go 'underworld' rafting through fabulous glow-worm caverns and to abseil down sheer rock faces. The subterranean world can also be explored as part of a guided caving tour; one such tour is called simply Te Tahi, 'The One' and involves descending 30m (100ft) down a vertical hole. The tour operators claim you will experience 'rebirth' on this one, perhaps, but what most people will want to experience is a stiff drink beforehand. It is worth mentioning, however, that there are easier ways to enter the many cave systems in the area.

Less strenuous than an adventure tour is a visit to one of Westport's other main attractions, the seal colony at Tauranga Bay, only 12km (7^1/$_2$ miles) away. Observation platforms atop the bluff behind the colony allow good views of the seals below. A nice walk along the coast, which starts here, is the Cape Foulwind Walkway (1^1/$_2$ hours).

The road to Karamea follows the coast for much of its way, though at Mokihinui it weaves inland through a beautiful area of native forest before touching the coast again at Little Wanganui. Close to Little Wanganui is the start of the Wangapeka Track (5 days).

Karamea marks the end of SH67. The only way to get further north is to walk the Heaphy Track to Golden Bay. Even for those who do not want to walk the entire track the beautiful coastal stretch of this walk to Heaphy Hut (5 hours) is well worth the effort. In any case there are plenty of excellent day walks in the area such as the Fenian, Mount Stormy and Karamea Gorge tracks. The Karamea Information and Resource Centre has more information on these and other walks.

A must when in the area is a visit to the Oparara Basin, a 12km (7^1/$_2$ miles) drive from the North Beach turn-off, north of Karamea. The main attractions here are the Honeycomb Caves and some spectacular limestone arches set in truly magnificent rainforest. It is possible to walk to the Oparara Arch and Little Arch but the caves can only be visited on a guided tour. This tour is worth the money however as the caves serve as a repository for a remarkable collection of bones belonging to birds that have long since become extinct in New Zealand. They include seven species of moa, a giant flightless goose and the giant New Zealand eagle (*Harpagornis*). Often referred to as Haast's eagle, after the man who first described it, this immense bird of prey had claws the size of a tigers and a wing-span of up to 3m (over 9ft).

Somewhat more modest in size but still to be found in the surrounding bush are snails of the genus *powelliphanta*. They are carnivorous, up to 70mm long and belong to a very ancient and primitive family of snails that is also present in Africa and Melanesia. Powelliphanta and paryphanta snails (another genus of carnivorous land snails found in New Zealand) feed on earthworms and lay eggs similar to those laid by birds. All these snails are protected and should not be disturbed!

The road from Westport to Punakaiki and Greymouth is undoubtedly one of the loveliest coastal drives in New Zealand. Undisputed highlights of the drive are the Pancake Rocks and lush rainforests of Paparoa National Park but a visit to Mitchell's Gully Gold Mine, near **Charleston**, is also worthwhile as it provides an interesting glimpse into the coast's lively goldmining past. Good views over the rugged coastal scenery can be had from Irimahuwhero Point.

Paparoa National Park

Punakaiki is the gateway to the national park and is situated right next to the famous Pancake Rocks. Wind and waves have sculpted these stratified limestone rocks into a surreal landscape of bizarre columns and ridges that rise impressively above the coast. At high tide blowholes become active at those points where the sea has undermined the rocks and is squeezed up through narrow fissures to produce a spectacular spray of water. The rocks can be reached along a track that starts just opposite the visitor centre.

Weird limestone formations do not stop at the coast however as the interior of the park is also a magnificent karst landscape of narrow rugged gorges, cliffs, and cave systems. All these geological features are cloaked in a primordial rainforest alive with native birds that is just waiting to be explored on one of the park's well defined trails or perhaps on a canoe trip up the Pororari Gorge. In summer, when the rata trees are flowering red, the lowland forests are especially beautiful.

Among the park's shorter walks are the Truman Track (30 minutes return) and Pororari River Track (3 hours). Both are located a few kilometres north of the Punakaiki visitor centre and serve as excellent introductions to the park's unique sub-tropical vegetation. Tree-ferns, nikau palms, yellow flowering kowhai trees and native forest giants such as rimu, matai and kahikatea are features of these tracks. An additional attraction of the Truman Track is the spectacular section of coastline where it ends. Longer walks include the Inland Pack Track (2-3 days) and Croesus Track (2-3 days), although the latter is not actually within the park's boundaries. As flooding can make some of the inland tracks impassable it is important to check at the visitor's centre before setting out. Detailed information about all the tracks mentioned here, and others as well, can be obtained from the centre.

Apart from walking the park and environs can also be explored by canoe, bicycle or on horseback. Kiwa Sea Adventures offer trips along the

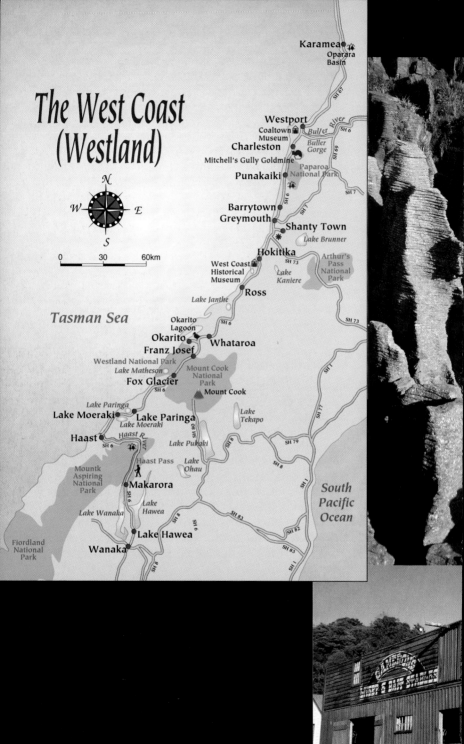

The West Coast (Westland)

N
W • E
S

0   30   60km

Tasman Sea

South Pacific Ocean

Karamea
Oparara Basin

SH 67

Westport
Coaltown Museum
Charleston
Mitchell's Gully Goldmine
Punakaiki
Buller River
Buller Gorge
SH 6
SH 69
Paparoa National Park
SH 7

SH 6

Barrytown
Greymouth
Shanty Town
Lake Brunner

SH 7

Hokitika
West Coast Historical Museum
Lake Kaniere
SH 73
Arthur's Pass National Park

Ross
Lake Janthe

SH 6
SH 73

Okarito Lagoon
Okarito
Whataroa
Franz Josef
Westland National Park
Lake Matheson
Fox Glacier
SH 6
Mount Cook National Park
Mount Cook

SH 1

Lake Paringa
Lake Moeraki
Lake Moeraki
Lake Paringa
Lake Tekapo
SH 80
Lake Pukaki
SH 77
SH 8

Haast
Haast R.
SH 6
Haast Pass
Lake Ohau
SH 79
SH 8

Mountk Aspiring National Park
Makarora
Lake Hawea
SH 6
SH 83
SH 1

Lake Wanaka
SH 8
SH 6
SH 82
SH 83

Fiordland National Park
Lake Hawea
Wanaka
SH 8

Shantytown near Greymouth

A grove of nikau palms

Pancake Rocks at Punakaiki

coast to see dolphins, fur seals and spotted shags. A real treat for bird-watchers is a visit to the world's only breeding colony of Westland black petrels (*Procellaria westlandica*). The best time to observe the birds is between June and October but note that the colony can only be visited on a guided tour with Paparoa Nature Tours. They also organise other bird-watching trips within the park.

From Punakaiki the road continues south through **Barrytown**, near the start of the Croesus Track, and a couple of other small settlements before reaching Greymouth on the Grey river. For those who wish to spend the night along this wild and romantic stretch of coast there is accommodation at Barrytown, at Sandie's Bed and Breakfast (☎ (03)731 1889) a bit further south, and of course at Punakaiki itself.

Greymouth is the largest town on the west coast and with a wide range of accommodation it serves as a good base for outdoor activities in the area. Visitors can try their luck at gold panning, go on a rafting adventure or join one of the scenic tours to old goldmining sites. There is plenty of good walking in the area and excellent trout fishing in the local rivers as well as at Lake Brunner further inland. In spring people can be seen netting whitebait at the mouth of the Grey River. Whitebait are tiny fish (actually the young of the *Galaxiidae* family of fish) that are considered a real delicacy not only on the coast but all over New Zealand. They are usually cooked in batter and well worth trying if one has the chance.

An interesting feature of town is the so-called 'Great Wall of Greymouth'. This stone barrier was erected in recent years to protect the town from the sometimes catastrophic flooding of the Grey River. But probably the biggest single attraction in the vicinity of Greymouth is **Shantytown**, 8km (5 miles) further south. This replica of a typical west coast gold-mining town gives a good feeling for pioneering life at the turn of the nineteenth century. It almost goes without saying that you can pan for gold here (they even guarantee that you will find some!) and a short ride on the quaint old steam train through native bush is also great fun.

For those who want to cross the Southern Alps to Christchurch there is a daily rail link from Greymouth with the TranzAlpine Express. There is also a bus link via Arthur's Pass (see Chapter 10) but in either case the trip over the Alps is quite spectacular. Otherwise this route along the coast continues to Hokitika.

In the 1860s, during the heady days of the west coast gold rushes, **Hokitika** was known as the 'Capital of the Goldfields'. The best place for visitors to inform themselves about the town's gold mining past is at the West Coast Historical Museum. It features a large collection of gold mining equipment, historic photographs and scale models of the various methods used to extract gold. A leaflet is available here (also at the information office) which describes a walk to places of historic interest such as the old wharf along Gibson Quay and the Custom House.

But although some gold is still being mined in the area the town is now better known as a centre for the processing of greenstone (jade) or *pounamu* as the Maori call it. Before the arrival of the Europeans greenstone was the hardest material known to the Maori and was highly prized both for ornaments and tools. As it is only found in the South Island the Maori of the North Island had to undertake long and perilous voyages before they could extract it from the swift-flowing rivers of the west coast. A major source of local greenstone is the Arahura river which enters the sea 8km (5 miles) north of town. Greenstone jewellery and sculptures can be bought at a number of shops in town and it is also possible to see it being cut and polished at Westland Greenstone on Tancred Street. In the same street The Gold Shop specialises in jewellery made from locally mined gold.

Like Greymouth the town is also a good base for outdoor activities such as white water rafting and kayaking. However a nice lazy way to enjoy the local scenery is to take a paddle boat cruise along Mahinapua Creek to Lake Mahinapua. To get to the place where the paddle boat departs take the Ruatapu Road a few kilometres south of Hokitika. If, however, a bit of exercise is called for then one of the best walking areas in the vicinity is around the shores of picturesque Lake Kaniere, only some 18km (11 miles) east of town.

Continuing south from Hokitika the main road passes through **Ross**, yet another of those west coast towns that can trace its history back to the goldrush days. It was near here that the largest gold nugget ever to be found in New Zealand was dug out in 1907. Two walkways, the Water Race Walk (1 hour) and Jones Flat Walk (1^1/$_2$ hours), lead through historic goldfields close to town.

Though the road winds inland after Ross the scenery loses nothing of its attractiveness and becomes, if anything, even more dramatic. On the northern shore of bush-clad Lake Ianthe a lovely picnic spot, with toilets provided, invites a break from driving. From here it is not much further to Whataroa and New Zealand's only breeding colony of white herons.

Just as Kaikoura owes its popularity (and economic recovery) to the marine mammals in its coastal waters so does **Whataroa** have reason to be grateful to the colony of white herons (the Maori name is *kotuku*) that enjoy refuge in a sanctuary on the banks of the Waitangitoana river. White Heron Sanctuary Tours conduct jet boat tours to the colony during the November to February nesting season. One can also see a nesting colony of royal spoonbills (*Platalea regia*) here.

Another worthwhile excursion for bird-watchers and for anybody who loves beautiful natural scenery is a kayak trip on Okarito Lagoon. Okarito Nature Tours operate guided boat tours but it is also possible to just rent a kayak and paddle off on your own. The turn-off to **Okarito** settlement is at The Forks, another 15km (9 miles) south of Whataroa. It was near Okarito, incidentally, that the Dutch explorer Abel Tasman first set eyes on New Zealand in 1642. A monument next to the Youth Hostel marks the event.

From The Forks turn-off it is not far, past the trout-rich waters of Lake Mapourika, to Franz Josef Village and the glaciers of Westland National Park.

Westland National Park

The glacial landscapes of this national park are so unique that it has earned the title of World Heritage Park from UNESCO. Nowhere else in the world do glaciers descend from alpine heights to end just short of luxuriant coastal rainforests. What is more, and contrary to world wide trends, the glaciers are advancing. At the moment they are roughly 12km

A typical West Coast landscape

(9 miles) from the sea with Franz Josef Glacier moving forward at a rate of some 30cm (11^1/$_2$ in) a day. How long this period of advance will continue is hard to say. Generally the last century has shown a pattern of steady retreat; in the distant past the glaciers once reached right down to the sea and even in the 1930s the terminal face was much closer to the coast than it is now.

Before setting out to explore Franz Josef and Fox Glaciers it is a very good idea to inform oneself about the park's natural history and geology at Westland National Park Headquarters in Franz Josef Village. Like all park visitor centres they have leaflets describing many of the walks, both long and short, in the area.

Both glaciers look a little bit disappointing from a distance so the only way to truly appreciate their dramatic beauty is to get as close as possible. The cheapest way to get close-up views of Franz Josef is to follow the unsealed access road a distance of 6km (3^1/$_2$ mile) to the car-park where there is an information kiosk. From here the Glacier Valley Walk ($1^1/_2$ hours return) leads to a viewpoint close to the terminal ice. Admittedly it would be even better to actually walk onto the glacier but this should only be done on a guided walk. Most expensive but certainly most spectacular of all are flights over the glaciers. A 'Grand Circle' flight takes in not only Fox and Franz Josef but also the mighty Tasman Glacier in Mount Cook

National Park. A snow landing on one of the glaciers allows visitors to experience a pristine world of snow and ice that is normally the exclusive preserve of experienced alpinists.

Fox Glacier Village is another 25km ($15^1/_2$ miles) further south. Access to the glacier is provided by two unsealed roads a short distance to the south of the village. The northern approach road (Fox Glacier Road) runs along the north bank of the Fox river and brings you closest to the glacier. From the car-park a track leads over rock debris to the impressive wall of ice that marks the terminal face. Once again visitors are warned not to venture onto the ice without a guide! The southern approach road (Glacier View Road) runs along the other side of the Fox river. The Chalet Lookout Walk (1 hour return) starts from the car-park and allows panoramic views of the glacier's lower reaches. However the views are even more spectacular if this track is combined with the Cone Rock Walk, a side track that branches off the Chalet route. The entire round trip would take about 3 hours. As at Franz Josef it is also possible to take a spectacular helicopter or ski-plane flight over the glaciers.

The road to Gillespies Beach runs west of the village and allows a detour to Lake Matheson. In the very early morning, on windless days, the lake's dark waters reflect a perfect mirror image of the snow-capped alps; one of the most famous picture-postcard panoramas in New Zealand. A walk around the lake takes $1^1/2$ hours. Even if wind or a late breakfast has ruined the chances of a stunning lake photograph it is worth continuing the scenic drive to the coast as it provides plenty of other photographic opportunities. From Gillespies Beach a 3 hour return walk leads to a large seal colony.

The most challenging walk in Westland National Park is without doubt the Copland Track (4 days). It starts 25km ($15^1/2$ miles) south of Fox Glacier near the Karangarua River bridge. Here a signpost points the way to Copland Valley. This alpine traverse links Westland to Mount Cook National Park and should on no account be attempted by the inexperienced. The Copland Valley section of the track is, however, quite easy walking. It is 6 hours from the road to Welcome Flat hut where there are hot springs. The springs together with some magnificent alpine scenery make the Copland Valley a very popular place in summer. For those who want to attempt the alpine crossing it is best to start from The Hermitage in Mount Cook National Park where a guide can be arranged (see Chapter 10).

The drive from Fox Glacier down to Haast is accompanied by magnificent scenery for the entire distance. After a brief interlude on the coast at Bruce Bay the road winds inland again to pass lakes **Paringa** and **Moeraki**. Surrounded by dense forest both offer good trout fishing but Moeraki is perhaps the more idyllic lake. Reasonably priced accommodation is provided by the Lake Paringa Heritage Lodge (☎ (03 751 0894) and the Lake Moeraki Wilderness Lodge (☎ (03)750 0881). A short walk through native forest leads from Lake Moeraki to the coast and Monroe's beach, where there is a breeding colony of Fiordland crested penguins (July-November). The road itself soons reaches the coast just south of Lake Moeraki and follows it the rest of the way to Haast, passing several good viewpoints en route.

Haast township is scattered over a wide area and comprises Haast (a small servicing settlement), Haast Junction on the main highway, and Haast Beach on the Haast Beach-Jackson Bay Road. Where exactly the centre of town might be is anybody's guess but more importantly this loose collection of fuel stations, hotels and shop (there is only one general store) is the gateway to a beautiful, wild region known simply as 'Haast'.

The wilderness area of Haast is part of the South-West New Zealand World Heritage Area (Te Wahipounamu). Established in 1990 Te Wahipounamu encompasses Westland, Mount Cook, Mount Aspiring and Fiordland National Parks; roughly 10 per cent of New Zealand's total area. The Haast region stretches along the coast south of Haast township to the Cascade river. This remote pocket of land between the sea and the Southern Alps preserves a unique natural environment composed of majestic kahikatea swamp forests, coastal lagoons, deserted driftwood-strewn beaches and beautiful rivers and lakes. At rocky points along the coast it is possible to view blue and Fiordland crested penguins and fur seals. Inland the lowland rainforests offer refuge to parakeets, kakas (bush parrots), kiwis and many other native birds.

A good base for activities in Haast would be the Haast Motor Camp at Okuru but there is also hotel/motel accommodation at Haast Junction and Haast Beach. Information about walks and adventure activities in the Haast region can be obtained from the South Westland World Heritage Visitor Centre at Haast Junction. They also have a useful pamphlet describing short walks along the Haast Pass Highway.

Though Haast Pass (563m/1,847ft) is the lowest of the three road passes linking the west coast to the east the journey along the glacially formed Haast River valley is nevertheless of great scenic beauty — but do not count on seeing snow-capped mountain peaks as they are often obscured by cloud. The western side of the pass is characterised by the lush rainforests so typical of the west coast but once the pass is crossed the dense forest vegetation soon gives way to the golden tussock grasslands of Central Otago. Along the way there are several waterfalls that can be reached on short walks from the road. Especially picturesque are Thunder Falls (5 minutes return) and Fantail Falls (5 minutes return).

At **Makarora** on the far side of the pass there is a visitor centre for Mount Aspiring National Park (the road over Haast Pass actually cuts through the northern extremities of the park) and a tearoom. The surrounding countryside offers some excellent walking, especially for those who prefer lesser known and less crowded tracks. However a great way to get to know the area if you have limited time is the Siberia Experience. This adventure tour starts from Makarora and involves a 25 minutes scenic flight to the remote Siberia Valley in Mount Aspiring National Park, a 3 hour bush walk (without a guide) and then a jet boat ride back to Makarora. The Makarora Tourist Centre (☎ (03)443 8372) offers the tour from mid-October to mid-April. People wishing to overnight in Makarora may choose between the motel or one of the simple DOC campsites to the north of town at Cameron Flat and Davis Flat.

From Makarora the road continues south past the shores of lakes Wanaka and Hawea to Wanaka township, the first place of any size since Fox Glacier. The superb scenery of the west coast has now been exchanged for a landscape that is perhaps even more spectacular; like sapphires adorning an emerald crown the Southern Lakes fringe the vast untouched forests of Fiordland.

The beautifully located motor camp at Fox Glacier

The spectacular Fox Glacier

Confluence of the Haast
and Landsborough

Additional Information

Accommodation & Eating Out

ACCOMMODATION
Franz Josef
Franz Josef Lodge *
SH6
☎ (03)752 0712

Franz Josef Glacier Hotel ***
SH6
☎ (03)752 0719

Greymouth
Living Streams Haven *
Cowper Street
☎ (03)768 7272

Australasian Hotel **
201 Main South Road
☎ (03)768 4023

Haast
Haast Highway Accommodation *
Marks Road
☎ (03)750 0703

World Heritage Hotel **
SH6
☎ (03)750 0828 Fax (03)750 0827

Punakaiki
(accommodation can be hard to find
here in summer)
Punakaiki Backpackers *
Corner Webb St and Dickenson Parade
☎ (03)731 1852

Punakaiki Motor Camp *
☎ (03)731 1894

Westport
Bazil's Hostel *
54 Russell Street
☎ (03)789 6410

Cosmopolitan Hotel **
Palmerston Street
☎ (03)789 6305

EATING OUT
Barrytown
All Nations Tavern *
Main Highway
☎ (03)731 1812

Franz Josef
D.A's Restaurant **
Main Road
☎ (03)752 0721

Steamers Café Bar **
58 Mackay Street
☎ (03)768 4193

Café Collage ***
115 Mackay Street
☎ (03)768 5497

Hokitika
PR's Coffee Shop Bistro *
Tancred Street
☎ (03)755 8379

Café de Paris **
19 Tancred Street
☎ (03)755 8933

Tasman View **
111 Revell Street
☎ (03)885 5344

Punakaiki
Nikau Palms Café *
Main Road
☎ (03)731 1841

Westport
Do Duck In Café *
194 Palmerston Street
☎ (03)789 7899

Diego Restaurant & Bar **
18 Wakefield Street
☎ (03)789 7640

Places to Visit

ROUTE 10
Charleston
Mitchell's Gully Gold Mine
Open: daily 9am-4pm

Greymouth
Shantytown
(8km south of town)
Open: daily 8.30am-5pm.

Hokitika
Westland Greenstone
34 Tancred Street
Open: daily 8am-5pm.

West Coast Historical Museum
Tancred Street
Open: daily 9.30am-5pm.

Westport
Coaltown
Queen Street South
Open: daily.

Travel Tips

ADVENTURE CAVING
Karamea
Adventures Unlimited
c/o Last Resort
PO Box 17
☎ (03)782 6617
Tours of Honey Comb cave system.

Westport
Norwest Adventures Ltd
41 Domett Street
☎ (03)789 6686
This company offers the Te Tahi cave tour and cave rafting.

BOAT TRIP
Scenic Waterways
Paddle Boat Cruises
Main South Road
PO Box 290
Hokitika
☎ (03)755 7239
Depart: 5km south of Hokitika. Daily 10.30am, 2pm and 6pm.

CANOE/KAYAK HIRE
Fox Glacier
Canoe Fox
Alpine Guides Building
Main Road
☎ (03)751 0825
Also canoe trips.

Karamea
Adventures Unlimited
C/o Last Resort
☎ (03)782 6617
Also kayaking trips in Oparara Basin.

Punakaiki
Pororari Canoe & Cycle Hire
☎ (03)731 1870

GLACIER WALKS
Fox Glacier
Alpine Guides Fox Glacier
Depart: daily 9.30am and 2pm.
Duration: 3 hours.
☎ (03)751 0825

Franz Josef Glacier
Franz Josef Glacier Guides
Depart: daily 9.15am and 2pm.
Duration: 3 hours.
☎ (03)752 0763

NATURE TOURS
Okarito
Okarito Nature Tours
The Strand
☎ (03)753 4014
Kayak trips on Okarito lagoon.

Punakaiki
Kiwa Sea Adventures
c/o Visitor Centre ☎ (03)731 1893

Paparoa Nature Tours
P0 Box 36 ☎ (03)731 1826

Whataroa
White Heron Sanctuary
White Heron Sanctuary Tours Ltd
PO Box 19 ☎ (03)753 4120
Season is November-February.

Scenic Flights
Franz Josef and Fox Glaciers
All the following companies offer snow
landings.

Fox Glacier Helicopter Services
☎ (03)7520 793 (Franz Josef) or
(03)7510 866 (Fox)

Glacier Helicopters
☎ (03)752 0755 (Franz Josef)
or (03)751 0803 (Fox)

Mount Cook Line Skiplanes
☎ (03)752 0714 (Franz Josef)
☎ (03)751 0812 (Fox)
Grand circle flights (60 minutes).

Hokitika
Wilderness Wings
Information Centre
☎ (03)755 8322

WHITE WATER RAFTING
Greymouth
Wild West Adventure Company
C/o Greymouth Information Centre
or ☎ (03) 768 6649
Also cave rafting.

Hokitika
Alpine Rafts
Kawhaka Station
☎ (03)755 8156

Westport
Buller Adventure Tours
Buller Gorge Road
☎ (03)789 7286
Buller, Karamea and other rivers.

Tourist Information &
Park Visitor Centres

Fox Glacier
Fox Glacier Visitor Centre
(Westland National Park)
State Highway 6, PO Box 9
Open: daily 8.30am-4.30pm. Longer
hours in summer.
☎ (03)751 0807

Franz Josef Glacier
Franz Josef Visitor Centre
(Westland National Park)
State Highway 6, PO Box 14
Open: daily 8am-5pm,
☎ (03)752 0796

Greymouth
Corner Herbert and Mackay Street
Open: Monday to Friday 8.30am-5pm,
☎ (03)768 5101

Haast
South Westland World Heritage Visitor
    Centre
State Highway 6
C/o Post Office Agency
Open: daily 8.30am-7pm (November to
April), otherwise 8.30am-4.30pm
☎ (03)750 0809

Hokitika
Westland Visitor Information Centre
Sewell Street
Open: Monday to Friday 9am-5pm, Mid-
December to March, also weekends.
☎ (03)755 8322

Karamea
Information & Resource Centre
PO Box 94
☎ and Fax (03)782 6652

Last Resort
PO Box 17
☎ (03)782 6617 Fax (03)782 6820

Paparoa National Park Visitor Centre
State Highway
PO Box 1, Punakaiki
Open: daily 8.30am-6pm early Novem-
ber to Easter. Otherwise 9am-4pm.
☎ (03)731 1895

Westport
Buller Visitor and Information Centre
1 Brougham Street
Open: daily 9am-5pm.
☎ (03)789 6658

The Sandfly

Scourge of the West Coast!

The adult sandfly measures only about 2.5mm long and has a hunch-back appearance. Various species of sandfly are found in many parts of the country but the ones along the West Coast and in Fiordland are particularly voracious. They are especially numerous close to streams and lakes because this is where the insect lives during the larval stage of its life-cycle. Only the adult female is a blood-sucker as she needs the hormonal stimulus that blood provides before she can lay her eggs. Normally sandflies would attack birds but any warm-blooded animal will do and they seem to find humans especially delectable.

By way of consolation it might help to add that sandflies are mostly active during the day and though their bite itches it is not dangerous. Local repellants are quite effective at warding them off and should be used if you want to have a relaxing day by the sea or a lake.

This 'giant sandfly' hangs outside the Bushman's Centre close to Lake Ianthe

Southern Lakes & Fiordland

8

Carved by glaciers many thousands of years ago lakes Wanaka, Hawea, Wakatipu, Te Anau and Manapouri are set in a landscape that is magnificent even by New Zealand standards. Hub of the region is Queenstown which not only enjoys a marvellous setting on the shores of Lake Wakatipu but also offers superb skiing in winter and a dazzling array of outdoor activities in summer. To the north and south-west of Queenstown are the untamed wilderness areas of Mount Aspiring and Fiordland National Parks. The former impresses with the splendour of its alpine scenery whereas the latter is renowned for its spectacular fiords and evergreen rainforests. Even if time does not allow for the walk along Fiordland's famous Milford Track no visitor should leave the region without taking a cruise on Milford Sound. The scenery is quite stunning and makes a visit to this fiord one of the absolute highlights of any trip to New Zealand.

Route 11• Wanaka to Manapouri and Beyond

So far **Wanaka** has been spared the great flood of tourists that descend on Queenstown, the region's principal tourist resort further south. Situated directly on the shores of Lake Wanaka the town serves as a relaxed base

above: Lake Hawea

for a whole range of outdoor activities in the midst of splendid scenery. Kayaking, rafting, paragliding, horse trekking and tramping are just a few of the sports that can be enjoyed here. In winter the town really comes alive as there is excellent downhill skiing at the Cardrona and Treble Cone fields. More experienced skiers have the chance to try some heli-skiing high up in the Harris Mountains, whereas the Waiorau ski area has been developed for cross-country skiing.

Gentler pursuits around Wanaka might include a round of golf at the Wanaka Golf Club, an aerial tour, a hovercraft trip on the lake or an attempt to solve the outdoor maze at the Maze and Puzzle Centre, a few kilometres out of town in the direction of Cromwell. But it might also be enough to simply go picnicking on the lake shore and to enjoy at leisure the unobstructed view of mountains and lake.

Like Lake Wanaka nearby **Lake Hawea** is a popular place for trout and salmon fishing. However this lake lacks Wanaka's beaches and gently sloping shoreline as they were drowned when the water level was raised in 1958 as part of a hydro-electric scheme. The lake is nevertheless still very picturesque and Lake Hawea township provides an even better place to get away from the tourist crowds than does Wanaka. But for those who want real solitude the only solution is to pull on the hiking boots and to bid farewell to civilisation for two or three days among the mountains and valleys of Mount Aspiring National Park.

Mount Aspiring National Park

With a total area of 289,000ha (713,830 acres) New Zealand's second largest national park covers a large chunk of the Southern Alps; from the Haast River in the north to where it joins Fiordland National Park in the south. At the heart of this park is Mount Aspiring (3,027m/9,928ft), a pyramid-like peak which has often been compared to the Matterhorn in the Swiss Alps. The Maori name for the region, *Titiraurangi* ('the land of many peaks piercing the clouds'), captures the essentially alpine character of a park that is as exhilarating for the tramper as it is for the mountaineer.

From Wanaka it is a 54km (33 miles) drive along the Mount Aspiring Road to the park's boundaries. The road heads west along the lake to pretty Glendhu Bay from where it soon enters the Matukituki valley, which is then followed to the road end at Raspberry Hut. On the way to Glendhu Bay those with surplus energy could scale Roy's Peak (1,585m/ 5,198ft) for splendid views of Mount Aspiring (5 hours return, signposted from road).

The track to Aspiring Hut (2-3 hours one way) starts from the carpark and follows the west branch of the Matukituki river. It would make a nice day's walk for those who do not have the time to explore this valley more thoroughly. There are however a number of side trips from this hut that would make a tour of 2 to 4 days very rewarding. One such trip is the track to Lucas Trotter Hut which leads to the glaciers around Mount Aspiring and some stunning alpine scenery. The track between Aspiring

Hut and Dart Hut via Cascade Saddle also guarantees magnificent alpine views but should only be attempted by the experienced.

Apart from the Matukituki Valley other access points to the park are from the Haast Road, Makarora (see Chapter 7) and Glenorchy near Queenstown. Glenorchy is in fact the starting point for some of the best known walks in the park such as the Routeburn and the Rees-Dart (see Queenstown). However walks in the central and northern regions of the park tend to be much less crowded and no less spectacular. A number of organised treks also start from Wanaka which enable trampers to reach areas of the park that are normally only accessible for the very experienced. Park headquarters in Wanaka can give advice on all the options available.

The direct route from Wanaka to Queenstown would be along the Crown Range Road via Cardrona, which is the highest main road in the country. But as this scenic mountain road is partly unsealed it does in fact take longer than the route via Cromwell on SH6. In winter the Crown Range Road may be closed and anyway it is an alternative that is best left for fine weather. However if you do venture along this way it is well worth stopping in at the historic Cardrona Hotel restaurant. It was built in 1868 and is a favourite eatery among skiers as it is close to the Cardrona skifield.

The main road to Queenstown passes **Cromwell** before entering the scenic Kawarau Gorge. Around Cromwell there are a number of roadside stalls where you can replenish the picnic hamper with nectarines, apricots, peaches and a variety of other fruits at bargain prices. If time allows the local museum is worth visiting for its interesting displays on the region's gold-mining days. What used to be 'Old Cromwell' is now covered by the waters of Lake Dunstan, an artificial lake that was created as part of a huge hydro-electric scheme. Some of the town's historic buildings were rescued however and can now be seen in the Old Cromwell historic village on Melmore Terrace.

In the Kawarau Gorge the Mining Centre is not only a place where visitors can see a genuine nineteenth-century goldfield but also where they can have a go at panning for gold themselves. Access to the site is across a footbridge over the gorge. Closer to Queenstown it is worth stopping to have a look at the bungy jumping from the old Kawarau suspension bridge (42m/137ft). Bungy jumping as a spectator sport seems to be as popular here as actually doing it and often tour buses will stop just to let people have a look.

At Arrow Junction a secondary road branches off the main road towards Arrowtown and then continues to Queenstown via Arthur's Point. For those who would rather save Arrowtown for later the main road continues directly to Queenstown past Lake Hayes, a very pretty little lake that looks particularly attractive when the trees that surround it are aglow with the colours of autumn.

With a main street lined by faithfully restored buildings from the nineteenth century **Arrowtown** is probably the most atmospheric of all New Zealand's old gold-mining towns. On top of this a good range of shops and accommodation makes the place a very pleasant alternative base for those who can do without Queenstown's nightlife. A good time to visit is definitely autumn when all the deciduous trees that have been planted around town are at their photogenic best.

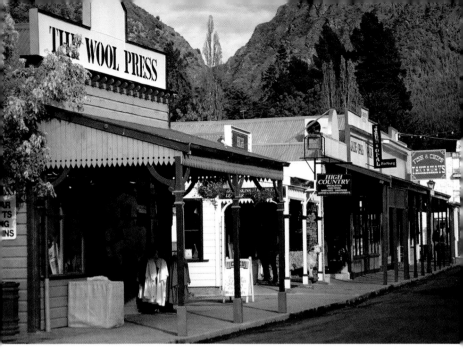

Arrowtown

Continental cafe in the Mall at Queenstown

The Lakes District Centennial Museum in Buckingham Street provides an excellent introduction to the town's gold-mining past. Once visitors have informed themselves here it is worth walking to the site of the old Chinese miners' settlement at the western end of Buckingham Street, adjacent to the Arrow River. The Chinese came to Otago in the 1860s to eke out a frugal existence searching for gold in the Shotover and Arrow gorges. Unfortunately they had to suffer the prejudice of their European neighbours and were forced to live apart from the main settlement. A few simple dwellings as well as a Chinese store have been preserved at the site.

An interesting excursion from Arrowtown is to Macetown, an old gold-miners' settlement that is now a ghost town. It is a long slog on foot (6 hours return) but the trip can also be done on a mountain-bike, on horse-back or most comfortably on a four-wheel drive tour — ask at the museum for details. It is a good idea to check about river levels in Arrowtown before walking or biking the route as there are 26 river crossings on the way!

Queenstown is set next to the shores of beautiful Lake Wakatipu with The Remarkables mountain range providing a magnificent backdrop from across the lake's deep blue waters. In autumn or winter, when the surrounding peaks are capped with snow, like icing sugar on a cake, the setting is more than picturesque, it is absolutely stunning!

Inevitably the South Island's premier holiday resort is as packed with tourists as it is with things to do but no first time visitor to New Zealand can afford to miss it on their itinerary. Queenstown does, after all, cater to all pockets: Backpackers can find plenty of budget accommodation to offset the expensive hotels and prices at many restaurants are surprisingly reasonable. However, any visitor wishing to take part in organised activities in Queenstown should be warned that some of these can be expensive. Still, in Queenstown the rule of thumb is that if you can pay for it you can do it and the range of activities is enormous; scenic helicopter flights, bungy jumping, ballooning, kayaking, jet boating, parapenting, rafting, river surfing (shoot the rapids on a boogie board) and the list goes on.

Though bungy jumping is now offered at a number of places in New Zealand it is still one of the most popular activities in Queenstown. The jumps are organised by bungy 'pioneer' A.J. Hackett who brought the bungy craze to the world when he jumped off the Eiffel Tower in 1987. With a rubber cord tied securely around the ankles the bungy jumper leaps into the void, reaching a top speed of around 150km (93 miles) an hour before the cord checks the fall. Apart from the Kawarau Bridge already mentioned it is also possible to jump off the more spectacular, and higher, Skippers Canyon Bridge (71m/232ft) on the upper reaches of the Shotover river. As proof that the deed has been done a video is taken of all jumpers as they plummet downwards. Transport to the bungy sites is arranged by A.J. Hackett Bungy.

Less of a test of courage but also very exhilarating are the jet boat trips on the Shotover, Kawerau and Dart rivers. A real favourite among many visitors is the ride with the famous Shotover Jet through the spectacular scenery of the Shotover river canyons but the trips offered by other companies such as Kawerau Jet and Dart River Jetboat Safari are certainly worth a try too.

White water rafting is also popular on the Kawarau and Shotover rivers, though the trip on the Shotover through the Oxenbridge Tunnel is meant to be the most exciting. Leisurely 3 day rafting tours are organised on the Landsborough river.

Although the Shotover river is the realm of jet boaters and rafters today its narrow gorges were once the scene of the country's largest gold rush. It had its beginnings in 1862 after two shearers discovered a large quantity of gold in the river. Before long thousands of fortune hunters had arrived to stake their claims. The diggings around Skippers Canyon were particularly productive but the cost of extracting gold from this difficult area were so high that large scale operations were brought to an end in 1907. Drivers who want to visit the area are warned that the road through the steep gorge of Skippers Canyon is narrow, unsealed and very winding. If a tour bus is encountered it can mean reversing considerable distances. Coaches make the trip regularly from Queenstown and this is probably the better alternative, even for those with their own transport. For more information about a bus trip to Skippers contact Mount Cook Line Travel Centre, Rees Street (☎ (03)442 7650).

Much more relaxing than jumping off bridges or shooting rapids is a lake cruise on the TSS *Earnslaw* (1912), a vintage steamer that once carried goods to and from isolated sheep stations scattered around the lake. In the mornings and afternoons passengers are taken on a 3 hour cruise to Walter Peak sheep station for a glimpse of life on a high-country farm. It is also possible to have lunch on board the boat during a short midday cruise and there are evening cruises with a meal at Walter Peak for the romantically minded.

Those who have missed a sailing can at least visit Underwater World on the pier at the end of the Mall — not far from the steamer wharf. An underwater viewing gallery allows a close-up look at the lake's inhabitants; native eels, along with rainbow and brown trout are attracted by automatic feeders. Quite often small ducks known as scaup put in guest appearances as they dive in search of food.

Other places to visit in town include the Queenstown Motor Museum with its collection of vintage cars and the Kiwi and Birdlife Park. Both are located near the lower terminal of the Skyline Gondola in Brecon Street. The gondola is an attraction in itself and the spectacular ride up Bob's Peak is not to be missed. At the top one can enjoy a splendid panorama of lake and mountains from the comfort of a licensed restaurant.

In winter Queenstown is no less active than in summer, the only difference being that the centre of activities has shifted to the surrounding ski fields. Closest to town are Coronet Peak and the Remarkables but daily shuttle buses also run to Treble Cone and Cardrona near Wanaka. The ski season lasts from about June to October.

Après-ski fans will appreciate that Queenstown's nightlife is somewhat more lively than in other New Zealand towns. There are a number of places where one can wine, dine and dance until late in the night. Live entertainment is offered at the Skyline Restaurant, Chico's Restaurant and Bar, the Lone Star Saloon and Vilagrad. A good cold beer can be enjoyed till the early hours at McNeill's Brewery Café, the Pig and Whistle or Eichardt's. Solera Vino is a wine bar which is meant to be good for a wild night on the town. All in all Queenstown has over 20 bars, 4 nightclubs and over 100 restaurants to choose from.

A nice excursion, or break, from Queenstown is to follow the unsealed road along the Wakatipu shoreline to **Glenorchy**, at the head of the lake. Glenorchy is the starting point for the Routeburn, Rees-Dart, Greenstone and Caples tracks. Of these it is the Routeburn, a magnificent 3 to 4 day hike through Mount Aspiring and Fiordland National Parks, that is most famous. Owing to its popularity the Routeburn has now joined the Milford as a bookable track and trampers must book their bunks or campsites before commencing to walk the track. (see Additional Information on page169). This route can be turned into a round trip by combining it with either the Caples or Greenstone Track. Though not as spectacular the Greenstone and Caples tracks have the advantage of being less crowded than the Routeburn and are usually done together as a loop walk in 4 or 5 days.

Least travelled of all these tracks is the Rees-Dart. This circular route through forest and dramatic alpine scenery can be walked in 4 days. An interesting option is to do the last section by inflatable canoe. The organisers bring trampers to the start of the track by van, from where they walk independently for three or more days through the Rees and Upper Dart Valleys. On the last day a guide meets trampers at Sandy Bluff in the Dart Valley for the canoe trip back to Glenorchy. This trip is advertised as the 'Fun Yak canoeing option'. For more information contact Danes in Queenstown, corner Shotover and Camp Streets, ☎ (03)442 7319. During the summer season transport to the starting points of all three tracks can be arranged from either Queenstown or Glenorchy.

Visitors who do not have their own transport, or want to save themselves the drive from Queenstown, can book a variety of day trips to Milford or Doubtful Sound. The trips include a cruise on the sounds and can be done with the bus, a combination of bus and plane or quickest of all by flying there and back. The journey using only the bus is certainly the cheapest but it makes for a long day: the Doubtful Sound trip takes 14 hours and the Milford trip takes 12 hours. Day trips are offered by Fiordland Travel, Mount Cook, Pacific Tourways and a few others. Shop around for the best deals.

The road south from Queenstown to Te Anau (177km/109 miles) is quite scenic with the first leg of the journey following the Wakatipu

Lake Wakatipu

The TSS Earnslaw is dwarfed by the rugged flanks of the Remarkables Range at Lake Wakatipu

Jet boating on the Shotover River

shoreline as far as **Kingston**, at the lake's southern tip. In the summer months an old steam train runs along the track between here and Fairlight, however at the time of writing the continued operation of this vintage locomotive was uncertain. At Five Rivers turn right off SH6 towards Mossburn. From here SH94 is followed to Te Anau and Fiordland.

Fiordland National Park

The largest of all New Zealand's national parks protects a vast, magnificent expanse of mountainous terrain covered by forests, penetrated by fiords and studded with glacially formed lakes. One of these lakes, Lake Te Anau, is surpassed in size only by Lake Taupo in the North Island. In view of all this it is hardly surprising that Fiordland forms a vital part of the South-West New Zealand World Heritage Area, one of the few places on earth that have survived the onslaught of civilisation in a virtually unspoiled state.

That Fiordland has been able to escape the devastating effects of the axe and plough is largely due to its remoteness and rugged character. These factors have also been important in enabling the survival of one of the country's rarest birds. In 1948 the takahe (*Notornis mantelli*) was rediscovered in a secluded valley in the Murchison Mountains. This flightless bird had been presumed extinct for more than half a century and its rediscovery aroused world-wide interest. The area in which the birds were found is now closed to the general public in order to ensure that the colony remains undisturbed.

Te Anau, on the shores of the lake of the same name, is the springboard for trips to Milford Sound and walks in Fiordland National Park. There is not a great deal to do in town itself but those with time to spare can choose from a variety of lake cruises or perhaps indulge in a scenic flight on a floatplane. About a ten minute walk from the visitor centre, in the direction of Manapouri, is the Te Anau Wildlife Centre. It is worth a look not only because it is free but also because this is one of the few places where visitors can get a close-up look at the rare takahe. Other native birds to be seen here include kakas, keas, tuis and parakeets.

A highlight of any Te Anau visit is the $2^1/2$ hour excursion to Te Ana-au Caves, the 'Caves of Rushing Water'. Though the caves were referred to in Maori legends their exact location had long been a mystery and it was not until 1948, after a search of several years, that they were rediscovered. Located on the lake shore, at the edge of the restricted takahe area, the cave system is accessible only by boat from Te Anau. A combination of footpaths and two short boat trips through spectacular limestone caverns lead visitors past underground waterfalls and to a glow-worm grotto.

There are many short day walks that can be started from Te Anau but the goal of most enthusiastic trampers is one of the big walks: the Kepler, the Hollyford, the Routeburn (see Glenorchy) or the famous Milford

Track. Vital equipment for all walkers on these tracks is good quality wet weather gear (Fiordland gets some of the highest rainfalls in New Zealand) and plenty of strong insect repellant to keep the sandflies at bay. 'Dimp' is a well known local brand of repellant but it also helps to wear long sleeve shirts and trousers.

Of the tracks mentioned above it is only the Kepler that forms a circular route. The track starts at the Lake Te Anau outlet control gates, a 45 minute walk from the Te Anau park visitor centre. Those who wish can also catch a shuttle bus to the start of the track or take one of the boat services from Te Anau to Brod Bay, thus saving three hours walking. The tramp, which takes 3 to 4 days, features splendid views from alpine ridge tops, lovely beech forest and a U-shaped glacial valley. The huts along the way are quite comfortable but camping is also permitted at Brod Bay and Iris Burn.

The Hollyford Track is a very long walk (112km/69 miles total distance) from Gunn's Camp on the Hollyford Road to the Tasman Sea at Martins Bay. The outward journey and return trip along the same route would take roughly eight days. However the time required to walk the track can be greatly reduced (4 days) by taking a pre-arranged jet boat across Lake McKerrow (the stretch of track along the lake is rather dull and difficult) and then flying out from Martins Bay. This can all be arranged through Hollyford Valley Walks in Te Anau. They also conduct guided walks along the Hollyford Valley which include the jet boat trip and the flight out as an optional extra. At remote Martins Bay there is a seal colony and Fiordland crested penguins may also be spotted.

Last but certainly not least is the Milford Track. Often described as 'the finest walk in the world' it is also New Zealand's most strictly controlled. The number of people who can walk the track in any one season is limited, it must be done within four days (50km/31 miles) and can only be walked in one direction. These controls, and others, are necessary to protect the track from overcrowding and to ensure that the natural environment remains intact.

In spite of all the limitations the walk is worth it. Waterfalls, lakes, mountain valleys carved by glaciers, luxuriant rainforest and stunning alpine views are all ingredients that combine to make the Milford Track so exceptional. One of the walk's most outstanding scenic highlights is the view of Sutherland Falls. With a drop of 580m (1,902ft) the falls are the highest in New Zealand and the fifth highest in the world. The only other way to see this spectacle is on one of the scenic flights from Te Anau or Queenstown — highly recommended if time is limited.

It is possible to do the Milford Track as an independent tramper or as part of a guided tour. Whereas the guided parties have everything provided independent walkers must carry all the gear and supplies they need themselves. The track starts at Glade House which is usually reached by boat from Te Anau or Te Anau Downs. A launch picks walkers up at the other end for the trip to Milford Sound township.

Mirror Lakes on the road to Milford

Bungy jumping

A launch trip through Milford Sound is one of the highlights of any visit to New Zealand

Everybody who wants to walk the Milford should book well in advance; this also applies to independent walkers as they require a permit for the track. These permits or accommodation passes can only be booked through the park visitor centre at Te Anau. Note that the track is only open from November to mid-April and that December, January and February are the months when demand is highest.

For those who have not been able to do the walk to Milford Sound then the road is the next best thing. Visitors without private transport can take the bus from Te Anau but if you are driving yourself try and pick up a copy of the free pamphlet describing the route which is available in Te Anau from either Fiordland Travel or the petrol station. As there are no fuelling stops on the 119km (73 miles) stretch of road between Te Anau and Milford Sound (a $2^1/_2$ hour drive) it is wise to make sure the tank is filled before departing.

Leaving Te Anau the road first follows the lake shore before swinging inland to enter the national park. In fine weather, which is by no means guaranteed, this drive is one of the loveliest in New Zealand. Worthwhile stops on the way to the Homer Tunnel include the Mirror Lakes, Cascade Creek (refreshments) and Lake Gunn.

If time allows the detour along the Hollyford Road to Gunn's (Hollyford) Camp is also rewarding. Near the start of the road is a track leading up to Lake Marian (4 hours return) and some fine alpine views. At Gunn's Camp there are simple cabins with coal-range stoves, bunks and electric light (only a few hours in the evenings). The camp's small museum is worth a look and there is also a shop with basic supplies. Most people who stay here are going to do the Hollyford Track but it would also be an alternative to accommodation in Milford for those with cars.

From the Hollyford turn-off the Milford Road climbs towards the Homer Tunnel. Rough hewn and almost forbiddingly dark the tunnel descends steeply for 1,219m (3,998ft) before it emerges dramatically into the magnificent upper reaches of the Cleddau Valley. Continuing its steep descent the road winds past a signpost pointing the way to the Chasm. A short walk (15 minutes return) leads through beautiful native forest to where the Cleddau River has carved its way through the rock, sculpting it into bizarre shapes and forming a chasm, some 22m (72ft) deep. From here it is just over 10km (6 miles) to Milford Sound.

Enclosed by walls of bare rock that rise vertically from the sea the 15km (9 miles) long fiord known as **Milford Sound** was formed by glacial action during the last Ice Age, some 1.5 million years ago. One of the fiord's most picturesque features is the sheer rock pinnacle of Mitre Peak which, rising as it does to a height of 1,694m (5,556ft), manages to stand out even in this landscape of superlatives.

The only way to really appreciate the majesty of Milford Sound is of course on one of the boat cruises that depart regularly from the large wharf complex. Apart from the spectacular scenery such a cruise also promises close-up views of seals and occasionally dolphins. Remember it can pay to book ahead in the summer season as these trips are very popular and furthermore do not be put off by wet weather! When it rains Milford's many waterfalls are at their most spectacular, especially the 154m (505ft) high Stirling Falls which can only be seen from the boat. An interesting variation on the day trips is the overnight cruise on the sailing boat *Milford Wanderer*. This trip, along with several others, can be booked through Fiordland Travel in Te Anau or Queenstown.

After the boat trip, which usually takes about 1 hour 45 minutes, it is worth making the short walk from the wharf to Lady Bowen Falls. The waterfall drops a spectacular 160m (526ft) from a hanging valley in the Darran Range. A large area at the foot of the falls is covered by a fine spray of water, including three old graves that must belong to the wettest in the world. The graves actually date back to the time of the early nineteenth century sealers and whalers who were sometimes marooned for many months on Fiordland's inhospitable shores. More information about other walks and the history of the area is available at the Milford Sound Hotel.

From Te Anau the way south continues via **Manapouri**, on the shores of beautiful Lake Manapouri. In the 1970s this idyllic piece of New Zealand was the subject of an intense environmental controversy. The government wanted to raise the level of the lake by 12m (39ft) to generate electricity for the aluminium smelter at Bluff. Massive protests prevented the worst and though the hydro-electric scheme went ahead the lake was not raised to levels that would have dramatically altered the local environment. Today it is possible to visit the hydro station; a trip that can be recommended even for environmentalists, if only because it is the most convenient way to visit isolated Doubtful Sound.

The trip to Doubtful Sound, dubbed 'Nature's Masterpiece', commences with a cruise on LakeManapouri to the underground power station at the end of the lake's West Arm. After leaving the launch a bus descends the 2km(1 mile) spiral of the access tunnel, deep into the bowels of the earth, to the power station's machine hall. Here visitors can admire the ingenuity that was required to carve this huge cavern from the solid granite. After the tour of the machine hall the bus leaves the power station to climb over Wilmot Pass (670m/2,197ft) to Deep Cove in Doubtful Sound, which is then explored on a catamaran.

For the very fit Manapouri also serves as a base for the challenging but uncrowded walk to Dusky Sound (10 days). The Dusky Track offers trampers an insight into the more remote reaches of Fiordland National Park as it threads its way through wild, rain-drenched forests and over alpine passes to reach isolated Supper Cove Hut on Dusky Sound. Because of the very rough nature of the terrain this track is only suitable for experienced parties but it can be shortened to 4 or 5 days by flying in or out of Dusky Sound. Instead of starting at Manapouri it is also possible to start from Lake Hauroko further south. Both variations of the tramp can be linked for a trip taking from 8 to 10 days.

The way south from Manapouri continues along the Southern Scenic Route. It starts in Te Anau, skirting the eastern borders of Fiordland

National Park to the coast, which it then follows part of the way to Invercargill. As the road nears the coast it is bordered by huge hedges of native flax that function as wind-breaks. Macrocarpa trees have also been planted along the road for the same purpose and many of them have been bent into incredible shapes by the prevailing wind. Just over 88km (54 miles) from Invercargill the small town of **Tuatapere** serves as a base for those who want to explore Lake Hauroko and the southern reaches of Fiordland National Park. Colac Bay and The Rocks near **Riverton** are safe areas for swimming. From Invercargill the Southern Scenic Route follows SH92 through the Catlins to where it ends at Balclutha. The section from Invercargill is described in the following chapter. A pamphlet with a map of the route is available from the tourist offices in Te Anau, Invercargill and Dunedin.

Additional Information

Accommodation and Eating Out

ACCOMMODATION

Arrowtown
New Orleans Hotel-Motel **
27 Buckingham Street
☎ (03)442 1745

Glenorchy
Glenorchy Holiday Park *
2 Oban Street
☎ (03)442 9939 Fax (03)442 9940

Milford
Milford Sound Lodge *
☎ (03)249 8071

THC Milford Sound ***
☎ (03)249 7926 Fax (03)249 8094
Queenstown

Bumbles *
Lake Esplanade
☎ (03)442 6298

McFee's Waterfront Hotel *
Shotover Street
☎ (03)442 7400 Fax (03)442 7403

Adelaide Street Guest House **
(Bed & Breakfast)
15 Adelaide Street
☎ (03)442 6207 Fax (03)442 7329

Queenstown Parkroyal ***
Beach Street
☎ (03)442 7800 Fax (03)442 8895

Te Anau
Anchorage Motel **
47 Quintin Drive
☎ (03)249 7256 Fax (03)249 7102

Wanaka
Pleasant Lodge Holiday Park *
Glendhu Bay Road
☎ and Fax (03)443 7360

EATING OUT

Arrowtown
The Stables **
22 Brougham Street
☎ (03)442 1818
Queenstown

Gourmet Express *
62 Shotover Street
☎ (03)442 9619

The Cow *
Cow Lane
☎ (03)442 8588
Bookings not taken.

Solera Vino **
25 Beach Street
☎ (03)442 6082
Bookings not taken

Saguaro's Mexican Restaurant **
Beach Street
☎ (03)442 8240

Skyline Restaurant ***
Brecon Street
☎ (03)442 7860"

Te Anau
La Toscana *
108 Town Centre
☎ (03)249 7756

Wanaka
Orient Express *
47 Helwick Street
☎ (03)443 7438

Anatole's Café **
34 Ardmore Street
☎ (03)443 7872

Ripples Restaurant ***
Pembroke Mall
☎ (03)443 7413
Places to Visit

ROUTE 11

Arrowtown
Lakes District Centennial Museum
Buckingham Street
Open: daily 9am-5pm.

Cromwell
Kawarau Gorge Mining Centre
In the Kawarau Gorge, 8km west
on SH6
Open: daily.

Cromwell Museum
44 The Mall
Open: daily 10am-4pm.

Queenstown
Kiwi and Birdlife Park
Base of the Gondola
Brecon Street
Open: daily 9am-5pm, during summer
until 9pm.

Queenstown Motor Museum
Base of the Gondola
Brecon Street
Open: daily 9am-5.30pm.

Underwater World
On the pier, end of The Mall
Open: daily.

Te Anau
Te Anau Wildlife Centre
On road to Manapouri
Open: daily. Admission is free.

Underground Trout Observatory
Lakefront Drive
Open: daily. Entrance is through a coin-
operated turnstile.

Wanaka
The Puzzling Place and Great Maze
On main highway, just south of Wanaka
Open: daily 8.30am-5.30pm. Entry to
Hologram Exhibition is free.

Travel Tips

BOAT TRIPS
Manapouri
Doubtful Sound Trip
Fiordland Travel
Pearl Harbour
☎ (03) 249 6602
Long trip: daily 10.30am (23 October-31
March).
Short Trip: daily 8.30am (1 October-31
March) and daily 10.30am (1 April-30
September.)
Fiordland Travel arranges connecting
coaches from Queenstown and Te
Anau.

Milford Sound
Fiordland Travel
Steamer Wharf
Queenstown
☎ (03)442 7500
This company offers a variety of cruises
on Milford Sound. The standard launch
cruise departs 11am & 1pm daily (all
year round) and also 3pm daily from
1 Oct-20 April. Overnight cruises take
place on the Milford Wanderer, a
motorised sailing vessel. The season for
these cruises is 1 Oct-30 April. Day
cruises are also offered on this boat at
10.45am (2´ hrs) & 1.30pm (1 hr 50
mins) daily from 1 Oct-30 April.

Red Boat Cruises
☎ (03)249 7926
Bookings can also be made at various
tour agencies in Queenstown
Departures: 11am & 1.30pm (all year
round) and 10.30am, 1pm & 3pm from 1
Oct-30 April.

Queenstown
TSS *Earnslaw*
Departs: Steamer wharf daily.

Te Anau
Te Ana-au Caves Trip
Fiordland Travel
Lakefront Drive
☎ (03)249 8900
Departures: daily 2pm and 8.15pm. The trip to the caves takes $2^1/_2$ hours.

Sinbad Cruises
15 Fergus Square
☎ (03)249 7106
Offer a variety of cruises on Lake Te Anau on board their yacht Manuska.

Wanaka
Hovercraft Cruise
Wanaka Lake Services
The Wharf
Departs: regularly for 15-45 min cruises.

BUNGY JUMPING
Queenstown
AJ Hackett Bungy
Queenstown Bungy Centre
Shotover Street
Open: office is open daily 7.30am-7.30pm. Bungy jumps take place daily, except Christmas Day. Bookings essential.
☎ (03) 442 7100

JET BOATING
Queenstown
Further details at the information centre Corner Camp and Shotover Streets.
Dart River Jet Boat Safari
☎ (03)442 9992
This trip lasts $5^1/_2$ hours.

Kawarau Jet
☎ (03) 442 6142

Shotover Jet
☎ (03)442 8570

Twin Rivers Jet
☎ (03)442 3257

Wanaka
Clutha River Jet
Wanaka Lake Services
The Lakefront
☎ (03)443 7495

MILFORD TRACK
Guided Walk: Bookings can be made through Te Anau Travelodge, 'Milford Track Guided Walk'
PO Box 185, Te Anau ☎ (03)249 7411 and Fax (03)249 7050.
Independent Walk: Bookings are made through Fiordland National Park Visitor Centre, PO Box 29, Te Anau
☎ (03)249 8514 or Fax (03)249 8515
Bookings for both walks should be made several months or even a year in advance.

SCENIC FLIGHTS
Queenstown
Scenic flights are popular and there are plenty to choose from. An interesting possibility is to take a fly/cruise/coach trip. This involves a scenic flight, a cruise on Milford Sound and a bus trip either to or from Queenstown. Companies offering such trips include Fiordland Travel and Amazing Tours (☎ (03)442 9437).

Te Anau
Air Fiordland
☎ (03)249 7505
The flight over Sutherland Falls is well worth it if you cannot do the Milford Track.
Southern Lakes Helicopters
☎ (03)249 7167

Wanaka
Aspiring Air
☎ (03)443 7943
Wanaka Aviation
☎ (03)443 1385

TRACK TRANSPORT
Fiordland National Park
Dusky Track: Waterwings Airways, Te Anau fly trampers to Supper Cove, thus saving the walk in. ☎ (03)249 7405 Fax (03)249 7939
Hollyford Track: Hollyford Valley Walks, Queenstown and Te Anau, arrange transport and also offer guided walks. ☎ (03)249 8012 (Te Anau) or (03)442 3760 (Queenstown).
Kepler Track: Te Anau Motor Park operates a shuttle bus to the track.

☎ (03)249 7777. The yacht *Manuska* (☎ 03 249 7106) and Lakeland Boat Hire (☎ 03 249 8364) bring trampers to Brod Bay from Te Anau Wharf.

Milford Track (independent trampers): Transport connections to and from the track can be booked with the application form for an accommodation pass that is available from the National Park Visitor Centre, Te Anau.
Please note that trampers must have transport arranged before they can pick up their accommodation passes.

Mount Aspiring National Park Routeburn Track: Glenorchy Holiday Park can arrange transport to this track and also Dart-Rees and Greenstone-Caples tracks. ☎ (03) 442 9939.
Backpackers Express runs from Queenstown and Glenorchy to the same tracks. ☎ (03)442 9939
Matuki Services provide a regular mini-bus service between Wanaka and the Matukituki Valley. ☎ (03)443 7980

WILD WATER RAFTING
Queenstown
Danes
Information Centre
Corner Shotover and Camp Streets
☎ (03) 442 7318

Kiwi Discovery Tours
Camp Street
☎ (03) 442 7340

Wanaka
Edgewater Adventures
☎ (03) 443 8311

Tourist Information & Park Visitor Centres

Fiordland National Park
Visitor Centre
Lakefront Drive
Te Anau
Open: daily.
☎ (03) 249 7924 or (03) 249 8514 (bookings for independent Milford Track walkers)

Mount Aspiring National Park
Visitor Centre
Corner Ballantyne Street and Main Road
Wanaka
Open: Monday-Friday 8am-5pm.
☎ (03) 443 7660

Queenstown
Travel and Visitor Centre Ltd
Corner Shotover and Camp Streets
PO Box 253
Open: daily from 7am.
☎ (03) 442 4100 Fax (03) 442 8907

Te Anau
Fiordland Travel Ltd
Te Anau Terrace
PO Box 1
☎ (03) 249 7419

Wanaka
Ardmore Street
PO Box 147
☎ (03) 443 1233

The Deep South & Otago

9

This chapter covers the region of Southland, including Stewart Island, in the far south of the South Island and all of Otago except for the lakes district around Queenstown. A natural border to the west is Fiordland National Park and to the north the Waitaki river. For those coming from Queenstown the quickest route to Invercargill is on SH6 but a much more interesting alternative is the Southern Scenic Route which starts at Te Anau (see Chapter 8).

Land's end, Bluff

Southland and South-East Otago are both areas that are relatively neglected by most visitors to New Zealand, many of whom get no further south than Queenstown or Milford Sound. Admittedly the weather is not as attractive as it is around Marlborough or Nelson (lots of rainy days and the country's lowest mean average temperatures) but the trip is still worth it, especially for those travellers who are interested in New Zealand's unique flora and fauna. East of Invercargill the beautiful Catlin's Forest Park shelters many different species of native birds as well as a variety of sea mammals along its rocky coastline. On Stewart Island nature still seems to reign supreme; there are hardly any roads, only a tiny resident population and most of the island is covered by dense forest. If you want to see a kiwi in the wild Stewart Island may be your best chance.

Otago is wedged in between Southland and Canterbury and is separated from the former by the Mataura river which enters the sea east of Invercargill. In general the climate is drier and sunnier than Southland's, especially in the area of Central Otago which lies in the rain shadow of the Southern Alps. In places like Dunback, St Bathans and Clyde the romance of the Otago gold rushes still lingers on whereas the Otago Peninsula awaits visitors with a rich diversity of wildlife and a Scottish baronial hall. Largest centre is Dunedin, a city as proud of its Scottishness as Christchurch is of its Englishness.

Route 12 • The Southern Scenic Route to Dunedin

Invercargill is a flat, sprawling city (population 52,000) in the far south of the South Island. It is the southernmost city in New Zealand and one of the southernmost settlements of any size in the world. The city's prosperity is based on the fact that it is situated in the midst of some of New Zealand's richest pasture lands, where a high but evenly spread annual rainfall allows the year-round growth of grass. But to Frederick Tuckett, who came to the South Island in 1844 to survey land for a proposed Scottish settlement, the area seemed distinctly lacking in potential. He described the present city site as 'a mere bog, and quite unfit for human habitation'. The Scots came anyway and today Invercargill's Scottish heritage is reflected in the fact that many of its streets are named after Scottish rivers.

The main place of interest is the Southland Museum and Art Gallery in Gala Street, near the main entrance to Queens Park. Housed in a building shaped like a large white pyramid the museum focuses on Southland's history and natural history. An important attraction is the Tuatara House where it is possible to see these rare and ancient reptiles in a setting that attempts to reproduce their natural environment as accurately as possible. Also well worth a look is the 'Roaring Forties Experience', an audiovisual that vividly portrays the flora and fauna of New Zealand's remote subantarctic islands.

After visiting the museum a pleasant place to stroll is through the manicured lawns and gardens of Queens Park. Within its spacious confines there are duck ponds, a play ground, a swimming pool and even an 18 hole golf course. Snacks and light lunches are provided by the tea kiosk which is open daily.

Invercargill's port is **Bluff**, 27km (16 miles) further south. The port's main claim to fame are the delicious oysters that are harvested from Foveaux Strait and which send New Zealand's seafood gourmets into raptures of delight. Oysters fresh from the sea can be sampled from 1 March until 31 August but the highlight of the season is undoubtedly the week-long Bluff Seafood Festival in mid-April. Those who wish can visit the oyster sheds during the season to watch skilled workers scooping the delectable molluscs from their shells. Although purists will prefer them raw the oysters are commonly disguised in a (hopefully) crisp batter and sold by the local take-aways as oysters and chips.

The pleasures of seafood aside there is not a great deal more to Bluff to distract the attention of visitors eagerly awaiting the departure of the Stewart Island ferry. One 'sight' that is impossible to miss is the rather unattractive industrial complex of the Tiwai Point Aluminium Smelter, just across the harbour. The smelter is one of the largest in the world and Southland's largest single employer. A free tour of the complex takes about two hours. Another place of interest is the unique Paua Shell House, a private home decorated with thousands of brightly polished paua (abalone) shells. At Stirling Point (follow SH1 through Bluff, along the coast) there is a restaurant with sea views and the start of a coastal walkway (2 hours). For the best views around either walk or drive to the top of Bluff Hill (265m/869ft).

Stewart Island

Separated from the South Island by Foveaux Strait Stewart Island is New Zealand as it once was: a thickly forested island where the sound of birds dominates over the sounds of human activity, where roads are less significant than forest tracks and where the light of stars on a clear summer night shine brighter than the modest lights of Oban, the island's only real concession to civilisation. On some clear nights visitors might even witness the *aurora australis*, the 'southern lights', a natural spectacle that perhaps explains the Maori name for Stewart Island which is Rakiura (heavenly glow). If one does not have the luck to see the fantastic shimmering of the southern lights then a brilliant blood-red Stewart Island sunset should be compensation enough.

Roughly the size of Singapore Stewart Island can only be appreciated in the course of a visit of several days and because there is not much more than 20km (12 miles) of road the best way to explore the island is on foot, along one of the island's many forest tracks. Day tours from Bluff or Invercargill are possible but can only be recommended for people who really are in a hurry.

The tiny settlement of **Oban** on the shores of Halfmoon Bay is the base

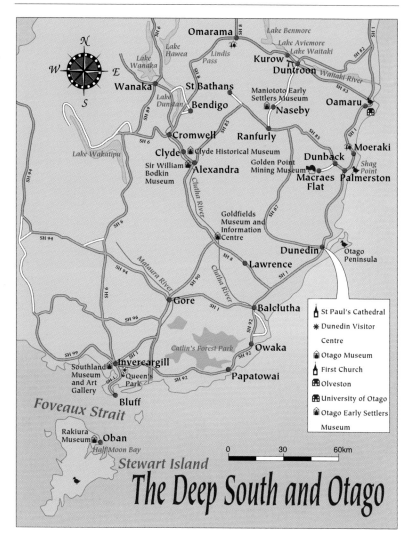

The Deep South and Otago

for all activities on the island. Near the ferry wharf the Visitors Information Centre can provide a list of all the accommodation possibilities as well as information on various walks. Of interest in Oban is the Rakiura Museum with its displays on the Maori and European history of the island and The Fernery, a craft shop and gallery set in a pleasant bush setting at the edge of town.

The two main walks on Stewart Island are the Rakiura Track (2-3 days) and the North-West Circuit (8-10 days). The Rakiura is by far the easier of the two and provides a gentle introduction to the island's virgin forests and isolated beaches. Though there are nice beaches along the circuit

South Island landscapes can be dramatic whatever the weather

track as well it can often mean crossing some very rugged and muddy terrain to get to them. Because the first stretch of the track is fairly easy and runs quite close to the coast many people only go as far as Christmas Village Hut (2-3 days one way) and then return the same way to Oban. Unfortunately the first few huts along the trail can get very crowded in summer so it might pay to bring a (mosquito-proof) tent. Trampers who want to save themselves some walking on the North-West Circuit can get dropped off at certain points along the coast by water taxi. However those who have endured the hardships of the entire 120km (74 miles) long track will no doubt feel justified in toasting their effort at Oban's only pub with a cold, locally brewed beer.

Those who are not so keen on walking could content themselves with some of the shorter tracks around Halfmoon Bay, for instance the 15 minute stroll to Observation Rock, or perhaps take a tour by bus or launch. The scenic minibus tour (☎ 03 219 1269) lasts about an hour and there are daily launch trips to Ulva Island bird sanctuary (a paradise for bird-watchers) and the salmon farms in Big Glory Bay. It is also possible to explore Stewart Island's fascinating coastline by sea kayak.

One activity that nobody should miss is kiwi spotting. Stewart Island is probably the best place in New Zealand to see kiwis in the wild. The local variety is known as the Stewart Island brown kiwi (*Apteryx australis lawryi*) and is unusual in that it is active during the day as well as at night. Because it is not purely nocturnal and likes to forage on the beaches instead of just in dense bush it is much easier to see than its North and South Island cousins. Phillip Smith of Bravo Adventure Cruises offers a guided kiwi spotting tour that includes a twilight boat trip and a short walk through native forest to where kiwi can be seen. Numbers are limited and the trip only takes place on alternate nights so it is probably necessary to book ahead. Trampers doing either the Rakiura or North-West Circuit tracks also have a good chance of seeing kiwi as well as penguins and fur seals on the more remote beaches.

But one does not have to go bird-watching, tramping, fishing or swimming to enjoy Stewart Island. It is a place where one can sit down and do nothing at all — and not feel guilty about it! A quiet evening on the beach enjoying the sunset, a beer and a yarn in the pub with the locals; that might be enough for frayed urban souls desperately seeking to 'get away from it all'.

From Invercargill the Southern Scenic Route (see Chapter 8) continues east along SH92 through the Catlins Forest Park to Balclutha and then Dunedin. The more direct route to Dunedin is along SH1 but SH92 is definitely the more picturesque alternative. However those who like fishing might consider a detour along SH1 to **Gore** as the area is famed for its brown trout. Anglers come from around the world to fish the waters of the Mataura river and it is claimed that it has the highest trout populations and catch rates of any river in New Zealand.

The Catlins

Described in tourist brochures as one of 'New Zealand's best kept secrets' the shaggy bush-covered hills of the Catlins region stretch from Nugget Point in Otago to Waipapa Point in Southland. Protected within the boundaries of the Catlins Forest Park is the largest remaining area of native forest on the east coast of the South Island. Here the southern beech forests reach their southernmost extremity and impressive stands of tall podocarps like totara, rimu, kahikatea and miro fringe the wild, rocky shores of the Catlins coast. Native birds abound (once the ancient Maori hunted the now extinct moa in this region) and ornithologists have registered around sixty different species within the forest park alone. On the coastal rocks it is possible to see fur seals, elephant seals, Hookers sea lion and the rare yellow-eyed penguin (*Megadyptes antipodes*). A trip through the Catlins gives a good idea of what the once densely forested east coast must have looked like before the timber-millers and farmers arrived.

After leaving Invercargill along SH92 the countryside is at first very flat and pastoral but it gradually takes on a hillier, more untamed aspect as the Catlins are approached. At Fortrose one has the choice of either following the partly unsealed coastal road to Curio Bay (35km/21 miles) or of continuing along SH92 (44km/27 miles).

Curio Bay is a beautiful, isolated little spot where the remains of a petrified forest are visible on a rocky platform at low tide. About 160 million years ago the fossilised tree stumps and fallen logs were part of a sub-tropical Jurassic forest. In neighbouring Porpoise Bay it is often possible to see Hector's dolphins playing in the surf. As the beach is safe for swimming there is nothing to stop visitors from joining them. For those who want to spend more time in the area there is a camping ground with basic facilities on the Porpoise Bay headland, just above the beach.

State Highway 92 enters Catlins State Forest Park shortly after the turn-off to Curio Bay. Though the road is now unsealed until near Owaka it should present no difficulty to motorists if appropriate care is taken. The first worthwhile detour along the way is to Cathedral Caves. This impressive cave system is only accessible at low tide but tide-tables are posted at the start of the dirt access road. From the car park at the end of the road (2km/1 mile) it is a 10 minute walk through lovely native forest and then another 10 minutes stroll along the beach to the caves.

Between Cathedral Caves and Papatowai are a few interesting scenic walks all of which are signposted from the main road. One track (15 minutes) leads to the splendid sandy beach at Tautuku Bay whereas another nearby leads to the forested shores of Lake Wilkie. The latter walk is really no more than a 10 minute stroll from the road and is especially worthwhile in summer when the rata trees flower red around the small lake.

At **Papatowai** there is a small service station with connected tearoom. Those who stop here for a snack will probably have noticed the large

New Zealand's Flightless Birds

Kakapo (*Strigops habroptilus*)

This nocturnal, flightless parrot is one of the world's rarest birds. When in danger the kakapo simply stands still and hopes that it will not be noticed. Unfortunately behaviour of this kind is of no help against introduced predators such as cats and weasels. Today the kakapo is virtually extinct on the mainland and only a few breeding pairs are found in Fiordland and on Stewart Island. Attempts are being made to resettle the bird on small off-shore islands that are free of predators. The current population of kakapos stands at around fifty.

Kiwi (*Apterygidae*)

New Zealand's national bird is nocturnal and rarely seen in the wild. To say that it is unique is something of an understatement. Its feathers resemble hair, it lays an egg that in relation to its size is disproportionately large (it weighs 450g) and has, for a bird, an excellent sense of smell. The kiwi's nostrils are situated at the tip of its long bill (also unusual for a bird) and this no doubt helps it in its search for insects and worms on the forest floor. There are three species of kiwi: the brown kiwi (*Apteryx australis*), the great spotted kiwi (*A. haasti*) and the little spotted kiwi (*A. oweni*). The kiwi is found only in New Zealand.

Moa (*Dinornithiformes*)

There were many different species of moa and they ranged in size from relatively small forest-dwelling birds to huge ostrich-like giants around 3m (10ft) tall and weighing up to 230kg (507lb). Though known to the early Maori the giant moa (*Euryapteryx gravis*) became extinct long before the arrival of the first Europeans. However it is believed that at least a few of the smaller species survived into the early nineteenth century.

framed photograph on the wall depicting Purakaunui Falls. As the photo suggests the falls are one of the area's scenic highlights. A few kilometres out of town a signpost points out the 10km (6 miles) detour necessary to get to them. Near the falls, which are reached along a forest path, is a pleasant picnic area with toilet facilities. There are other waterfalls in the vicinity but these ones are certainly the most photogenic. A tip: the best photographs are taken in the late morning.

Takahe (*Notornis mantelli*)
The takahe was believed to be extinct for many years until its rediscovery in 1948. It is a member of the rail family and is powerfully built with bright blue and green plumage. The introduction of deer, which eat the same plants as the takahe, are thought to be the main reason for the bird's declining numbers. Today the takahe is only found in the Murchison Mountains of Fiordland National Park. The present population consists of around 200 birds.

Weka (*Gallirallus australis*)
Wekas are neither shy nor endangered and are often seen by trampers in New Zealand's national and forest parks. The birds, which are about the same size as a chicken, have a predominantly brown colouring and are omnivorous. Like the kea parrot the weka has a weakness for shiny objects and will run off with anything that is left lying around.

The flightless Weka has a penchant for shiny objects and will steal anything left lying about

Further north another detour can be made to Jacks Bay Blowhole by following the road along Catlins Lake (actually an extension of the Catlins river) towards the coast. The blowhole lies in the middle of farmland and is connected to the sea by a 200m (656ft) long subterranean tunnel. The plume of sea-water that spurts out of the 60m (196ft) deep hole is at its most impressive at high tide and in stormy weather. However if the weather is fine there is no need to feel disappointed as the beach at Jacks Bay is one of the finest around.

Continuing along the main road it is not long before the small settlement of **Owaka** is reached. This is the main town of the Catlins district and it has all the essential facilities, including a Department of Conservation (DOC) visitor centre. This is the place to go for information about walks in the area. Among the more interesting walks is the Catlins River Walk (5 hours) which passes through pretty silver beech forest and can be started from the Tawanui camping area west of Owaka. Another good walk for those interested in the local flora is the Pounawea Nature Walk (45 minutes). It starts from the Pounawea Motor Camp just to the southeast of Owaka. There is a good chance of spotting white-faced herons, pied shags, paradise ducks and other aquatic birds along this loop track.

Before finally leaving the Catlins it is well worth making the detour to Nugget Point. Here visitors may see fur seals, elephant seals and the rare Hooker's sea lion. Shortly before the car park at the road end is another parking spot from where a track leads down a steep bank to the yellow-eyed penguin viewing platform. As it is not permitted to go beyond the platform when the penguins are ashore it is a good idea to bring a pair of binoculars. Photographers will need at least a 500mm telephoto lens for a close-up shot of these small birds. Yellow-eyed penguins can usually be observed on shore after about 3pm. Other sea-birds that may be spotted include little blue penguins, gannets, sooty shearwaters and spotted shags. At the end of the point is a stone lighthouse that was built in 1870.

From Nugget Point it is possible to follow the road via Kaka Point and Port Molyneux to Balclutha. This town on the banks of the Clutha river marks the 'official' end of the Southern Scenic Route but the remaining kilometres to Dunedin are not without interest.

State Highway 1 continues on from Balclutha via Milton to Dunedin. To the north-west of Milton, near the town of **Lawrence**, is Gabriel's Gully. In 1861 Gabriel Read discovered a rich deposit of gold here and in so doing sparked off the Central Otago gold rushes. Within a couple of months there were over 11,000 prospectors in the district, searching feverishly for a quick fortune in the ground. Today there is still some evidence of the old workings around Gabriels's Gully and those wishing to know more about the gold rush can visit the small museum in Lawrence which also doubles as the local information centre.

Dunedin, the South Island's second largest city after Christchurch, was originally a mainly Scottish settlement and is still often referred to as the 'Edinburgh of the South'. Today the city's Scottish roots are most obviously reflected in its name (Dun Edin was the old Gaelic name for Edinburgh) the country's only kilt shop, the large statue of the Scottish bard Robert Burns and, almost inevitably, the only whisky distillery in New Zealand. A slight rolling or at least burr of the 'r', that may be heard throughout Southland and Otago, also hints at an ancestry reaching back to the 'bonny hills of Scotland'.

The first boatload of Scots arrived at Port Chalmers, Dunedin's port, in 1848 to take up land that had been bought from the local Maori for about a penny an acre. Though the first settlers were mainly Scottish and Presbyterian by faith there were also enough Englishmen around to allow some scope for traditional frictions to come to the fore. Job advertisements sometimes carried the line 'Englishmen need not apply' and the early settlement's leader, Captain William Cargill, once directed an English gentleman to go back to Canterbury (a predominantly English settlement) 'where he belonged'.

In the 1860s the Otago gold rushes brought sudden prosperity to the town. They stimulated not only a dramatic increase in population but also provided a firm economic basis for the rapid development of industry and agriculture. For many years Dunedin was the most important manufacturing and commercial centre in the country. Legacies of this early wealth are the city's many fine old Victorian buildings and the country's first university and medical school. Though still an important industrial centre (heavy engineering) it is in the role of a university town that Dunedin now commands most recognition. The 14,000 or so students have a pervasive influence on the city's day-to-day life, as is reflected in the many student pubs, the cheap cafés and the vibrant local arts and entertainments scene.

The best place to start exploring is from the **Octagon**, an eight-sided garden area in the heart of the city. As proud of its Scottish heritage as Dunedin is it is not surprising to find that the Octagon is presided over by the statue (1887) of Robert Burns, Scotland's national poet. Behind the statue rises **St Paul's Anglican Cathedral**, which was built of Oamaru stone in 1915. It is worth a look inside because of the impressive stone vaulted ceiling, some fine interior woodwork and the stained-glass windows. Located within the recently refurbished Municipal Chambers (1880) nearby is the excellent **Dunedin Visitor Centre**. In Stuart Street, just above the Octagon, and not far from the cathedral, are a number of decorative terrace houses from the Victorian period.

At the lower end of Stuart Street, in the direction of the harbour, is Dunedin's **Edwardian railway station** (1904). Decorated with stained-glass windows and a magnificent mosaic floor the station foyer vividly reflects the city's early wealth and optimistic belief in a prosperous future. A few of the old steam locomotives that once puffed their way into the station are on display at the **Otago Early Settlers Museum** in Cumberland Street, a short distance away. The **Presbyterian First Church** is situated to the north-west of the museum in Moray Place. Dedicated in 1873 it has been described as 'a masterpiece of Gothic revival'.

To the north-west of the Octagon, at 42 Royal Terrace, is **Olveston**. Built in 1904-06 as a home for the wealthy businessman David Theomin its beautifully furnished rooms can be visited in the course of an hour-long guided tour. Crammed as it is with valuable antiques and early New Zealand paintings Olveston provides a fascinating insight into the lifestyle of a cultivated turn-of-the-century family.

Cathedral Caves, Catlins

The **Otago Museum** can be reached from the Octagon along Great King Street. Especially worth seeing here are the excellent southern Maori and Pacific Island exhibits and the natural history displays. Of note among the other exhibits is a surprisingly good collection of art and sculpture from classical Greece, Rome and the Middle East. A recent addition to the museum is 'Discovery World', where working exhibits introduce children and adults alike to the world of science.

A little further east of the museum is the **University of Otago** campus. Founded in 1869 New Zealand's oldest university began its life with a roll of only 81 students and a staff of three professors. The original nineteenth-century building complex has been retained and is worth taking a stroll around. Particularly photogenic is the turreted clock tower. Guided walking tours are available for those who want to know more about the university and its history.

As a change from history and architecture visitors with a penchant for the local beer or whisky might enjoy taking part in tours of either Wilson's whisky distillery or Speights Brewery. Both tours last about an hour and, most importantly, include a sampling of the wares. On a sweeter note are tours of the Cadbury chocolate factory. Children in particular will enjoy the free samples offered at the end of this 1 hour tour.

Otago Peninsula

When in Dunedin do not leave without making the side trip to Otago Peninsula. Though within easy reach of the city the peninsula is unique in that it provides a breeding habitat for such rare or seldom seen birds as the royal albatross and yellow-eyed penguin. There is enough to see and do here to keep most visitors occupied for a full day but at least a half day is necessary for the main attractions. A pleasant circular tour of the peninsula can be made by first following the coast road (Portobello Road) and then Highcliff Road back to Dunedin. Those without private transport can join a bus tour from Dunedin. Contact Newtons Coach Tours, ☎ (03) 477 5577.

As far as the peninsula's natural attractions are concerned it is the famous royal albatross colony at Taiaroa Head that draws most attention. With a wing-span of over 3m (9ft) the royal albatross (*Diomedea epomophora*) is the world's largest sea-bird. Nowhere else on the globe do they breed so close to human habitation. In fact except for here and a few remote subantarctic islands they are rarely seen on land as they spend the greater part of their solitary lives gliding over the oceans of the Southern Hemisphere. When they do come ashore it is only to breed. The single egg laid in November hatches in January and by September the young birds are ready to depart the colony. It will be eight to ten years before these birds are ready to breed themselves but with a life-span of well over sixty years plenty of time remains to produce offspring.

The albatross colony can only be visited as part of a 1 hour guided tour which needs to be booked in advance at the Dunedin Visitor Centre. A slightly longer tour ($1^1/_2$ hours) also includes a visit to Fort Taiaroa where the main attraction is a historic Armstrong 'disappearing gun'. Placed on the headland in 1888 to counter a feared Russian invasion (which did not eventuate) the gun was only raised above ground when it was ready to fire.

From the albatross colony follow the signs to get to Penguin Place, a privately run conservation reserve. The best chance of viewing the yellow-eyed penguins that breed here is during the last few hours of daylight when the birds come ashore to their nests. Apart from the penguins it is also possible to see a fur seal colony.

Tours of the penguin colony start from McGrouther's Farm, at Penguin Place, on a daily basis throughout the season (October to August). A longer tour (8 hours) run by Wild South Limited also includes a visit to the ornithological section of Otago Museum, the albatross colony and other points of related interest around the peninsula. It starts from and can be booked through the Dunedin Visitor Centre. Participants may be interested to know that the penguin reserve is funded entirely through profits gained from these tours.

On the way back to Dunedin it is well worth making the short detour off Highcliff Road to see Lanarch Castle. New Zealand's only 'castle' was built by William Lanarch, a wealthy financier and politician, for what was then the immense sum of £125,000. Construction began in 1871 but in spite of the fact that 200 labourers were working on the house it took five years before the family could move in. The entire building was constructed using only the very best materials available and Lanarch did not even shy from the expense of importing European craftsmen to do some of the interior work. Outstanding features of the house include the hanging staircase with a handrail carved from solid kauri, the beautifully carved foyer ceiling and the huge ballroom.

Other attractions on the peninsula include Glenfalloch Gardens, which are at their most attractive from September to October, and the Trust Bank Aquarium which features local marine life as well as a tuatara. Saturday is feeding day at the aquarium and visitors are welcome to help feed the fish. Both attractions are clearly signposted from Portobello Road.

The last, but not the least of, Dunedin's many attractions to be mentioned here is the trip on the Taieri Gorge Railway. One of New Zealand's great train journeys this 4 hour return trip from Dunedin to Pukerangi goes through rugged, spectacular scenery that cannot be seen from the road. There are two or three photo stops along the way and refreshments are available on board. At certain times of the year a longer version of this trip ($5^1/_2$ hours) is offered to Middlemarch, 83km (51 miles) north-west of Dunedin on SH87.

From Dunedin SH1 continues north to **Palmerston** where the traveller is presented with two alternatives: either follow SH1 further north to Oamaru and then turn inland along the Waitaki river to Omarama or follow SH85 north-west through Central Otago and then continue north over the Lindis Pass to Omarama. Both routes have their scenic attractions but the drive through the Lindis valley is particularly beautiful. From Omarama it is not far to Mount Cook National Park and the lakes of southern Canterbury.

Route 13 • Oamaru and the Waitaki Valley

Like Taiaroa Head and Penguin Place on the Otago Peninsula **Shag Point**, just over 8km (5 miles) north of Palmerston, is a great place for anybody interested in wildlife. Though aptly named for the hundreds of shags that perch on the rocky islets off-shore it is the large colony of fur seals and a small yellow-eyed penguin colony that attract most visitors here. It is possible to venture quite close to the fur seals while they bask on the rocks but visitors should not attempt to get close views of the penguins as they are easily disturbed.

Further up the coast, near the fishing village of **Moeraki**, are the famous Moeraki boulders. Strewn like giant marbles across the sand of Hampden Beach the spherical boulders are not in fact the product of erosion but of a natural chemical process. They were formed some 60 million years ago by the gradual accumulation of lime salts around a central lime crystal core. These septarian concretions, as geologists prefer to call them, gradually appear from the cliffs behind the beach as the soft mudstone in which they are embedded is eroded away by the sea. Some of the concretions are over 4m (13ft) in circumference and weigh several tons. In a strategic position near the boulders is a large reasonably priced restaurant with great views over the sea.

Next stop on the coast is **Oamaru**. Though the town lacks the Mediterranean flair of art deco Napier it too can boast some of the country's most interesting architecture. Oamaru's historic buildings generally reflect the classical styles favoured throughout New Zealand during the nineteenth century. What makes them distinctive however is the widespread use of local limestone; a material that is soft enough to be quarried with a circular saw but which gradually hardens when exposed to air.

Many of these old limestone buildings are to be found in the Tyne-Harbour Street Historic Precinct, the only complete example of a nineteenth century commercial area in New Zealand. Some of the noble old premises are at present a bit dilapidated but a restoration scheme is under way that will hopefully return them to their former grandeur in the not too distant future. On holiday weekends a steam train runs through the Historic Precinct to provide that extra touch of nostalgia (check at the information centre for details).

Within walking distance of the Historic Precinct and downtown Oamaru is, surprisingly enough, a blue penguin colony. The world's smallest penguins have built their nests around the harbour area and a

A Fur Seal at Shag Point

The famous Moeraki boulders at Moeraki

section of foreshore has been set aside as a refuge for them. From the viewing platforms at the end of Waterfront Road the dapper little birds can be seen just after dusk as they return from a day's fishing at sea. The yellow-eyed penguin site at Bushey Beach can be reached by following Graves Walkway (2 hours return) from the blue penguin colony.

Those in a hurry to get north might prefer to travel directly from Oamaru to Christchurch on SH1 but a much more scenic alternative is to follow SH83 inland along the Waitaki Valley to Omarama. En route the road passes lakes Waitaki, Aviemore and Benmore, all of which were created as part of a major hydroelectric scheme on the Waitaki river. Well stocked with trout and salmon the lakes are as popular with anglers as they are with water sports enthusiasts. Worth a brief stop is the small settlement of **Duntroon**. In town the historic blacksmith shop can be visited whereas a few kilometres outside town, in the direction of Kurow, there are some Maori rock drawings to be seen. Signposted from the main road the Takiroa rock drawings were probably executed by pre-European Maori between AD1000 and 1500. Another 20km (12 miles) away **Kurow** is the starting point for jet boat trips on the Waitaki river.

Omarama, on the fringe of the Mackenzie country, has a wide reputation as a gliding centre due to favourable thermal air currents in the locality. There is plenty of accommodation in town and a reason for visitors to stay longer is the rare opportunity of going on a scenic flight with a glider (☎ 03 438 9621). Not to be missed if the weather is right are the beautiful Clay Cliffs. In certain light conditions the bizarrely eroded cliffs can display a remarkable range of colours, giving them an almost surreal atmosphere. The Clay Cliffs are signposted from SH8 on the way to Lindis Pass but an organised tour (☎ 03 438 9428) can be arranged for those without transport.

Route 13a • The Goldfields Route (Pigroot) to Lindis Pass and Omarama

The Pigroot was the route to the goldfields of Central Otago, a route now followed by SH85 as it winds its way from Palmerston towards Ranfurly on the Maniototo plains. Some claim that the name for the route described the early road's bad condition, whereas others claim that it derives from the name given to a hill by a certain John Thomson who was surveying the locality in the 1850s. Thomson, a man with a marked fondness for naming geographical locations after farmyard animals, is supposed to have chanced upon a tame wild boar and commemorated the event by naming the hill on which he found it 'Pigroot Hill'.

The tiny settlement of **Dunback** is situated just over 10km (6 miles) north-west of Palmerston. To the north of town a turn-off to the left leads to **Macraes Flat**, the site of a modern gold mine as well as the historic Golden Point Mining Battery. Tours of the gold mine can be arranged from Stanley's Hotel, a century-old pub at Macraes Flat.

From Dunstan the road continues over the Horse range before eventually descending to the Maniototo plains and **Ranfurly**, the largest town (population 994) in the area. There is not a lot to Ranfurly but there is a railway station and of course a pub. For tourists the most interesting fact about the place is that it is centrally located and makes a useful base for visits to the gold-mining towns of Naseby and St Bathans.

Naseby lies to the north of Ranfurly. Once the largest gold-mining town on the Maniototo it is now a sleepy little place with only a few old buildings left to conjure up an impression of the wild gold rush days. Worth visiting is the Maniototo Early Settlers Museum as well as the old watchmaker's shop to which it is connected. In winter the local ice rink is popular among followers of the sport of curling.

The unsealed road that heads north-west from town leads past the Kyeburn Diggings, where miners gouged away the cliffs in a fevered search for gold, to the historic Dansey Pass Hotel. Built in the 1880s to serve the goldminers the hotel still offers food and accommodation in the remotest of surroundings. Continuing on from Dansey Pass it is another 48km (29 miles) to Duntroon and the Waitaki valley (see Route 13).

About 40km (24 miles) further west of Naseby, on a loop road off SH85, is the former gold-mining township of **St Bathans**. Strung along the main street are a number of buildings that date from the nineteenth century gold rushes. In those days the town had a loud, hard-drinking community of 2,000 miners who were catered for by no less than thirteen pubs. Of these only the Vulcan Hotel (1869) has survived but it has no trouble catering to the needs of St Bathan's present population of around twenty. Blue Lake, a popular picnic spot close to town, was formed by miners sluicing for gold.

Continuing along SH85 from Ranfurly it is another 88km (54 miles) to **Alexandra**. Located in what is now a rich fruit growing region Alexandra was also a mecca for those smitten by gold fever. Thousands of diggers flocked to work the nearby Dunstan fields but this rush proved short lived and it was not until the gold dredging boom of the 1890s that the town was really able to prosper.

More information on gold dredging is available at the Sir William Bodkin Museum on the corner of Thompson and Walton streets. An excellent viewpoint over Alexandra, from where the old dredge tailings are clearly visible, can be reached by turning off Tarbert Street at the north-east end of town and then following Little Valley Road to the top of Tucker Hill. It is also worth stopping in at the information centre as they have plenty of tips on other things to see and do in the region. They take bookings for four-wheel drive safaris into the Dunstan mountains and Old Man range; trips definitely worth considering if you want to see the more remote areas of Central Otago. They also have an excellent collection of brochures detailing walks or cycle tours for those who prefer to explore under their own steam.

Only a short distance up the road from Alexandra is **Clyde**. The many stone buildings that still line Clyde's streets are reminders of the days when the town was at the centre of the Dunstan Gold-rush (1863). Located in the stone courthouse of 1864 is the Courthouse Museum. It mainly concentrates on the history of the early goldfields whereas the Briar Herb Factory nearby displays historic herb processing machinery and has exhibits illustrating the pioneering days in general. Those who want to enjoy a nice meal in historical surroundings should try Oliver's Restaurant. It is housed in what used to be a general store that served the gold miners.

From Clyde SH8 follows the shores of Lake Dunstan, by-passing Cromwell (see Chapter 8) on its journey northwards to Lindis Pass and the lakes of South Canterbury. Near the northern end of Lake Dunstan a loop road leaves the main highway and leads to the ghost town of **Bendigo**. All that remains of this old quartz mining town are a few ruined stone dwellings and the vague sense of melancholy that clings to such places. Logantown and Welshtown, also ghost towns, are in the near vicinity. Take extreme care when exploring as there are many unmarked mine shafts in the area.

The Lindis Pass links Central Otago to the Mackenzie Country and Mount Cook and provides a magnificent exit from the region. The drive over the pass to Omarama is especially beautiful in the late afternoon when the tussock-covered hills glow in subtle hues of gold and bronze. The effect can be overwhelming; on some clear days it is as though the entire landscape is bathed in an enchanted, almost otherworldly light, so intense are the colours. Painters and photographers will love this route. From Omarama it is less than 100km (62 miles) to the start of Route 14 at Mount Cook.

Additional Information

Accommodation and Eating Out

ACCOMMODATION

Alexandra
The Willows **
(Bed & Breakfast)
3 Young Lane
☎ (03) 449 2231

Dunedin
Elm Lodge *
74 Elm Row
☎ (03) 474 1872
Law Courts Hotel **
Corner Stuart and Cumberland Streets
☎ and Fax (03)477 8036

Quality Inn ***
Upper Moray Place
☎ (03) 477 6784 Fax (03) 474 0115

Invercargill
Coachman's Inn **
705 Tay Street
☎ (03)217 6046 Fax (03)217 6045
Also cheap cabins.

Oamaru
Anne Mieke Guest House *
(Bed & Breakfast)
47 Tees Street
☎ (03) 434 8051

Oban
(Stewart Island)
Stewart Island Backpackers *
Halfmoon Bay
PO Box 103
☎ (03) 219 1230

Pub at Naseby

An historic watchmaker's shop, Naseby

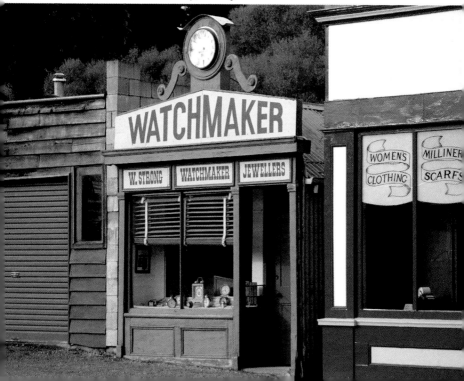

South Sea Hotel **
Elgin Terrace
☎ (03) 219 1059 Fax (03) 219 1120

Omarama
Omarama Hotel *
Main Road
☎ (03) 438 9713
Owaka

Pounawea Motor Camp *
On Catlins Estuary
☎ (03) 415 8483

EATING OUT
Alexandra
Dandelion Wine Bar *
12 Limerick Street
☎ (03) 448 8704
Light meals, live entertainment Sundays.

Fruitlands Gallery *
SH8 13km south of Alexandra
☎ (03) 449 2192
Light lunches.

Clyde
Oliver's Restaurant ***
34 Sunderland Street
☎ (03) 449 2860

Dunedin
Mega Bite *
388 George Street
☎ (03) 477 7343

Thai Cuisine *
205 King Edward Street
☎ (03) 455 8212

The Terrace Café **
118 Moray Place
☎ (03) 474 0686

Bell Pepper Blues ***
474 Princes Street
☎ (03) 474 0973

Invercargill
Zookeepers Café *
50 Tay Street
☎ (03) 218 3373

Gerrard's ***
3 Leven Street
☎ (03) 218 3406

Oamaru
The Last Post ***
12 Thames Street
☎ (03) 434 8080

Places to Visit

ROUTE 12
Bluff
Paua House
Corner Marine Parade and Henderson
Street
Open: almost always open.
Tiwai Point Aluminium Smelter
Open: guided tours Monday-Friday at
10am. Bookings essential. Minimum age
is 12.
☎ (03) 218 5999

Dunedin
Cadbury Confectionery Ltd
(chocolate factory)
280 Cumberland Street
Open: guided tours. Bookings essential.
☎ (03) 474 1126

Lanarch Castle
(Otago Peninsula)
Open: daily 9am-5pm.
Olveston
42 Royal Terrace
Open: Guided tours (1 hour) daily at
9.30am, 10.45am, 12noon, 1.30pm,
2.45pm and 4pm.

Otago Early Settlers Museum
220 Cumberland Street
Open: Monday-Friday 10am-5pm,
weekends 1-5pm.

Otago Museum
419 Great King Street
Open: Monday-Friday 10am-5pm,
weekends 1-5pm.

Speights Brewery
Rattray Street
Open: guided tours ($1^3/_4$ hours) at
10.30am Monday-Thursday. Bookings
essential.
☎ (03) 477 9480

Trust Bank Aquarium
Portobello
(Otago Peninsula)
Open: daily 1 December-1 March
12noon-4.30pm.

University of Otago
Open: for guided walking tours contact
Dunedin Visitor Centre.

Wilson Distillers
(whisky distillery)
Open: guided tours, book at Dunedin
Visitor Centre.

Invercargill
Southland Museum and Art Gallery
Gala Street, Queens Park
Open: Monday-Friday 9am-5pm,
weekends 1-5pm.

Lawrence
Goldfields Museum
Ross Place
Open: daily 10am-4pm.

Oban
(Stewart Island)
Rakiura Museum
Ayr Street
Open: Tuesday and Thursday 10am-
12noon; Monday, Wednesday and
Friday 10am-2pm; Saturday 11am-
12noon and Sunday 1-2.30pm.

Roaring Forties Brewery
(Southernmost brewery in the world)
Open: tours on request.
☎ (03) 219 1269

The Fernery
400m from Post Office
For opening times ☎ (03) 219 1453

ROUTE 13
Oamaru
Blue Penguin Colony
Oamaru Harbour
Open: September-March, evenings
Tyne-Harbour Street Historic Precinct
Open: Guided tours of Oamaru's historic
buildings can be arranged by contacting
the visitor information centre.

ROUTE 13a
Alexandra
Alexandra Museum
(Sir William Bodkin Museum)
Walton Street
Open: by arrangement, contact visitor
information centre.

Clyde
The Clyde Historical Museums
(Dunstan Courthouse and Briar Herb
    Factory)
Open: Tuesday-Sunday 2-4pm.

Macraes Flat
Macraes Gold Mine
Open: guided tours weekends and
public holidays at 1.30pm (May-August,
first weekend in month only).
Contact Stanleys Hotel, Macraes Flat.
☎ (03) 465 2400

Naseby
Maniototo Early Settlers Museum
Open: November-April daily (except
Monday) 1.30-3.30pm.

Travel Tips

BOAT TRIPS
(see also nature tours)

Dunedin
Monarch Cruises
Corner Wharf and Fryatt Streets
PO Box 102
☎ (03) 477 4276
Otago Harbour cruises and wildlife
cruises

Stewart Island
Moana Charters
☎ (03) 219 1202
Offer half day cruises to Ulva Island
and salmon farms as do several other
operators (contact DOC office for more
addresses).

JET BOATING
Alexandra
Riverside Hostel
☎ (03) 448 8152

Kurow
Waitaki Jets and Tours
Liverpool Street
☎ (03) 436 0778

NATURE TOURS
Catlins
Catlins Wildlife Trackers
PO Box 2192
Dunedin
(or C/o Dunedin Visitor Centre)
☎ (03) 455 2681
Depart Dunedin for 2 day safaris
through the Catlins. Winners of 1993
NZ Ecotourism Award.

Otago Peninsula
Penguin Place
(yellow-eyed penguins)
Wild South Ltd
PO Box 963
Dunedin
☎ (03) 476 1443

Royal Albatross Colony
Taiaroa Head
Open: guided tours daily (24 November-
16 September). Prior bookings necessary.
Contact Dunedin Visitor Centre.

Stewart Island
Bravo Adventure Cruises
PO Box 104
☎ (03) 219 1144
Offer guided kiwi spotting. Includes
boat cruise.

Thorfinn Charters
PO Box 43
Halfmoon Bay
☎ (03) 219 1210
Guided bird watching and nature walks.

KAYAKING/CANOEING
Alexandra
Central Outdoor Adventures
☎ (03) 448 6360
Rentals, guided trips and also mountain
bike hire.

Stewart Island
Inne's Backpackers
Argyle Street
PO Box 32
☎ and Fax (03)219 1080
Rentals and guided tours.
Stewart Island Connections
Air: daily flights from Invercargill with
Southern Air, ☎ (03) 218 9129.
Boat: Foveaux Express (catamaran)
departs Bluff (summer season) Mon-
day-Friday 9.30am and 5pm, Sunday
5pm. Winter sailings (21 May-23
August) Monday, Wednesday, Friday
and Sunday. Trip takes 60 minutes.
☎ (03) 212 7660.

TRAIN TRIP
Dunedin
Taieri Gorge Railway
Dunedin Railway Station
PO Box 140
☎ (03) 477 4449
Timetables are available from Dunedin
Visitor Centre.

TRACK TRANSPORT
Stewart Island
Stewart Island Water Taxi
☎ (03)219 1394
Drops trampers off at various points
along coast. Several other operators offer
the same service. Contact DOC office.

Tourist Information & Park Visitor Centres

Alexandra
Central Otago Visitor Information
Centre
22 Centennial Ave
PO Box 56
☎ (03) 448 9515

Catlins
DOC Visitor Centre
Corner Ryley and Campbell Streets
Owaka
☎ (03) 415 8341

Dunedin
48 The Octagon
PO Box 5457
Open: Monday-Friday 8.30am-5pm,
weekends 9am-5pm.
☎ (03) 474 3300

Invercargill
Victoria Avenue
PO Box 1012
Open: Monday-Friday 9am-5pm,
weekends 1-5pm.
☎ (03) 218 9753

Lawrence
17 Ross Place
☎ (03) 485 9222

Oamaru
Severn Street
Private Bag 50058
Open: Monday-Friday 9am-5pm,
weekends 10am-5pm.
☎ (03) 434 5643

Omarama
On SH83
☎ (03) 438 9808

Stewart Island
DOC Visitor Centre
Main Road
Half Moon Bay, PO Box 3
☎ (03) 219 1218

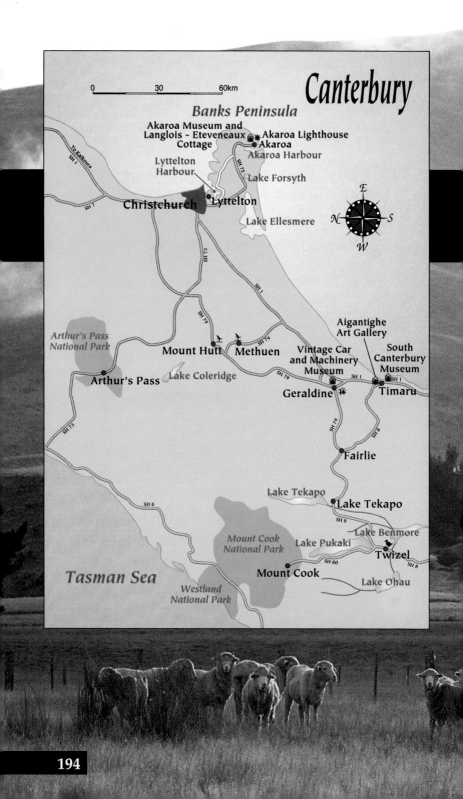

Canterbury

Banks Peninsula

Akaroa Museum and
Langlois - Eteveneaux
Cottage

Akaroa Lighthouse
Akaroa
Akaroa Harbour

Lyttelton
Harbour

Lake Forsyth

To Kaikoura
SH 1

SH 75

SH 7

Christchurch Lyttelton

Lake Ellesmere

SH 73

SH 1

*Arthur's Pass
National Park*

SH 79

Aigantighe
Art Gallery

SH 74

Mount Hutt Methuen

Vintage Car
and Machinery
Museum

South
Canterbury
Museum

SH 79

SH 1

Arthur's Pass

Lake Coleridge

Geraldine

Timaru

SH 73

SH 79

SH 8

Fairlie

SH 6

Lake Tekapo

Lake Tekapo

SH 8

Lake Benmore

*Mount Cook
National Park*

Lake Pukaki

Twizel

SH 80

SH 8

Tasman Sea

Mount Cook

Lake Ohau

*Westland
National Park*

Canterbury

Sheep farming is still a mainstay of the economy

10

This region features two dramatically different landscapes: the broad flat expanse of the Canterbury Plains and the alpine majesty of the Southern Alps. The main centre is Christchurch, a place with a distinctly English flavour to it. To the south-east of the city is lovely Banks Peninsula and the old French settlement of Akaroa. Here baguette and wine hold a slight edge over tea and scones. The Alps form the region's western boundary and are best explored in the vicinity of Mount Cook and Arthur's Pass National Parks, both areas of stunning natural beauty.

Route 14 • Mount Cook to Christchurch

Mount Cook Village can be reached by bus or plane from Christchurch or Queenstown. For those driving from Christchurch the quickest route (around 5 hours) is to follow SH1 south via Ashburton and then turn off onto SH79 via Fairlie and lakes Tekapo and Pukaki. More scenic however is the route along state highways 79 and 72 as described here from Mount Cook. From Omarama at the end of Route 13 it is not much more than an hour's drive.

Mount Cook National Park

Mount Cook National Park is part of the World Heritage Area (see Chapter 7) and protects some of the most spectacular alpine scenery in the Southern Alps. Within the park's boundaries are five major glaciers and more than 140 peaks over 2,000m (6,560ft). But rising above them all, at a height of 3,754m (12,313ft) is Mount Cook, the highest mountain not only in New Zealand but in all of Australasia. Only a few years ago Mount Cook was even higher but in December 1991 a gigantic landslide removed more than 10m (32ft) from the peak. The mountain acquired its European name in 1851 when the captain of a survey ship named it after the explorer Captain James Cook. However to the Maori it has long been known as Aoraki, after a figure in Maori mythology whose name translates as 'cloud in the sky'.

In spite of the rugged alpine character of the park there are a number of short walks in the vicinity of Mount Cook Village that can be undertaken by most people. Starting from the Hermitage hotel are the Hooker Valley (4 hours), Kea Point (3 hours) and Sealy Tarns (4 hours) walks. The popular Hooker Valley walk leads to a lake at the terminal face of Hooker Glacier whereas both the Kea Point and Sealy Tarns walks impress with dramatic views of glaciers and mountain peaks. An added attraction of the Sealy Tarns track is the abundance of alpine flowers in summer. The most famous of these flowers is the Mount Cook lily, the world's largest buttercup. Keep an eye out also for keas, New Zealand's mountain parrot.

Full day or overnight trips in the park are generally restricted to those with mountaineering experience but the tracks to Mueller and Hooker huts can be attempted by the fit and properly equipped. Anybody doing an overnight trip should inquire first at the visitor centre as to the degree of difficulty and make sure they sign the park intentions book. Note that the Copland Pass Track over the Alps is definitely not for the inexperienced.

From the end of the Tasman valley road there is a track along the side of the mighty Tasman Glacier to Ball Shelter. With a length of 27km (16 miles) this glacier is the longest in New Zealand and one of the largest anywhere in the world outside the polar regions. Though walking the track allows some excellent views of the glacier's lower reaches it is only by taking a scenic flight that one can appreciate its beauty to the fullest. Some of these flights include a landing on the glacier whereas others also take in Fox and Franz Josef glaciers in neighbouring Westland National Park. Those who want to combine a scenic flight with a bit of adventure can ski the Tasman. This all day tour is an unforgettable experience and one does not need to be a champion skier to take part.

However the more sedentary among us need not fear: it is neither necessary to walk, climb or fly to get a wonderful view of mountain scenery. All one needs is a seat in the air-conditioned comfort of the Hermitage Hotel's Panorama Room. The vista of snow-capped peaks, including Mount Cook, that greets the eye through generously proportioned windows is perhaps compensation enough for the rather expensive menu they set before you.

Accommodation within Mount Cook Village is provided by the luxury Hermitage Hotel, the slightly cheaper Glencoe Lodge Motel, Mount Cook Chalets and the Mount Cook Youth Hostel. Cabins, camping and caravan sites are provided at the Glentanner Park motor camp, about 20km (12 miles) from the village on the shores of Lake Pukaki. Heliskiing trips also start from here. Cheapest of all is the White Horse Hill camping area, to the north of the village, where the facilities are accordingly basic; running water and toilets but no electricity or showers.

Twizel is located about 58km (35 miles) south of Mount Cook Village and offers itself as an alternative place to stay. Born in 1968 as a base town for the Upper Waitaki Hydroelectric Power Development Scheme, Twizel would have been bulldozed once work was completed were it not for the tourist potential of the area and the tenacity of the residents who wanted to remain. Close to town are lakes Pukaki, Ohau, Ruataniwha and Benmore. Apart from the fishing and water sport activities that these lakes provide there is also a unique attraction in the form of a black stilt breeding centre 3km (1$^1/_2$ miles) south of town. The black stilt has the unfortunate reputation of being the world's rarest wading bird; there are only around seventy of them living in the wild. Visitors can observe stilts in the rearing aviaries from a specially constructed viewing hide.

Most South Island roads are free of heavy traffic

Church of the Good Shepherd, Tekapo

The tussock-covered plains of which Twizel marks the centre are popularly known as the Mackenzie country. The region is named after the legendary sheep thief James McKenzie, who was caught with a large flock of stolen sheep on the fringes of the basin that now bears his name. McKenzie was accused of stealing the sheep from a run near Timaru in March 1855, a charge which he denied. Though convicted of the crime he always proclaimed his innocence and he was eventually pardoned in 1856. The current theory is that McKenzie may really have been innocent but whatever the truth may be the mystique of this man, about whom little is known, continues to live on as part of the country's folklore.

Still within the Mackenzie Country and just over 50km (31 miles) north-east of Twizel, is beautiful Lake Tekapo. The waters of this glacial lake have an exquisite turquoise colouring that contrasts magnificently with the bronzed, almost treeless, surroundings. This unique colouring is produced by rocks that have been ground to a fine powder by glacial action and which now hang suspended, as 'rock flour', in the water. Though the water looks inviting the lake is as chilly as the glaciers that feed it so a swim is something only the bold should attempt.

The township of **Lake Tekapo** is located at the lake's southern end. On the lake shore a short distance from town is the Church of the Good Shepherd, a simple stone building that was erected as a memorial to the pioneer runholders of the Mackenzie. Not far away is the bronze statue of a sheepdog, a fitting tribute to an animal which played, and continues to play, an indispensable role in the grazing of the high-country.

Although the desolate beauty of the scenery which surrounds the lake can be enjoyed for free it is nevertheless worth considering spending a dollar or two on the scenic flights which start from here. The 'Grand Traverse' offered by Air Safaris is a 50 minute scenic flight around Mount Cook and Westland National Parks which takes in Franz Josef, Fox and Tasman Glaciers. The same company also offers roughly the same tour from Glentanner Park, near Mount Cook. In any case these flights are great value for money and a bit cheaper than those offered by other airlines at Mount Cook.

From Tekapo SH8 curves its way eastwards through vast tussock grasslands until, at Burke Pass, the wide-open spaces of the Mackenzie are abruptly left behind for an altogether gentler landscape. The rolling downs on which towns like Fairlie and Geraldine are situated are a first hint of the Canterbury Plains, one of the most prosperous farming regions in New Zealand.

Fairlie, the 'Gateway to the Mackenzie' for those coming from Timaru or Christchurch, is noted for its pretty tree-lined avenues and makes a good base in winter for those skiing at either Fox Peak or Mount Dobson in the Two Thumb range. If time is pressing it is probably best to leave Fairlie on SH8 for Timaru and then follow SH1 directly to Christchurch through the middle of the Canterbury Plains. However a more scenic and leisurely alternative is to follow state highways 79 and 72 via Geraldine and Mount Hutt.

Geraldine is a nice little town with a few interesting things to see and do in the vicinity. About 20km (12 miles) north of town is Peel Forest Park, one of the few remaining stands of native forest in the area. There is a nice camping ground here for those who enjoy a secluded setting, as well as some lovely picnic spots in the forest. Some of the park's well marked trails lead to waterfalls but the Big Tree Walk (1 hour) leads, appropriately enough, to a huge totara tree with a circumference of over 9m (29ft). At the end of the road that leads on from the forest park is Mesopotamia, a sheep run once owned by the great English writer Samuel Butler, who briefly tried his luck as a sheep farmer back in the 1860s. In Geraldine itself the Vintage Car and Machinery Museum is worth a look for those interested in things technical and just out of town, in the direction of Fairlie, visitors can enjoy the taste of elderberry wine at Barker's Wines.

Probably the best time to visit the port of **Timaru**, south of Geraldine, is when the Christmas Carnival is held at Caroline Bay. The carnival starts on 26 December and lasts about 10 days. In town the Aigantighe Art Gallery is of interest along with the South Canterbury Museum. The museum has among its exhibits a replica of the plane designed by pioneer aviator Richard Pearse, who may have been airborne a few months before the Wright brothers.

The main route continues north of Geraldine towards Mount Hutt. The **Mount Hutt** ski field is regarded as one of the best in the Southern Hemisphere. Reliable snowfall means that the season here can last for as long as six months. There are slopes suitable for beginners but the experienced can go higher up to enjoy the challenges of off-piste heli-skiing. All the necessary amenities are available, including a large ski school. Other ski fields within reasonable driving distance are Mount Dobson, Craigieburn and Porter Heights.

The base for winter activities at Mount Hutt is **Methven**, a few kilometres off SH72. Obviously this town is at its liveliest during the winter months when tourists with sun-tanned faces strut down the main street looking for the best place to enjoy their après-ski. However there are things to do in summer too when trendy ski clothes are exchanged for the gumboots and check-shirts of a small farming town. Apart from a beautiful 18-hole golf course there is good walking (Mount Hutt Forest) and fishing in the vicinity, as well as the possibility of jet boat rides through the dramatic Rakaia Gorge. A walkway allows a more leisurely look at the gorge (3-4 hours return).

At the intersection of state highways 72 and 73 the traveller can either choose to go left for a last close look at the Alps in the vicinity of Arthur's Pass or turn right on the road to Christchurch. For those who are starting their exploration of the South Island from Christchurch the Arthur's Pass Road can be highly recommended as a very scenic route to the 'Wild West Coast' (see Chapter 7).

Arthur's Pass National Park

Arthur's Pass township is the gateway to the national park and only 4km (2 miles) from the 924m (3,030ft) pass itself. Here there is accommodation as well as a park visitor centre. The centre has detailed information about all the tracks and inexperienced trampers should seek advice from the staff as to the difficulty of the walks they intend to do. The weather here can change very rapidly, making many normally 'safe' walks quite dangerous.

The national park spreads over both sides of the Southern Alps, covering an area of 98,408 hectares (243,067 acres). Dry tussock grasslands and mountain beech forest dominate in the east, whereas the park's western slopes, where rainfall is much higher, are characterised by dense, tangled rainforests of podocarp, beech and broadleaved trees. The alpine regions are also rich in flora; in fact more than 50 per cent of the alpine species found in New Zealand occur within the boundaries of this national park.

Such a diversity of vegetational zones also supports a wide range of native birds. Most common are wood pigeons, riflemen, bellbirds and silvereyes. In the alpine regions keas amuse trampers with their antics. Less commonly seen are parakeets, yellowheads and blue ducks. Great spotted kiwis are also found throughout the park but due to their nocturnal habits they are more often heard than seen.

The walks within this mountainous park vary from easy strolls to demanding tours of 4 or 5 days. Short walks close to the township include the Dobson Nature Walk ($1^1/2$ hours return), Devil's Punchbowl Falls Walk (1 hour return) and Bridal Veil Track ($1^1/2$ hours return). An excellent 2 day tramp which crosses from the eastern beech forests to the rainforests of the West Coast is the Mingha-Deception Track. It starts only 5km (3 miles) south of the village at Greyneys Shelter. Also within easy reach the Temple Basin Track (3 hours return) is hard to beat for magnificent views of alpine peaks, some of which exceed 2,000m (6,560ft). In winter a ski field operates here.

Christchurch

Christchurch is frequently described as 'the most English city outside England' which, however true the statement may or may not be, is at least partly reflected in its Cathedral Square, punting on the willow-lined Avon river, some noble old stone buildings and the very English traditions of Christ's College secondary school for boys. The first settlers in the area (organised settlement took place in the 1850s) were certainly English to the core and brought with them not only their Anglican faith but also their cricket bats. Christchurch has been the headquarters for New Zealand cricket ever since. The city was named, incidentally, after Christ Church College at Oxford, where one of the early settler leaders had studied.

Cathedral Square, at the centre of town, is a good place to start a walk around the inner city. For those who are driving (and who have success-

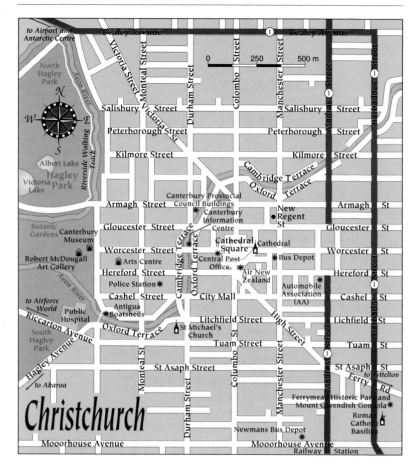

fully negotiated the one-way street system) there is parking at the corner of Gloucester and Manchester Streets.

Dominating the square is the neo-Gothic cathedral. For an elevated view of the surroundings the energetic can climb halfway up the 63m (206ft) tower to the observation balconies. During the week at 1pm, weather permitting, the city's most eloquent eccentric comes to harangue crowds in the square with his view of the world. Famed throughout the country as 'the Wizard', and dressed in flowing robes, he is an 'official' attraction with his postcards and upside-down maps of the world available from the tourist information centre.

From the square continue west along Worcester Boulevard towards Rolleston Avenue. Just before crossing a bridge over the Avon river it is worth stopping at the **Canterbury Information Centre** which is housed in an attractive old red brick building. Here visitors can get all the information they need on the many things to do in and around Christchurch.

Christchurch Cathedral

New Regent Street, Christchurch

Apart from town plans they also have a pamphlet describing various walks around the central city. Opposite the information centre is a statue of the Antarctic explorer Robert Falcon Scott, who set off from here on his ill-fated expedition to the South Pole.

At the end of Worcester Boulevard, on Rolleston Avenue, is the **Canterbury Museum**. Among the most interesting displays is the reconstruction of a Christchurch street from the pioneer days and the Hall of Antarctic Discovery where exhibits chart the trials and tribulations of antarctic exploration. The recently opened gallery Iwi Tawhito — Whenua Hou (Ancient People — New Land) takes visitors far back into New Zealand's pre-European past, to a time when the now extinct giant moas were hunted by the early Polynesian ancestors of today's modern Maori. Directly behind the museum the **Robert McDougall Art Gallery** has large permanent collections of New Zealand and international art.

Access to the art gallery is through the **Botanic Gardens** which, combined with the adjacent South and North Hagly Parks, spread out behind the museum like a green oasis in the middle of the city. Bordered by the gently flowing Avon river with magnificent old trees providing shade, and luxuriant flower beds adding a splash of colour, the gardens make a very pleasant setting for a relaxing stroll. A tea kiosk offers light refreshments.

Just across the road from the Botanic Gardens and museum, in the former Canterbury University buildings, is the **Arts Centre**. Once cloaked in the sober mantle of academia the dignified stone buildings are now a gathering place for artists, musicians and craftspeople. Live entertainment, craft shops, galleries and good restaurants ensure that there is plenty to see and do here. Especially popular is the weekend market where a colourful melange of stalls sell everything from handicrafts to exotic foods.

The **Antigua Boatsheds** at the southern end of Rolleston Avenue, hire out single and double canoes for those who want to paddle themselves along the Avon. If you prefer someone to do the work for you punts, complete with a boatman wearing his boater, depart from the Canterbury Information Centre, the Town Hall Restaurant and the Thomas Edmonds Restaurant; all of which are within walking distance of Cathedral Square.

From the boatsheds follow Cambridge Terrace back to Worcester Boulevard and Cathedral Square. This part of the walk is particularly nice as it follows the tree-lined banks of the River Avon. On the way the very impressive wooden structure of **St Michael's Church** (1872) can be seen across the river.

The **Canterbury Provincial Council Buildings** (1859-65), which are considered to be the best examples of neo-Gothic architecture in the country, can be reached from Cathedral Square by going north along Colombo Street and then turning left into Armagh Street. The most interesting feature of the complex is the magnificent high Victorian Gothic interior of the Stone Council Chamber. Further afield but also of great interest to architecture buffs is the **Roman Catholic Basilica** (1901- 05) in Barbadoes Street. The Irish playwright George Bernard Shaw (1856-1950) was greatly impressed by this cathedral and it is generally regarded as New Zealand's finest neo-Renaissance church.

Some of the city's other attractions are best reached with either the bus or car. The **International Antarctic Centre** is located out near the airport. It offers an insight into the Antarctic research programmes that are being carried out by American and New Zealand scientists. Christchurch is in fact the US headquarters for 'Operation Deep Freeze', as the aerial supply link to their main Antarctic research station at McMurdo Sound is known. Multimedia special effects and the fascinating *Great White South* audio-visual presentation make the trip here a memorable experience.

Air Force World is an imaginatively arranged museum, only a 15 minute drive from the city centre. Pride of place is taken by sixteen vintage aircraft that have seen service in the New Zealand Air Force over the years. A special attraction is the chance to fly in a Tiger Moth biplane. Roughly the same distance away, but this time to the south-east of the city centre, the **Ferrymead Historic Park** focuses on transport and technology. Visitors who passed on the role (and expense) of being a World War I flying ace at the previous museum can at least ride on a steam train or tram here. Only a few minutes away the **Mount Cavendish Gondola** offers spectacular views of the Southern Alps and Banks Peninsula on its way up to the top of the Port Hills.

Banks Peninsula

The rugged hills of Banks Peninsula stand in dramatic contrast to the flat plains surrounding Christchurch. These hills are in fact the heavily eroded flanks of two offshore volcanoes that formed millions of years ago and were eventually linked to the mainland by an accumulation of shingle that was washed down from the Alps. Around 15,000 years ago the huge twin craters filled with sea-water to form the natural harbours at Lyttelton and Akaroa.

The quickest way to get to the peninsula, as well as Christchurch's port at Lyttelton, is to take Ferry and then Tunnel Road through the road tunnel. An alternative is to go south on Colombo Street and over Dyers Pass. This route offers excellent views and allows the possibility of a stop at the Sign of the Takahe, an impressive medieval-looking stone building that houses a restaurant. Those without their own transport can take advantage of the Akaroa Shuttle, a minibus that runs between Akaroa and Christchurch (☎ (03) 304 8600).

Probably the most interesting thing to do in **Lyttelton** is to take one of the harbour cruises that start from here. Apart from that there is not much else to engage one's interest except for a small museum and the Timeball Station. For many years the lowering of a timeball at precisely 1pm enabled mariners in the harbour to adjust their chronometers.

Bank of New Zealand building, Akaroa

Akaroa's origins as a French settlement are commemorated in many of the street names

St Patrick's, Akaroa

The road from Lyttelton to Akaroa is narrow, winding and very pictur-esque. After passing Governors Bay and Allandale you can choose be-tween two routes for the onward journey. The easiest to drive is the one over Gebbies Pass Road which then links with SH75 to Akaroa. The other road is less busy but partly unsealed and goes via Port Levy and Pigeon Bay.

Akaroa was originally intended as a French colony but to the dismay of the colonists who arrived from France in 1840 the Treaty of Waitangi had already been signed and New Zealand was now under British sover-eignty. The French stayed on, nevertheless, and the Gallic influence per-sists in many of Akaroa's street names (Rue Jolie, Rue Benoit) and the French flavoured menus of some local restaurants.

The town itself is quite charming; it stretches along a palm fringed harbour with quaint little cottages dotted here and there. The oldest house in town, and possibly Canterbury, is Langlois-Eteveneaux Cottage (1841-45). Behind the cottage is a museum that deals with Akaroa's colourful history. Other places of interest are the picture-postcard Church of St Patrick (1864) and the historic Akaroa lighthouse (1878). But apart from viewing any specific sights it is also nice to just wander about town and enjoy the relaxed atmosphere of the place. For those who linger a perfect way to end the day would be with a bottle of (New Zealand) wine and a seafood meal at the Pier Café, or any of the other restaurants in town for that matter. Akaroa is, all in all, a great place to while away a few days.

Many of the little bays and inlets on Banks Peninsula can be reached by car, including lovely **Okains Bay** where there is an excellent Maori and Colonial Museum. However the really secluded places are only accessi-ble on foot. One of the peninsula's most interesting walks is the 4 day Banks Peninsula Track. It begins and ends in Akaroa and covers 30km (18^1/$_2$ miles) of remote coastline. The track offers spectacular coastal scenery, safe swimming beaches and the chance to see penguins, seals and rare Hector's dolphins. For more information about the track and hut bookings ☎ (03) 304-7612. The tourist office in Akaroa should also have a few useful pamphlets about this and other walks.

From Akaroa SH75 winds its way back to Christchurch past Lake Forsyth and Lake Ellesmere. Both lakes serve as breeding grounds for hundreds of black swans and provide a habitat for around 150 other species of bird as well.

Before finally leaving the South Island's largest city it is worth men-tioning the TranzAlpine Express. The route this train takes over the Southern Alps via Arthur's Pass is quite spectacular and some consider it to be one of the world's finest train journeys. The train departs daily from either Christchurch or Greymouth (on the west coast). The trip can also be done as part of a package tour that combines a ride on the TranzAlpine Express with a jet boat ride and a visit to a high country sheep farm (Contact Pacific Tourways ☎ (03) 359-9133).

State Highway 1, on which this long exploration of New Zealand began, is the road now followed for all those who are returning to Auckland for the flight home. The main place of interest on the way to Picton is Kaikoura and those who took the direct route to the west coast as described in Chapter 7 have the chance of stopping here now.

As a footnote it is worth mentioning one final place: 860km (533 miles) east of Christchurch is a remote group of islands known as the Chathams.

The Chatham Islands

Windswept and about as far off the beaten track as most tourists are likely to get the Chathams are home to a small community of fishermen and farmers. Most of the thousand or so islanders live on Chatham Island (90,000ha/222,300 acres), the largest of the 10 islands in the group. The only other island that is inhabited is tiny Pitt Island where the population stands at around fifty. A feature of the main island is the large central lagoon which, together with many shallow lakes, covers almost a quarter of its entire area.

The European discoverer of the islands was the British naval officer Lieutenant William Broughton, who landed in 1791 at Kaingaroa, near the north-eastern tip of Chatham. His encounter with the island's original inhabitants, the Moriori, was less than satisfactory and resulted in one of the Moriori being shot during a dispute. After him the islands were visited periodically by sealers and whalers but a serious attempt at European settlement did not begin before the 1840s.

When and from exactly where the Moriori came is not known for certain. Some theories maintain that these Polynesians arrived here before the Maori settlement of New Zealand whereas others suggest that the Moriori migrated here from the South Island. Whatever the case may be the Moriori evolved, isolated as they were, a culture which differed in many respects from that of the mainland Maori.

At the time of European discovery there were about 2,000 Moriois living on the Chathams. However in the early nineteenth century an invasion by mainland Maoris, along with diseases introduced by sealers and whalers decimated the population. The last supposedly full-blooded Moriori died in 1933.

Not much remains as a reminder of these people but those who are interested in the Moriori can visit the small museum at **Waitangi**, on Chatham, where there are a few Moriori artefacts and early photographs of the islands. Also of interest are the Moriori tree carvings (dendroglyphs) near the old Te Hapupu airfield. Researchers have yet to unravel the significance of these carvings which have no equivalent on the New Zealand mainland.

But as fascinating as the mysteries of Moriori culture may be the reason more and more people are beginning to visit the Chathams is to go bird-watching. The rarest of the eighteen species of bird that are unique to the islands is the black robin. Once there were only five of these birds in the world but successful breeding techniques have rescued them, for the moment, from the brink of extinction. On the other hand introduced birds like black swans and wekas are so common that they feature in the local cuisine along with freshly caught seafood such as crayfish.

Other activities on the islands include horse-riding, diving and tramping. It is also possible to hire four-wheel drive vehicles on Chatham Island which, apart from walking, are the only way to get around as there is no public transport. But having said all this it might be added that a great deal of the charm of these islands lies in the simple fact of their isolation and the chance they offer of getting an insight into what it is like to live in a community remote from the mainland's comforts and distractions.

Those who want to visit this tiny insular world of lagoons, peat bogs, rugged coastlines and deserted beaches should plan well ahead. Though there are weekly flights from Napier, Wellington and Christchurch demand is high and seats are very limited. There is no passenger boat service from the mainland but those with the money could join one of the cruises organised by Southern Heritage Expeditions. This company also specialises in trips to New Zealand's subantarctic islands.

Additional Information

Accommodation and Eating Out

ACCOMMODATION

Akaroa
Chez La Mer *
Rue Lavaud
☎ (03) 304 7024

Lavaud House **
(Bed & Breakfast)
83 Rue Lavaud
☎ (03) 304 7121

Christchurch
Dreamland *
21/23 Packe Street
☎ (03) 366 3519

Ambassador's Hotel **
(Bed & Breakfast)
19 Manchester Street
☎ and Fax (03) 366 7808

Kingsgate Christchurch Hotel ***
766 Colombo Street
☎ (03) 379 5880 Fax (03) 365 4806

Mount Cook
Glentanner Park *
SH80 (at head of Lake Pukaki)
☎ (03) 435 1855 Fax (03)435 1854

The Hermitage Hotel ***
☎ (03) 435 1809 Fax (03) 435 1879

Lake Tekapo
Lake Tekapo Motels **
Lake Side Drive
☎ (03) 680 6825 Fax (03) 680 6824
Also cheap cabins.

Methven
Pudding Hill Chalets **
SH72 (5km from town)
☎ and Fax (03)302 8416
Also tent sites.

Waitangi
(Chatham Islands)
Hotel Chathams **
Waterfront Road
☎ (03) 305 0048 Fax (03) 305 0097

EATING OUT

Akaroa
La Rue **
6 Rue Balguerie
☎ (03) 304 7658

Jacque's French Café and Bar ***
Beach Road
☎ (03) 304 7421

Arthur's Pass
The Chalet ***
Main Road
☎ (03) 318 9236

Christchurch
Dux de Lux *
Corner Hereford and Montreal Streets
☎ (03) 366 6919

Bardelli's **
98 Cashel Mall
☎ (03) 353 0000

Thomas Edmonds Restaurant **
Corner Cambridge Terrace and Manchester Street
☎ (03) 365 2888

Bridge Restaurant ***
128a Oxford Terrace
☎ (03) 366 9363

Geraldine
Papillon Chinese Restaurant *
40 Talbot Street
☎ (03) 693 9722

Timaru
Golden Palace Chinese Restaurant **
84 Evans Street
☎ (03) 684 4180

The 'Bold As' Brasserie **
335 Stafford Street
☎ (03) 688 3981

Places to Visit: Christchurch

Air Force World
Main South Road
Bus: No. 25 or 8. A courtesy bus leaves Christchurch Information Centre 3 times daily.
Open: daily 10am-4pm.

Arts Centre
2 Worcester Boulevard
Open: daily Monday-Friday 8.30am-5pm, weekends 10am-4pm.

Canterbury Museum
Rolleston Avenue
Open: daily 9am-4.30pm. Free guided tours 10.15am, 11.30am, 1.15pm and 2.30pm. Admission is free (donations welcome).

Canterbury Provincial Council Buildings
Durham Street
Open: Monday-Friday 10am-4pm. Guided tours Sunday 2-4pm. Admission is free except for guided tours.

Cathedral of the Blessed Sacrament
(Roman Catholic Basilica)
Barbadoes Street
Open: daily 8am-4pm. A 15 minutes walk from the Square.

Christ Church Cathedral
Cathedral Square
Open: tower is open Monday-Saturday from 8.30am, Sunday 11.30am. Free guided tours Monday-Friday at 11am and 2pm, Saturday 11am and Sunday 11.30am.

Ferrymead Historic Park
269 Bridle Path Road
Heathcote
Bus: No. 3
Open: daily 10am-4.30pm.

International Antarctic Centre
Orchard Road
Open: daily 9.30am-8.30pm (1 October-31 March), 9.30am-5.30pm (1 April-30 September).

Robert McDougall Art Gallery
Rolleston Avenue
(Access via Botanic Gardens)
Open: daily 10am-4.30pm. Guides available 11am-3pm daily.

Useful Information: Christchurch

Area Code: (03)

Consulates
UK: Tel. 365 5440
USA: Tel. 379 5795

Important Telephone Numbers
Emergency Chemist: ☎ 366 4439
Emergency Medical: ☎ 365 7777
Taxis: ☎ 379 9799

Post Office
Chief Post Office is on Cathedral Square.

Punting/Canoeing
Antigua Boatsheds
Rolleston Ave
Open: daily 9.30am-6pm.
☎ 366 5885
Single and double canoes for boating on
the Avon.

Punting
Punts depart daily 9am-6pm, in winter
10am-4pm.
Departure points: Canterbury-
Christchurch Information Centre,
corner Worcester Street and Oxford
Terrace, the Town Hall Restaurant
(corner Colombo Street and Kilmore
Street) and Thomas Edmonds Restau-
rant (Cambridge Terrace).

Transport

Airport
Bus from city to airport leaves from
Tower Building, Cathedral Square.
They depart half hourly from 6am-6pm,
then less frequently until 9.45pm. For
exact times: ☎ 366 8855
Super Shuttle offers a door-to-door
service to airport, ☎ 365 5655

Bus Services
For local bus timetables enquire at Bus
Kiosk, Cathedral Square, ☎ 366 8855
Mount Cook Landline Coach Terminal
is at 40 Lichfield Street. Reservations:
☎ 379 0690
Intercity Coachlines Terminal is at 471
Moorhouse Avenue, by railway station,
☎ 379 9020.
Bookings for long distance buses can
also be made through Christchurch
Information Centre.

Mount Cavendish Gondola
10 Bridle Path Road
Open: Monday-Thursday 10am-11pm;
Friday and Saturday 10am-midnight;
Sunday 10am-9.30pm.

Trains
Railway Station is off Clarence Street.
Reservations ☎ (0800) 802 802

Places to Visit

ROUTE 14
Akaroa
(Banks Peninsula)
Akaroa Lighthouse
Beach Road
Open: Sun 1-4pm (daily during Jan.)

*Akaroa Museum & Langlois-Eteveneaux
    Cottage*
Corner Rue Lavaud and Rue Balguerie
Open: daily 10.30am-4.30pm.

Geraldine
Barker's Wines
Off SH79
(8km from Geraldine)
Open: Monday-Saturday until 6pm.

Vintage Car and Machinery Museum
174 Talbot Street
Open: daily 10am-12noon, 1.30-4pm
(Labour weekend to Queen's Birthday
weekend).

Lyttelton
Lyttelton Museum
Gladstone Quay
Open: 2-4pm Tuesday, Thursday and
weekends (December-February),
otherwise only weekends 2-4pm.

Timeball Station
Reserve Terrace
Open: Monday-Friday 10am-4pm,
weekends 10am-5pm.

Okains Bay
(Banks Peninsula)
Maori and Colonial Museum
Open: daily 10am-5pm.

Timaru
Aigantighe Art Gallery
49 Wai-iti Road
Open: Tuesday-Friday 11am-4.30pm,
weekends 2-4.30pm.

South Canterbury Museum
Perth Street
Open: Tuesday-Sunday 1.30-4.30pm.
Admission is free.

Twizel
Black Stilt Breeding Centre
Off SH8
Open: guided tours Monday-Friday at
10.30am and 2pm, weekends 3pm.
Bookings must be made beforehand at
Visitor Information Centre, Wairepo
Rd, Twizel.

Waitangi
(Chatham Islands)
Chatham Islands Museum
South Road
Open: daily.

Travel Tips

BOAT TRIPS
Akaroa
(Banks Peninsula)
Harbour Cruises
MV *Canterbury Cat*
Office opposite wharf
☎ (03) 304 7641
Daily at 11am and 1.30pm.

Lyttelton
Harbour Cruises
☎ (03) 328 8368
Daily 2.45pm.

Mount Cook
Glacier Explorers
PO Box 18
Offer glacial lake tours ($2^1/_2$ hours).

CANOE/KAYAK HIRE
Akaroa
(Banks Peninsula)
Banks Peninsula Sea Kayaks
114 Rue Jolie
☎ (03) 304 8776
Also guided tours.

Lake Tekapo
Lake Tekapo Motels & Motor Camp
PO Box 43
☎ (03) 680 6825

CHATHAM ISLANDS
CONNECTIONS
Flights to the Chatham Islands depart
from Wellington, Napier and
Christchurch. For bookings contact
Ansett New Zealand ☎ (09) 376 950

(agent for Air Chathams) or Mount
Cook Airline ☎ (03) 379 0690
(Christchurch) or (09) 309 5395 (Auck-
land).

Southern Heritage Expeditions offers a
cruise to the Chathams and New
Zealand's subantarctic islands. The trip
takes 14 days. Contact:
New Zealand
PO Box 22
Waikari
☎ (03) 314 4393

UK
Naturetrek
Chautara
Bighton
Hants. SO24 9RB
☎ (0962) 733051

USA
NZCRO
6033 West Century Blvd
Suite 1270
Los Angeles CA 90045
☎ (310) 395 7480

GUIDED WALKS
Lake Tekapo
Alpine Recreation Canterbury Ltd
PO Box 75
Lake Tekapo
☎ (03) 680 6736 Fax (03) 680 6765
Offer the Mackenzie High Country
Walk, an easy 3 day alpine walk.

Mount Cook National Park
Alpine Guides Ltd
Mount Cook
☎ (03) 435 1834
Can provide a guide for the Copland
Pass Track.

Alpine Recreation Canterbury Ltd
(see above)
Offer a 2-3 day alpine crossing over Ball
Pass in the national park. A good
standard of fitness is required. No
mountaineering experience necessary.

HELISKIING
Mount Cook
Heliskiing is offered by the Helicopter Line (see Scenic Flights) in association with Alpine Guides and Glentanner Park. Bookings are essential for heliskiing and the Tasman Glacier ski trip, ☎ (03) 435 1834

JET BOATING
Christchurch
Jet Stream Tours
☎ (03) 352 2961
On Waimakariri river.

Methven
Windwhistle Jets
Darfield, near Methven
☎ (03 318 6850
Through Rakaia river gorge.

SCENIC FLIGHTS
Lake Tekapo
Air Safaris
☎ (03) 680 6880
Offer Grand Traverse flight around Mount Cook and Westland National Parks.

Mount Cook
Mount Cook Airline
☎ (03) 435 1848
Offer snow landings on Tasman, Fox and Franz Josef Glaciers.

The Helicopter Line
Glentanner Park
☎ (03) 435 1855
Similar trips to those offered by Mount Cook Airline.

Tourist Information & Park Visitor Centres

Akaroa
80 Rue Lavaud
PO Box 80
Open: daily.
☎ (03) 304 8600

Arthur's Pass National Park
Main Road
PO Box 8
Open: daily 8am-5pm.
☎ (03) 318 9211

Christchurch
Christchurch/Canterbury Information Centre
Corner Worcester Street and Oxford Terrace
PO Box 2600
Open: Monday-Friday 8.30am-5pm, weekends 8.30am-4pm.
☎ (03) 379 9629

Visitors' Information Centre
Christchurch International Airport
PO Box 14-001
Open: times coincide with arrival of international flights
☎ (03) 353 7783/4

Visitors' Information Centre
Domestic Terminal
Harewood
PO Box 14-001
Open: 6.30am-10.30pm. Saturdays 6.30am-8pm.
☎ (03) 353 7774/5

Geraldine
Talbot Street
☎ (03) 693 8597

Methven
Mt Hutt Road
☎ (03) 302 8955

Mount Cook National Park Visitor Centre
Bowen Drive
PO Box 5
Open: daily 8am-5pm.
☎ (03) 435 1818

Twizel
Wairepo Road
Private Bag
Open: daily.
☎ (03) 435 0802

Fact File

11

Accommodation

There is a wide range of accommodation from the cheap motor camps and backpacker hostels to modern motels and luxury hotels. The *Where to Stay Guide* published by the NZTB lists many of New Zealand's motels, hotels, guest houses and motor camps and is available from New Zealand's overseas tourist offices.

There are also a number of publications available locally which list the various forms of accommodation. Some of these are available free of charge at tourist information centres, motor camps, motels or at railway stations and airports. *AA Accommodation Guides* published by the Automobile Association (AA) are free to overseas visitors who belong to an affiliated automobile club. These guides are available from AA offices throughout the country. *Jason's* accommodation guides are available in bookshops but some are also distributed free, as for instance *Jason's Budget Accommodation* which can be picked up at many motor camps.

Camping

New Zealand has some of the best camping facilities in the world. Camping grounds are well spread around the country and are often called 'motor camps', though some of the larger ones are called 'holiday parks'. Most camping grounds have not only tent sites but also powered sites for campervans and caravans and cabins. There are a number of free booklets available in New Zealand which list camping grounds, for instance the Holiday Accommodation Parks directory, published by the Camp and Cabin Association of New Zealand.

The kitchens at camping grounds are usually very well equipped with stoves or microwave ovens, toasters, electric jugs and hot water for washing up. All you need to supply is your own crockery and pots, etc. Hot water showers and laundry facilities are also available.

Many camping grounds offer cabins. The simplest are the standard cabins which are not much more than a bunk, a mattress and a roof over the head. There are a few better grades of cabin but the best of the lot are the tourist flats which may be equipped with TV, shower and cooking facilities. Usually you have to bring your own sleeping bag or blankets, though they can sometimes be hired. Even the simplest cabins will usually have an electric heater.

Cabins are excellent value for the budget traveller and can cost as little as NZ$20 for two persons. Tourist flats hover around the NZ$45-$50 mark.

There are also camping sites run by the Department of Conservation (DOC) which are situated in national, maritime or forest parks as well as in various forest reserves. Some of these sites are serviced (hot showers, etc) but others are very simple and might only have a toilet and water supply. The brochure *Conservation Campsites* lists these sites and is available from DOC offices or by writing to DOC, PO Box 10420, Wellington, New Zealand.

Hostels

YHA hostels and private or backpacker hostels are found throughout New Zealand and cater to budget conscious travellers. Many have single or double rooms as well as dormitory style accommodation. Fully equipped communal kitchens and laundry facilities are generally available. Many hire out bicycles and will also help organise outdoor activities. Some hostels offer a pick-up service if they are located outside town. Reservations are recommended for all hostels in the summer season. Average price for a double room is about NZ$15 per person.

YHA Hotels (Hostelling International)

In New Zealand there is no age limit, no curfew, no duties and 24 hour access for guests. Bedding is supplied. YHA members are also entitled to discounts on travel in New Zealand with Air New Zealand, Ansett New Zealand, certain bus services and long-distance trains. You can join the YHA in New Zealand. For more information contact:

YHA New Zealand, National Office
PO Box 436
Christchurch
☎ (03) 379 9970
Fax (03) 365 4476

National Reservation Centre
PO Box 68-149
Auckland
☎ (09) 309 2802
Fax (09) 373 5083

Backpackers Hostels

Have similar services and facilities to YHA hostels but are more likely to have private or double rooms, at least at the moment. Premises are open all day and there are no membership fees. The optional VIP Backpackers Discount Card entitles holders to discounts similar to those available to YHA members.

Booklets listing backpacker accommodation are available at information centres or the hostels themselves. For more information contact:

A.T.A
PO Box 8
Kaikoura
☎/Fax (03) 319 5916

Backpackers Resorts of New Zealand Ltd
PO Box 991
Taupo
☎/Fax (07) 377 1157

Budget Backpackers Hostels NZ Ltd
99 Titiraupenga St
Taupo
☎/Fax (07)377 1568

Guesthouses and Bed & Breakfasts

These vary a lot in price and in the standard of accommodation offered. In the cheaper guesthouses you may have to share bathroom facilities but the more expensive places have private facilities. The breakfasts at the B&Bs can be very good value and they generally provide a more personal touch than motels or hotels. Lists of B&B accommodation are available at the guesthouses themselves or from the tourist information centres.

Hotels, Motels and Motor Inns

Hotels can be quite cheap and basic or offer all the luxury one could ever wish (to pay) for. They are usually centrally located, often have an attached café or restaurant, guest lounge and laundry facilities. New Zealand's traditional 'pub' hotels are licensed to sell alcohol and may have both lounge and public bars. Many of the smaller hotels also offer budget or backpacker rooms. These budget rooms are normally without private bathrooms and TVs, etc.

Motel units are equipped with bathrooms and always provide tea or coffee making facilities. Bedding is usually provided. Many have very well equipped kitchens with everything necessary to prepare a proper meal. Other facilities include television, radio, heating and electric blankets. Sauna, spa and swimming pool may also be available.

Motor Inns are a cross between a motel and hotel. They usually have a bar and a public restaurant. All rooms have attached bathrooms and tea or coffee making facilities are usually provided. A few rooms might also have kitchens. As is the case with a motel it is possible to park very close to your room.

Farmstays and Homestays

These places offer foreigners a chance to get to know a New Zealand family in either a rural, town or city environment. On the farmstays it is possible to participate in such typical farming activities as milking or rounding up sheep. Rooms may be in the family's house or in a separate cottage. Costs for this type of accommodation vary greatly. Some farm and homestays are listed at the back of the *Where to Stay Guide* mentioned earlier, otherwise contact one of the tourist information centres or:

Homestay Ltd	Rural Holidays New Zealand Ltd
PO Box 25 115	PO Box 2155
Auckland	Christchurch
New Zealand	☎ (03) 366 1919
☎ (09) 575 5980	Fax (03) 379 3087
Fax (09)575 9977	

WWOOF

A cheaper way to stay on a farm than a farmstay is to join Willing Workers on Organic Farms (WWOOF). Members receive a list with organic farms throughout New Zealand. In exchange for your work the farmer provides food and accommodation. To join contact: WWOOF, PO Box 10-037, Palmerston North, New Zealand ☎ (06) 355 3555

Arrival and Customs

All visitors to New Zealand need to have valid passports to enter the country and the passport must be valid for at least 3 months beyond the time of your intended stay. Holders of British, Canadian, USA or Australian passports do not require a visa. British passport holders are permitted to stay for up to 6 months, Canadian and USA passport holders are given a permit on arrival that enables a stay of 3 months and Australian citizens can stay in New Zealand indefinitely.

Apart from a passport it is necessary to be able to produce a return or onward ticket to a country that you are permitted to enter and evidence that you have sufficient funds to support yourself during the time of your stay. This is usually NZ$1000 per month; often it is enough to produce one of the major credit cards (Visa, Amex, MasterCard, Diners Club, Bankcard).

Vaccination certificates are not required.

As entry requirements are subject to change it is always wise to check the current situation with your airline, travel agent or a New Zealand embassy or consulate before departing.

Customs Regulations

New Zealand has so far managed to remain relatively free of many of the animal and plant diseases that affect other countries. The accidental introduction of such diseases could have disastrous effects on the nation's economy which still relies heavily on agriculture. Because of this the interiors of all planes arriving

Climate in New Zealand

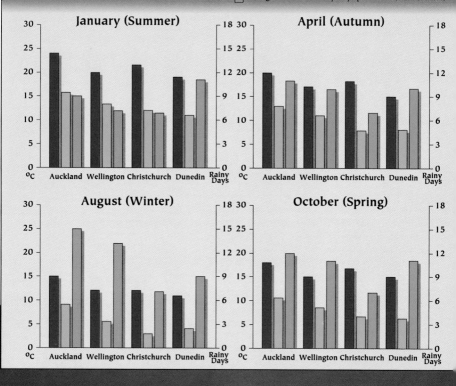

Legend:
- Average Daily Maximum Temperature
- Average Daily Minimum Temperature
- Average Number of Rainy Days per Month (1mm or More)

January (Summer)

°C — Auckland, Wellington, Christchurch, Dunedin — Rainy Days

April (Autumn)

°C — Auckland, Wellington, Christchurch, Dunedin — Rainy Days

August (Winter)

°C — Auckland, Wellington, Christchurch, Dunedin — Rainy Days

October (Spring)

°C — Auckland, Wellington, Christchurch, Dunedin — Rainy Days

from overseas are sprayed with an insecticide (harmless to humans) before passengers can alight. Furthermore all arriving passengers must fill out a form declaring whether or not they are carrying any plants, animal products or foodstuffs.

All personal belongings (clothing, cameras etc) needed for a visit are duty-free. The following goods are duty free for persons over 17 years of age: 200 cigarettes or 250g tobacco or 50 cigars (or a mixture of all three that does not exceed 250g); 4.5 litres of wine (e.g. six 750ml bottles) or 4.5 litres of beer and one bottle of spirits of no more than 1,125ml.

Visitors are warned against bringing illegal drugs into the country.

Banks

Open Monday to Friday 9am-4.30pm. Overseas exchange services are available at international airports for all incoming and outgoing flights.

Business Hours

Shops are generally open Monday to Friday 9am-5.30pm, Saturdays 9am-12.30pm and some shops (especially in the cities) may be open all day Sunday. On late shopping nights (Thursdays or Fridays) the hours are 9am-9pm. Some large supermarkets remain open 7 days a week.

Chemists

Chemist shops are found in all towns and cities. They keep normal business hours but in larger towns and cities there is also an after hours emergency service. Telephone numbers of Emergency Chemists are given in the Useful Information sections for Auckland and Wellington.

Apart from medicaments the chemist shops also sell a wide range of products from cosmetic articles to photo accessories.

Climate

When to Come and How Long to Stay

New Zealand has a mild climate but temperatures are at their warmest between October and April. The months June to August are cooler, especially in the south of the South Island, but in Northland the temperatures can still be quite pleasant.

As the European winter falls in the New Zealand summer this is the time when most people decide to visit New Zealand. However it is probably better to avoid the months December to January as this is when most of New Zealand is on holiday too. Early and late summer are pleasant times to travel in New Zealand as is autumn. If you are in New Zealand in autumn make sure you visit the area of Queenstown. The light and the colours at this time of the year are simply fantastic!

If you visit New Zealand in winter you are probably headed for the excellent ski fields of the South Island. But even if this is not the case there are still many things to see and do and accommodation will be quite a bit cheaper — at least outside the main ski centres.

It is possible to whizz around New Zealand in two weeks but most people find this far too short. Four weeks or more is much better. If you do have only limited time then it is best to stick to the main attractions and to fly as often as possible — check the airline discounts! It might even be worth considering taking one of the many tours around the country that are offered.

Currency and Credit Cards

New Zealand has a decimal system based on dollar and cent denominations. Dollars come in notes to the value of $5, $10, $50 and $100. There are 5c, 10c, 20c, 50c, $1 and $2 coins.

There is no limit on the amount of money that you can bring in or take out of New Zealand. New Zealand dollars can be exchanged for any foreign currency at the going rate.

All major credit cards (American Express, Bankcard, Mastercard, Visa and Diners Club) are widely accepted. The same applies to travellers' cheques. Banks will give a cash advance on Mastercard/Eurocard and Visa. Those with American Express credit cards should go to an American Express office.

Electricity

The mains electricity supply operates at 230 volts (AC), 50 hertz and three pronged plugs are used.

Embassies

Main foreign Embassies in New Zealand:

Australia
Australian High Commission
72-78 Hobson Street
Thorndon
Wellington
☎ (04) 473 6411

Canada
Canadian High Commission
61 Molesworth Street
Wellington
☎ (04) 473 9577

UK
UK High Commission
44 Hill Street
Wellington
☎ (04) 472 6049

USA
29 Fitzherbert Terrace
Wellington
☎ (04) 472 2068

For a complete list of embassies and consulates refer to 'Diplomat and Consular Representatives' in the Yellow Pages.

Main New Zealand embassies overseas:

Australia
New Zealand High Commission
Commonwealth Avenue
Canberra, ACT 2600
☎ (6) 270 4211

Canada
New Zealand High Commission
Suite 801
Metropolitan House
99 Bank Street
Ottawa, Ont. K1P 6G3
☎ (613) 238 5991

UK
New Zealand High Commission
New Zealand House
The Haymarket
London SW1Y 4TQ
☎ (71) 973 0366/63

USA
New Zealand Embassy
37 Observatory Circle NW
Washington DC
☎ (202) 328 4848

Emergencies

For police, fire and ambulance ☎ 111 and tell the operator which service you require.

Facilities for the Disabled

Facilities for disabled persons are available at airports and many other public buildings such as theatres, museums, shopping centres and public toilets. Some of the more modern hotels and motels also have facilities for the disabled and this is sometimes indicated in the *Where to Stay Guide* published by the NZTB and available from overseas tourist offices. Some short walks in the national parks are suitable for people in wheelchairs and the park visitor centres can provide the necessary information. For general information about disabled facilities in New Zealand contact: Disability Resource Centre, PO Box 24-042, Royal Oak, Auckland ☎ (09) 625 8069, Fax (09) 624 1633

Festivals

Listed here are only some of the more important or interesting festivals and local events. Local information centres will have more details.

Auckland • Fiesta Week: mid-March

Blenheim • Marlborough Food and Wine Festival: second weekend in February.

Hamilton • Ngauruawahia Regatta for Maori Canoes: March
New Zealand Agricultural Field Days: June

Hastings • Highland Games: April

Hokitika • Wildfoods Festival: 12 March, food and entertainment.

Masterton • Golden Shears Sheep Shearing Contest: March

Taihape • Gumboot Day: Easter Tuesday. Main event is the Gumboot throwing competition.

Wellington • International Festival of the Arts: February to March in even numbered years only.
Summer City Programme: January to February

Health

New Zealand is a clean and safe country and travellers have no particular health problems they need worry about. However the sun can be a problem. Because of the dramatic thinning of the earth's ozone layer over New Zealand the sun's harmful UV rays are more dangerous here than elsewhere. Make sure that you use a strong sunscreen and wear a hat if spending more time outdoors. The amount of time that you can spend outdoors without risking sunburn (the 'burn-time') is broadcast on local radio over the summer months. Note you can get sunburned even on cloudy days.

Health Insurance

Travellers are advised to get a travel insurance policy that adequately covers them in the event of falling ill in New Zealand. It is written in some booklets put out by the New Zealand Tourist Board that the country operates a no-fault accident compensation scheme which covers both residents and visitors. This basically means that if you suffer personal injury through an accident you are entitled to compensation for 'reasonable' expenses related to that accident. As this situation could change it is wise to check with your travel agent or New Zealand tourist offices or embassies in your home country before setting out. Medical treatment not related to an accident is **not** free of charge.

Language

The two official languages are English and Maori, though English is the language that is most widely spoken. In spite of the fact that visitors are rarely required to speak Maori it can nevertheless help to know a few words as many of New Zealand's towns and geographical features have Maori names. Maori place-names are either descriptive or refer to an event, real or legendary, that may have occurred at that particular spot.

Space precludes a detailed description of Maori pronunciation but it helps to know that in Maori 'wh' is normally pronounced like the English 'f' and that 'ng' is pronounced like the 'ng' in singer.

A few common greetings:

Haere mai — welcome
Haere ra — goodbye (spoken by the person staying to the person going).
Ka pai — thank you
Kia ora — hello

Words commonly encountered in Maori place-names:

ao — cloud	*papa* — flat rock
awa — river or valley	*puke* — hill
ika — fish	*rangi* — sky
iti — small	*roa* — long
kai — food	*roto* — lake
manga — stream or tributary	*rua* — two, cave
maunga — mountain	*tapu* — sacred
moana — sea or lake	*te* — the
motu — island	*wai* — water
nui — big	*whanga* — bay, body of water
pa — fortified settlement	*whenua* — land or country
one — sand, beach	

Taumatawhakatangihangakoauauotamateapokaiwhenuaakitanatahu or Taumata for short. A hill 8km south of Porangahau in Hawke's Bay. This is not even the longest version of the name which would then, beyond any doubt, be the longest place-name in the world. It roughly translates as 'after Tamatea's brother was killed in battle near here, Tamatea climbed this ridge and played a lament on his flute'.

Maori Cultural Tours

The Maori have a unique cultural heritage and those visitors who wish to learn more about this Polynesian people can do so on one of several cultural tours. Other tours are listed in the NZTB brochure *Maori Cultural Heritage Guide*.

Tall Tale Travel 'N Tours Ltd
PO Box 403
Kaitaia
☎ (09) 408 0870
Fax (09)408 1100
A guided visit to Pukepoto Marae
Kaitaia

Tamaki Tours
PO Box 1492
Rotorua
☎/Fax (07) 346 2823
Overnight stay on marae, hangi
and concert.

Te Rehuwai Safaris
Ruatahuna
☎/Fax (07) 362 7641
Learn about the Maori people
(Tuhoe) of Te Urewera National
Park. Horse treks and marae visit
included.

Tuwharetoa Tourism
145 Tongariro Street
Taupo
☎ (07) 378 0254
Fax (07)378 3714
Marae stays with full traditional
welcome.

Maps

Good road atlases and maps can be bought from any bookshop. *Pathfinders*
maps are quite good for travelling around as are *Wises* maps. Particularly good
are the AA road maps, which are free to AA members and to members of motor
clubs overseas that are associated with the New Zealand AA. These maps are
available at any AA office.

Measurements

The metric system is used in New Zealand:
1 kilogram (1,000 grams) = 2.2lb
1 litre = $1^3/_4$ pints
4.5 litres = 1 gallon
1 kilometre = 0.62 miles (10km = approximately 6 miles)

Nature Tours

Nature tours in New Zealand cover everything from bird-watching to whale
watching. Some nature tours are listed in the Additional Information sections at
the end of each chapter. A useful booklet published by the NZTB is the *Natural
Heritage Guide*. It lists a wide variety of nature tours throughout New Zealand.
Nationwide operators include:

New Zealand Nature Safaris
PO Box 5035
Port Nelson
☎ (03) 542 3159
Fax (03) 542 3190

Nature Quest New Zealand
PO Box 6314
Dunedin
☎/Fax (03) 489 8444

National Park Visitor Centres

Park visitor centres are located near the main entrances of all national parks.
They not only offer all the necessary practical information about walking and
other activities in the parks but also function as 'mini' natural history museums
specialising in the local flora and fauna. Maps, brochures and books concerning
the park in question can be bought here. These park books are excellent value

and because they are superbly illustrated with colour photographs they also make nice souvenirs of your visit.

Another source of information about both national and forest parks are the Department of Conservation (DOC) offices. These offices are found in many towns and cities and can also provide you with maps, brochures etc.

The DOC runs summer visitor programmes for 3 months from Christmas at many of the national parks. These highly informative programmes include half day and full day field trips as well as evening talks on natural history. Their addresss is: DOC Information Centre, Central Office, 59 Boulcott Street, PO Box 10420, Wellington ☎ (04) 471 0726.

The addresses of National Park Visitor Centres are listed at the end of the relevant chapters.

Post Offices

Open Monday to Friday 9am-5pm. Mail can be sent poste restante to post offices all over the country. In cities address poste restante to the chief post office (CPO). Mail is held for 30 days.

Public Holidays

1 and 2 January — New Years Day and day after New Year
6 February — Waitangi Day (New Zealand Day)
March/April — Good Friday and Easter Monday
25 April — Anzac Day
First Monday in June — Queen's Birthday
Fourth Monday in October — Labour Day
25 December — Christmas Day
26 December — Boxing Day

The main school holidays are from mid-December until January. There are also school holidays in May and August. The provinces (Northland, Otago, etc) also have their own anniversary day holidays.

Restaurants and Tearooms

Restaurants in New Zealand are divided into BYO (Bring Your Own) or licensed establishments. Only licensed restaurants may serve alcohol but the BYOs, which are often cheaper, allow you to bring your own bottle of wine, etc. A corkage fee is charged for opening the wine bottle and providing glasses. Pubs often have restaurants attached which offer simple but reasonably priced food. Vegetarian restaurants are most likely to be found in the cities. Many Indian restaurants have at least a few vegetarian dishes.

The small tearooms which are found all over the country are the traditional New Zealand equivalent of the café. Though some are rather low on atmosphere they are usually very reasonably priced. The better ones offer excellent home-made cakes (the carrot cakes are especially good) along with piping hot tea or coffee. Devonshire teas, which are served in the mornings and afternoons, consist of a pot of tea with a hot water refill and a couple of scones or muffins with cream and jam. Many tearooms along the main tourist routes are combined with a handicrafts shop.

Souvenirs

With all those sheep it is not surprising that most souvenir shops make sure that they have a good stock of woollen jerseys or sheepskin rugs. Hand-knitted jerseys are usually of very high quality but they are not cheap. More affordable are woollen walking socks (Norsewear is a good brand), scarves and hats.

A woollen garment that is favoured by many Kiwi trampers because of its robust quality is the Swann-Dri or 'Swannie' for short. They are also fairly expensive but will probably last longer than any other piece of clothing you have ever bought.

Traditional Maori carvings in either bone, wood or greenstone (jade) are also popular souvenirs. The famous Maori tiki (a stylized human figure) is often carved from both greenstone and bone. Paua (abalone) shell is, like greenstone, used for various items of jewellery but unfortunately it is often wasted on many pieces of kitsch.

Generally speaking New Zealand handicrafts are of a very high standard and it is worth browsing through the many local arts and crafts shops for original souvenirs.

Especially good is the pottery, weaving and wood carving. Articles range from objects of everyday usage to those that may be described (without any exaggeration) as works of art.

New Zealand-made outdoor equipment belongs to the world's best and if you need a new backpack, sleeping bag or tent it might pay to investigate one of the many sports shops throughout the country. Towards the end of summer it is often possible to get some good deals.

Other souvenirs might include one of the glossy *New Zealand is Beautiful* picture books, a cassette of traditional Maori music or perhaps a T-shirt decorated with a kiwi-bird motif.

Sports and Pastimes

The scope for outdoor activities and sports in New Zealand is virtually unlimited. Not all the sports and pastimes available are listed below but more information is available from NZTB offices overseas and of course the local tourist information centres. A very useful booklet published by the NZTB is *Adventure New Zealand*, it lists a wide range of adventure activities ranging from dolphin swimming to tandem sky diving. Background information about some of the most exciting (and unusual) outdoor adventures is contained in the excellent book *Classic New Zealand Adventures* by J. Kennett, J. Mulheron, G. Carlyon and M. O'Neill (GP Publications, Wellington).

Angling
Some people come to New Zealand just for the fishing, it is that good! Trout, salmon, perch and a few other fresh water species have all been introduced to New Zealand and seem to thrive in the country's rivers and lakes, often reaching record sizes. For trout the best places to go are Lake Taupo and the Tongariro river near Turangi but Gore in the South Island is also renowned for its excellent trout fishing. Salmon fishing is also good in many parts of New Zealand, though Southland and Otago are the regions where the fishing is meant to be at its best.

The main centres for big game fishing in New Zealand are Paihia and Russell in the Bay of Islands, Whitianga on the Coromandel and Tauranga and Whakatane in the Bay of Plenty. Launches can be chartered in these places and the sort of fish one is likely to catch include hammerhead shark, blue marlin, striped marlin, tuna and broadbill. The season for marlin and tuna is January-May, whereas sharks may be fished throughout the year.

For angling in lakes and rivers it is necessary to obtain a permit. Permits are usually issued for a particular area and may be valid for a day, week, month or an entire season. Special tourist fishing permits that are valid throughout New Zealand for a month are available from the larger sports shops or from Tourism Rotorua. For more information about permits and regulations contact the appropriate tourist information office.

Guided fishing trips are available in Turangi, Taupo, Rotorua and a number of other places as well.

Bungy Jumping
(See also Queenstown in main text)
Throwing oneself off a bridge with a rubber cord tied around the ankles might not be everybody's cup of tea but there are still plenty of people only too happy to pay for the experience. The main centre for bungy jumping is Queenstown but it is also offered at Hanmer Springs in the South Island and Taupo, Mangaweka, Masterton and Auckland in the North Island. Safety standards are very high but the rush of adrenalin through your body is probably even higher.

Canoeing and Kayaking
With so many rivers and lakes and so much coastline it almost goes without saying that New Zealand is a great place to go canoeing or kayaking. If you have never done it before you can learn it here and you will love every moment of it!

Canoes and kayaks can be hired at a number of places around the country and many of the companies that rent them out also offer guided tours. Tourist information centres can supply the necessary details.

One of the best rivers in the country for canoe/kayak trips is the Whanganui in the North Island. If you only have the time to canoe one river then do this one. It is suitable for beginners and the stretch between Taumarunui and Pipiriki offers some superb scenery.

Sea kayaking is something that the authors cannot recommend highly enough. Explore New Zealand's fascinating coastline and discover lonely bays and beaches accessible only by water! Great places for sea kayaking include the Bay of Islands, Coromandel, the Marlborough Sounds and along the coast of Abel Tasman National Park. Sea kayaks can be hired and guided trips are offered in all these areas.

Cycling
In spite of all the hills New Zealand is getting more and more popular among cyclists. Even on the main roads there is not too much traffic, the landscape is beautiful and varied and there are plenty of camping grounds along the way.

Mountain bikes can be hired in many towns and it is also possible to book guided mountain bike tours with all equipment provided if you so wish. Bikes are hired by the day, week or even on a monthly basis. It is often possible to hire equipment for touring as well. The local tourist information centres can provide the necessary addresses.

Trains and the main long distance bus companies will transport bicycles but only if there is enough room in their luggage compartments. The Kiwi Experience bus (☎ 09 366 1665) and other so-called 'alternative bus companies' are rather more generous in this respect and endeavour to make sure that there is always room for cyclists and their bikes.

In New Zealand it is compulsory to wear a helmet and it is forbidden to cycle along the tracks in the national parks.

Golf

Golf is a very popular sport in New Zealand and just about every town seems to have at least one golf course. There are in fact over 400 golf courses to be found spread throughout the country — more per head of population than in the USA! Most clubs welcome visitors and a few will also hire out the necessary equipment.

Not only are many of the country's golf courses of a very high standard but some can be counted among the most beautiful in the world. The American *Golf Digest* has included Wairakei International near Taupo in its list of the twenty five top courses outside the USA. Other top golf courses include Titirangi Golf Club (Auckland), Waitangi Golf Club (Bay of Islands), Paraparaumu Beach Golf Club (near Wellington) and Queenstown Golf Club, Kelvin Heights and Millbrook Resort (near Arrowtown, the country's first luxury golf resort. The Rotorua Golf Club's Arikikapakapa Course is worth a visit if you like a bit of volcanic activity to accompany your game. However those golfers who misjudge the 15 hole course may well find that their ball has been irretrievably lost in a boiling hot pool.

Horse Trekking

An interesting way to explore New Zealand is on horse-back and horse treks to suit all levels of experience are offered at many places throughout the country. Some of the longer treks may last well over a week but there are also plenty of half day and full day trips being offered. A few addresses:

North Island

Rangihau Ranch
Rangihau Road
Coroglen, Whitianga
☎ (07)866 3875
Book at Whitianga
Information Centre
1 hour and overnight treks
into the Coromandel ranges.

Waitomo Horse Trekking
Juno Hall
Waitomo Caves
☎ (07)878 7649
1 hour rides and overnight treks.

Whananaki Trail Rides
Hales Rd, RD1
Hikurangi, Northland
☎ (09)433 8299
2 hour and overnight treks

Windyglen Farm
Peter & Lynda Wilson
Bertrand Rd, RD43
Waitara, Taranaki
☎ (06)752 0603
1 hour and full day treks.

South Island

Ardachy Trail Rides
Leila Graham
Private Bag
Hindon, Dunedin
☎ (03)489 1499
1 hour, half day and full day
treks in Otago hill country.

Cape Farewell Horse Treks
Golden Bay
Book at Farewell Spit
    Visitor Centre
☎ (03)524 8454 or 524 8031
1 hour rides to 6 day treks on
West Coast.

Clarence Alpine Rides
David King
Clarence Bridge
Kaikoura RD1
☎/Fax (03)319 4339
1-4 day treks through river
valleys and alpine regions.

Mount Vernon Stables
Rue Balguerie
Akaroa
☎ (03)304 7180
$^1/_2$ - $2^1/_2$ hour rides.

Jet Boating

Racing down a narrow river canyon at breakneck speed in a boat that can execute a 360° spin just when a collision seems imminent is, in essence, what jet boating is all about.

Jet boating is offered just about everywhere in New Zealand where there is a river or lake. Popular jet boating rivers in the North Island are the Motu river near Opotiki and the Whanganui river. In the South Island the rivers around Queenstown are the location of some of New Zealand's most exciting jet boat trips.

Mountaineering

The best area for mountaineering is of course the Southern Alps. Mountaineering centres within this region are Mount Cook National Park, Mount Aspiring National Park and Arthur's Pass National Park. All these parks offer climbs suited to all levels of experience. Mountain huts are provided as are mountaineering guides. For those who wish to learn mountaineering skills there are climbing schools at both Mount Cook and Mount Aspiring.

Scuba Diving

Favourite diving areas in the North Island include Goat Island Marine Reserve north of Auckland, the Poor Knights Islands and the Bay of Islands. The fiords of Fiordland in the South Island attract divers because there is no other place in the world where black and red corals grow so close to the surface. Normally black coral is only found at depths of over 120m (394ft) but in the clear water of the fiords it may be seen at depths of just 6m (19ft).

Scuba divers also have plenty of historic shipwrecks to explore from the days when sailing ships plied the sometimes treacherous coastal waters. Of more recent vintage is the wreck of the *Rainbow Warrior*. After having been sunk by the French secret service in 1985 it was towed out to its final resting place near the Cavalli islands off the Northland Coast. Regular diving tours to the Cavalli's are offered from the Bay of Islands and Matauri Bay.

Another wreck worth exploring is that of the Russian cruise ship *Mikhail Lermontov*. It sank in the Marlborough Sounds in 1986 and it is claimed that it is the largest easily accessible wreck in the world. Tours to this wreck can be booked at diving shops and travel agents throughout the country.

Diving equipment can be hired from the various diving or sports shops. At some of the more popular diving areas there are also diving schools. Divers should remember to bring their diving licence and logbook. For details about diving in New Zealand contact: New Zealand Underwater Association, PO Box 875, Auckland 1 ☎ (09)895 456, Fax (09)897 051

Skiing

New Zealand offers some of the best skiing in the Southern Hemisphere. The large ski fields have all the necessary facilities and ski equipment can be hired. The season varies from place to place but it is usually from June to October.

In the North Island the best fields are to be found within Tongariro National Park. Whakapapa and Turoa ski fields both lie on the slopes of Mount Ruapehu, an active volcano. Needless to say the slopes will be closed if there is any chance of an eruption!

In the South Island the best skiing is in the vicinity of the Southern Lakes, around Queenstown and Wanaka. The skiing is fantastic and the scenery even more so. The main ski areas are Coronet Peak and The Remarkables near Queenstown and Treble Cone and Cadrona near Wanaka. Treble Cone is more suited to experienced skiers whereas Cadrona has a number of runs suitable for beginners. Another excellent ski region is Mount Hutt, not too far from Christchurch. Mount Hutt has the longest ski season in the country. It lasts from the end of May to the start of November. Even closer to Christchurch is the Porter Heights ski area.

Apart from the commercial fields there are also a number of smaller club fields. Facilities here are generally simpler than at the commercial fields but they tend to be cheaper and the skiing can be just as good. Club fields close to Christchurch include Temple Basin, Craigieburn, Broken River, Cheeseman and Mount Olympus. Mount Robert is located inside Nelson Lakes National Park and Amuri is near Hanmer Springs.

Club fields in the North Island are Manganui on the slopes of Mount Egmont (Taranaki) and Tukino on Mount Ruapehu.

The Waiorau Nordic ski area is situated in the Pisa range near Wanaka. This is New Zealand's only commercial cross-country ski area and offers around 25km (15 miles) of prepared trails.

Heliskiing is possible from Wanaka, Queenstown, Mount Cook, Fox Glacier and Methven. Companies offering heliskiing trips include Harris Mountains Heliskiing, Wanaka (☎ (03)443 7930), Mount Hutt Helicopter, Methven (☎(03)302 8401) and Alpine Guides Westland, Fox Glacier (☎ (03)751 0825).

Tramping (Trekking)

New Zealanders refer to trekking in their national and forest parks as tramping. The main tracks are usually very well marked and there is a good system of huts providing simple accommodation in both types of park. Some of the more popular tracks can get rather overcrowded during the summer but there are plenty of lesser known and often equally beautiful tracks that can be walked instead.

New Zealand's most popular walks are classified as 'Great Walks'. They are: Lake Waikaremoana, Te Urewera National Park (NP); Tongariro Northern Circuit, Tongariro NP; Abel Tasman Coastal Track, Abel Tasman NP; Heaphy Track, Kahurangi National Park (formerly North-West Nelson Forest Park); Routeburn Track, Mount Aspiring/Fiordland NP; Kepler Track, Fiordland NP; Rakiura Track, Stewart Island. The Milford Track is certainly a 'Great Walk' but is in a class all of its own — see Chapter 8.

The huts in New Zealand's national, maritime and forest parks are divided into four categories. Category One is the best and these huts have stoves, bunks with mattresses, toilet and washing facilities and maybe even lighting and other 'luxuries'. Categories two and three have at least toilets, bunks and a water supply but category four is not much more than a (at least free) roof over the head.

In the national parks wardens collect hut fees from November to April. However huts can be paid for in advance at any park visitor centre or DOC office. Hut fees should always be paid whether a warden is present or not. The back country hut tickets (what you get if you pay for huts in advance) that can be used on most walks are not valid on the Great Walks. These require a special Great Walks Pass for the walk in question. Such passes are available at DOC offices or park visitor centres near each walk. The use of huts is on a first come first served basis, therefore it is a good idea to bring a tent during the peak season. Camping, however, is only allowed at designated camping sites — contact local DOC offices.

To go tramping in New Zealand you need to have the right equipment. A pair of good quality walking boots, a backpack that is comfortable to wear even when it is fully loaded, wet weather gear and warm clothing (even in summer) are all essential equipment for longer walks in the national parks. As the huts on some walks are quite far apart it is wise to carry a tent or at least a fly in case you do not make it to the hut in daylight. Also important to carry is a torch, eating utensils, candles, a first aid kit and a portable stove — the firewood provided in the huts should only be used when really necessary. Enough food should be carried to last for the duration of the walk as you cannot buy food at the huts. The food should be high in energy and as light as possible. Bring extra rations in case of unforeseen delays.

Safety tips: Giardia parasites have been found in many of New Zealand's rivers and lakes so it is important to treat the water before you drink it.

- Always fill out the intentions form at a DOC office or park visitor centre before setting out on a walk.
- Check the difficulty of a track before you set out. If you have doubts about a certain track get advice from the local DOC or park visitor centre.
- Do not tramp alone.
- Before setting out on a walk it is important to have a good topographical map showing the track in question. These maps are available from DOC offices, local bookshops and park visitor centres. There are walking maps for each national park.

This book cannot and does not attempt to replace a good tramping guide. Inexperienced trampers are strongly advised to buy one of the tramping manuals or guides that are available in bookshops all over New Zealand. They have detailed descriptions of many of the country's most interesting tracks as well as tips on safety, what to take, etc.

White Water Rafting

For those who like to get wet while having their thrills then white water rafting is ideal. It is offered on many of the country's rivers, both in the North and South Islands. Some of the most exciting rivers to raft include the Motu river near Opotiki in the North Island and the Karamea river in the South Island. The rivers are graded from 1 to 6, though grade 6 is only of theoretical interest as rivers of this grade are considered unraftable.

Telephones

Most new public telephones accept either phone cards, coins or credit cards. Phone cards are available from any shop that displays the 'phone cards sold here' sign. In some rural areas where only coin-operated phones are available it is useful to have a pocketful of 20c coins. A local call made from a public booth costs 20c a minute. Local calls from private telephones cost nothing.

In New Zealand area codes are known as STD codes. The STD codes in the North Island are: Auckland and Northland (09), Coromandel Peninsula, Bay of Plenty and Central North Island (07), East Coast (East Cape), lower central North Island and Taranaki (06) and for the Wellington region (04). For all the South Island and Stewart Island the STD code is (03). STD codes are used when calling long distance within the country and even within a region if the town you are calling is some distance from you. 0800 numbers are toll free numbers.

International

For international calls it is most convenient to use a card phone or private phone. Instructions for direct dialling are in the phone directories but in principal it is very easy. Simply dial the international code you require and drop the first zero of the number you are ringing.

There are reduced telephone call rates to a number of countries outside New Zealand. The times when these rates are applicable vary from country to country but they are all listed in the telephone directory. Call rates to the UK are cheaper from midnight to 8am Sunday to Friday and all day Saturday; the same days apply to Australia but the hours are 11pm to 8am; to the USA and Canada the cheap rates are from 10pm to 8am Monday to Saturday and all day Sunday.

Main international direct dialling codes are:

Australia 0061	Other services:
Britain 0044	National Directory 018
Irish Republic 00353	International Directory 0172
New Zealand 0064	National Tolls 010
USA and Canada 001	International Tolls 0170

To make a price-required call to another country dial 0160 instead of 00 when beginning the call.

Time

New Zealand is 12 hours ahead of Greenwich Mean Time, however daylight saving during the summer in New Zealand and in other countries means that this can vary.

Daylight Saving Time in New Zealand starts on the last Sunday in October and finishes on the first Sunday of March. The clocks are put ahead 1 hour.

During Daylight Saving Time (New Zealand) when it is 12 noon in New Zealand it is: 11pm in London •10am in Sydney • 3pm in San Francisco • 6pm in New York • 5pm in Chicago • 6pm in Montreal

Tipping

Is not customary in hotels or restaurants.

Tourist Offices

Local Offices

Opening times have only been given for the more important visitor centres. As a rule of thumb one can expect that they (and National Park Visitor Centres) will usually be open between 8.30am and 5pm, Monday to Friday. In summer many are often open at weekends, especially in the larger centres.

The main New Zealand Tourism Board Offices (NZTB) are:

Australia	Level 19	Prudential Finance House
Ground Floor	Como Office Tower	84 Pitt Street
288 Edward Street	644 Chapel Street	Sydney
Brisbane	South Yarra	New South Wales 2000
Qld 4000	Melbourne	☎ (2)221 7333
☎ (7)221 3176	Victoria 3141	Fax (2)235 0737
Fax (7)221 3178	☎ (3)823 6283	
	Fax (3) 823 6276	

Canada
Suite 1200-888
Dunsmuir Street
Vancouver, BC
V6C 3K4
☎ (604)684 2117
Fax (604)684 1265

New Zealand
NZTB Head Office
PO Box 95
Wellington
☎ (04)472 8860
Fax (04)478 1736

UK
New Zealand House
Haymarket
London SW1Y 4TQ
☎ (071)973 0363
Fax (071)839 8929

USA
1825 North Lincoln Plaza
Suite 603
Chicago IL 60614
☎ (312)587 1190
Fax (312)587 1192

501 Santa Monica Blvd #300
Santa Monica
CA 90401
☎ freephone 1 800 388 5494
(this number may be called from
anywhere in the USA for
information about New Zealand)
Fax (310)295 5453

Travel

To New Zealand

Most people arrive in New Zealand by air. The main entry point is Auckland International Airport but there are also international airports at Wellington in the North Island and Christchurch in the South Island.

The flight from Britain via the USA/Canada or South-east Asia takes about 30 hours. Because it is such a long, tiring flight it is a good idea to plan a stop-over en route. Air New Zealand offers stop-overs in Fiji, West Samoa, Tonga and a number of other destinations as well. Other interesting stop-overs can be made with Cathay Pacific in Hong Kong; Singapore Airlines in Singapore; Thai Airways in Bangkok; Malaysian Airlines in Kuala Lumpur; United Airlines in San Francisco, Los Angeles or Hawaii; Qantas in Sydney or Melbourne and Canadian Airlines in Toronto or Hawaii. All these options and others are best discussed with your local travel agent.

Another very interesting possibility is a 'Round the World' ticket. They do not cost much more than a normal return ticket and give you an even greater choice of stop-over destinations. Most importantly take the time and shop around for the best deals. Prices can vary substantially. The so-called bucket shops are often quite a bit cheaper than the regular travel agents.

Note that baggage allowance is much more generous on flights that go via the United States than those via Asia.

Travellers from the USA and Canada will find the 'Circle Pacific Tickets' good value. These tickets link the American west coast with destinations in Australia, New Zealand, the Pacific Islands and Asia; in other words you circle the Pacific region. An excellent way to see the South Sea Islands is on Air New Zealand's 'Coral Route'. Departure point is Los Angeles. Possible stop-overs include Hawaii, Tahiti, Fiji, Tonga, and the Cook Islands. Your local travel agent will have all the details about these tickets and the restrictions that apply.

Departure Tax: For international flights is NZ$20.

Within New Zealand
Domestic Air Services

The main domestic airlines are Air New Zealand and Ansett New Zealand. Mt Cook Airline is partly owned by Air New Zealand. There are regular flight connections between Auckland, Wellington, Hamilton, Palmerston North, Christchurch, Dunedin and Invercargill. Ansett and Mt Cook airlines also fly the popular tourist route Rotorua — Christchurch — Mount Cook — Queenstown. This is obviously a good alternative to travelling overland if you have limited time.

There are a number of discounts available on inland flights which can make flying within New Zealand reasonably economical. The Air New Zealand 'Explore New Zealand Airpass' can only be bought outside the country and is valid on all inland flights with Air New Zealand or airlines belonging to 'Air New Zealand Link' (Mt Cook Airline, Air Nelson and Eagle Air). Though the route and number of flights have to be fixed before departure the times for the flights can be decided on arrival. Ansett's 'New Zealand Airpass' can be bought overseas or in New Zealand. Those who buy it overseas save $12^1/_2$ per cent GST (Government Service Tax) tax. The advantage of Ansett's airpass is that it is possible to change your itinerary within New Zealand at any time. All you are required to do is to pay a (not too expensive) surcharge. With Air New Zealand you can only alter your flight route up to the point where you take your first flight. After that you have to stick to the routes you have chosen. Other discount fares include Air New Zealand's 'Thrifty Fares' (35 per cent discount on off-peak flights) and Mount Cook Airlines 'Kiwi Air Pass'. The latter is valid for 30 days and allows you to fly once in each direction on each sector of the Mount Cook Airline schedule network. As details of the above can change please check with your travel agent.

Both Air New Zealand and Ansett Airlines offer substantial discounts (50 per cent) to holders of International Student Identity Cards, YHA cards and VIP Backpackers cards. These discounts only apply to standby flights but you usually have a good chance of getting one. Even if you do not intend staying at YHA hostels or backpackers hostels it could be well worth your while getting one of these cards.

If funds allow take one of the spectacular scenic flights that are offered in New Zealand. 'Flightseeing' trips over the volcanoes of Tongariro National Park and the Southern Alps are especially rewarding. The Additional Information sections at the end of each chapter in this book have details about especially interesting flights.

Air New Zealand
Head Office
29 Customs Street West
Auckland
☎ (09)379 755
Fax (09)388 075

Ansett New Zealand
PO Box 4168
Auckland
☎ (09)309 6235
Fax (09) 309 6434

Mount Cook Airline
PO Box 4644
Christchurch
☎ 0800 800 737 (toll free)

By Road

BUS

The main bus companies in New Zealand are InterCity, Newmans and Mount Cook Landline. Of these it is InterCity that offers the most extensive service. Virtually all of the country's larger towns can be reached by bus. In addition to the main bus companies there are a number of smaller operators who offer services within a particular region.

Off the main routes travel by bus can be rather slow as one often has to change buses and this can result in lengthy waits.

All the main bus companies publish free timetables which also have details on the many discounts available. It pays to be aware of these discounts as travel by bus can be rather expensive. Holders of YHA and VIP Backpackers cards are entitled to 30 per cent discounts on the main bus lines. Discounts of 30 per cent are also available to persons over 60 years of age and for the disabled. If you travel overnight between Auckland and Wellington with an InterCity bus you can also save money. Ask for the 'Starlighter' ticket.

'Backpacker' or 'alternative' buses provide a tour rather than just a simple bus connection along the routes they follow. Budget accommodation along each route is pre-booked and there are plenty of stops for the sights and activities along the way. The atmosphere on these buses is very relaxed and they are definitely better tailored to the needs of independent or budget travellers than are the normal buses. Backpacker buses in New Zealand include the 'Kiwi Experience', 'Magic Bus' and 'West Coast Express'. The first two operate in both the North and South Islands, whereas the latter only operates between Nelson and Queenstown along the West Coast. For more information and bookings contact the visitor information centres or the various YHA and backpacker hostels in New Zealand. Some of these buses run tours (with pre-booked rather than just a simple bus connection) but they can be great value for people without their own transport.

'Backpacker'/'Alternative' Buses:
(a selection)
Green Beetle Bus Co
PO Box 31-228
Auckland 1330
☎ (09) 358 4874
Fax (09) 354 4871
5-6 day tours around Northland

Kiwi Experience
36 Customs Street East
PO Box 1553
Auckland
☎ (09) 366 1665

Magic Bus
☎ (09) 358 5600

West Coast Express
YHA Nelson
☎ (03) 548 8817

Local and Shuttle Buses:
North Island
Alpine Scenic Tours
PO Box 519 Taupo
☎ (07) 386 8918
Fax (07) 377 0576
Operate between National Park, Turangi and Rotorua. Will take trampers from Turangi to Tongariro National Park.

C Tours
43 Egmont Street
New Plymouth
☎ (06) 758 1777
Connecting services to Rotorua. On the regular buses this west to east route through the central North Island is very time consuming.

East Cape Shuttles
To get around the East Cape on the coastal road you need the services of a number of local bus companies:

Opotiki to Hick's Bay
Eastland Backpackers, ☎ (07) 315 4870 operate a passenger service to Hick's Bay as do Hick's Bay Backpackers Lodge, ☎ (06) 864 4731

Hick's Bay to Gisborne:
Fastway has a daily courier service to Gisborne
☎ (06) 868 9080

Gisborne to Opotiki:
Super Shuttle operates a daily service (except Saturday) from Gisborne to Opotiki and Rotorua
☎ (07) 349 3444

South Island
Coast to Coast Bus
☎ 0800 800 847 (toll free)
Christchurch to Hokitika and
Greymouth via Arthur's Pass.

Coast Shuttle
Blenheim Taxis
☎ (03) 578 0225
Fax (03) 578 0224
Picton to Greymouth.

Collingwood Bus Services
Tasman Street
Collingwood
☎ (03) 524 8188
Collingwood-Takaka-Nelson

Nelson Lakes Transport
Nelson
☎ (03) 548 6858
Nelson to Nelson Lakes
National Park

Main Bus Companies:
InterCity
Auckland InterCity Travel Centre
Central Railway Station
Beach Road
☎ (09) 358 4085
Fax (09)270 5383

Mount Cook Landline
PO Box 4644
Christchurch
☎ 0800 800 737 (toll free)

Newmans Coachlines
PO Box 90 821
Auckland
☎ 0800 733 500 (toll free)

CAR
A car is a good way to get around New Zealand if you plan to do a lot of travelling. The main roads are generally very good though minor roads may be unsealed. These unsealed or 'metalled' roads are only covered by gravel and are much slower to drive.

The distances between petrol stations (especially in the South Island) can be considerable. It is best to fill up the tank before it gets too low.

Breakdown
The AA (Automobile Association) have emergency breakdown services available to their members or members of affiliated motor clubs overseas. Short-term membership (6 months) is available for foreigners. AA offices are found throughout New Zealand. Some local garages also have their own tow-trucks.

If you do breakdown and are a long way from any phone then do not despair. Eventually some passing motorist is bound to stop and offer you help. New Zealanders are renowned for their friendliness and what is (in this case) more important their practical ways.

Automobile Association (AA)
33 Wyndham Street
Auckland
☎ (09) 377 4660

Driving Regulations
Australian, UK, American and Canadian drivers only require their valid national driving licences. This enables the motorist to drive for a period of up to one year in New Zealand.

New Zealanders drive on the left-hand side of the road. At intersections you must give way to all traffic crossing or approaching from your right. If you yourself are turning you must give way to all traffic not turning. The New Zealand road code is readily available from most bookshops or AA offices.

The speed limit on the open road is 100kph (62mph), in urban areas it is 50kph (31mph). The sign LSZ stands for 'Limited Speed Zone'. This is an area where the speed limit is usually 100kph but when visibility, etc, is low a 50kph speed limit applies. Road signs in New Zealand generally keep to the international standards and should present no problem for overseas motorists.

Seat belts are compulsory. The legal limit for alcohol while driving is .08. The penalties for drinking and driving are very high.

CAR HIRE

To rent a car you must be at least 21 years of age and you need to have held your driving licence for at least one year. Car insurance is obligatory for rental cars. Remember: it always pays to read the small print before signing the contract.

The main car hire firms are Avis, Budget and Hertz. These companies have offices in all New Zealand's main cities, towns and airports. Apart from them there are also many local firms which can sometimes be cheaper.

Depending on the season, duration of rental and so forth, prices can vary greatly from dealer to dealer so shop around.

If you wish to drive on both main islands it pays to find out whether or not you have to take your car on the ferry or whether you can leave it in Wellington and pick up another one in Picton. One-way rentals can be very practical when possible. For instance you could hire your car in Auckland and then hand it over in Christchurch or Queenstown and fly back north. This saves all the driving and you do not have the expense of the Cook Strait Ferry. Often it is only the larger companies that offer such one-way rentals.

Avis	Budget	Hertz
Building 4	83 Beach Road	Auckland
Central Park	Auckland	☎ (09) 303 4924
666 Great South Road	☎ (09) 379 6768	
Auckland	Fax (09)366 0212	
☎ (09) 525 1982		

Campervans

Travelling by campervan is a very popular way of getting around New Zealand. Prices vary greatly according to the season. Note that it can be cheaper to travel by car and to stay at camping grounds or hostels. Reservations for campervans are necessary in the high season (December to March).

Campervan Hire:	Maui	Newmans
(a selection)	Auckland	Auckland
Horizon	☎ (09) 275 3013	☎ (09) 303 1149
Auckland	Fax (09) 275 9690	
☎ (09) 307 8226		

Carshare

Sharing not only the ride but also the petrol costs with private motorists is an interesting alternative to hitch-hiking. Travelpool — Travelshare in Auckland and Wellington organise carshares to destinations anywhere in New Zealand.

Telephone Auckland (09) 307 0001 or Wellington (04) 473 5558 (daily 8am-9pm) for details.

Inter-Island Ferries

The Interislander ferry operates between Wellington on the North Island and Picton on the South Island. The ferry takes cars as well as passengers. From Wellington there are three to four sailings daily and the crossing takes about three hours. In the high season (December to January) and holiday periods it is necessary to book well ahead if you are taking a car.

As the trip with the ferry takes you through the picturesque Marlborough Sounds it is best to do the crossing in daylight. Bear in mind that the crossing can be quite rough.

There is a free bus service between the Wellington Interislander terminal and Wellington Railway Station. Buses leave Platform 9 at the railway station 35 minutes before scheduled sailings between 8am and 6.40pm. In Picton a free bus service is provided for passengers connecting with Coastal Pacific Express to Christchurch. However this service only applies to the 10am sailing from Wellington.

For bookings and enquiries ☎ (04) 498 3999 or 0800 658 999 (toll free).

Train

New Zealand Rail's long distance trains link the main centres and are quite modern and comfortable. They often travel along particularly scenic routes and snacks are served on board. Most rail services also have a buffet car.

North Island

The Overlander is the daytime daily rail service between Auckland and Wellington.

The Northerner does the overnight run between Auckland and Wellington. Sunday to Friday.

The Kaimai Express runs daily between Tauranga and Auckland.

The Geyserland runs twice daily between Auckland and Rotorua.

The Bay Express runs daily between Wellington and Napier.

South Island

The Coastal Pacific runs daily between Christchurch and Picton. The 10am Interislander Ferry from Wellington connects with Coastal Pacific. The Coastal Pacific departs Christchurch at 8.15am to connect with ferry departing Picton at 2.20pm.

The TranzAlpine runs daily between Christchurch and Greymouth. This is a spectacular trip across the Southern Alps.

The Southerner runs between Christchurch and Invercargill, Monday to Friday.

For more information and bookings contact:

Passenger Group
New Zealand Rail Ltd
Private Bag
Wellington
(Correspondence)

New Zealand Rail
Central Reservations Centre
☎ 0800 802 802 (toll free)
Fax (04)498 3721

Index